"Reichl understands that food lies at the center of human sociality. As the title of her memoir suggests, her interest goes beyond all the recipes, all the talk about ingredients, tableware and restaurant décor. At the heart of her book is love (however laced with conflict) for her friends and family, and her wish to extend their number by having a child. You know that kid's going to eat very well."
    —*The New York Times Book Review*

"Food writer Ruth Reichl's memoir, *Comfort Me with Apples*, proved so tasty, I can barely resist wearing out the fawning-praise button on my computer keyboard. . . . The book's charm emerges from Reichl's writing, her observations and her amazing ability to capture people in a few memorable sentences. . . . In a literary landscape groaning with memoirs of really action-packed lives, it's hard to explain why *Comfort Me with Apples* proves so compelling. . . . You just have to read it."
    —*USA Today*

"Despite her breezy tone, there's any underlying tartness that gives Reichl's narrative a satisfying complexity. Subtly but effectively, she contrasts the story of the education of her senses with that of the gradual disintegration of her marriage to her first husband. . . . 'I have this idea that I could write reviews that were like short stories,' Reichl writes at the beginning of her book, and the three hundred swiftly moving pages that follow amply testify to a real writerly gift. (You have no trouble believing that her first ambition was to write novels.) The author knows how to convey mood and setting with efficient, sometimes really poetic, strokes. . . . *Comfort Me with Apples* . . . reminds you of a really great meal, well balanced and well seasoned, leaving you satisfied and yet somehow wanting more."
    —*New York*

"Reichl made her reputation by chronicling not just the sensory attributes of food but its emotional and psychosocial qualities as well. She brings those same skills to writing about life in *Comfort Me with Apples*. The stories [here] are delicious reads: witty, reflective ac-

counts of her experiences in, around and through food. They are perfectly balanced meals accompanied by recipes."
—*Time*

"Reichl's irresistible charms should be savored."
—*Us Weekly*

"In this follow-up to the excellent memoir *Tender at the Bone,* Reichl (editor in chief at *Gourmet*) displays a sure hand, an open heart and a highly developed palate. As one might expect of a celebrated food writer, Reichl maps her past with delicacies. . . . Recipes are included, but the text is far from fluffy food writing. . . . Like a good meal, this has a bit of everything, and all its parts work together to satisfy."
—*Publishers Weekly* (starred review)

"[*Comfort Me with Apples*] takes readers on a delectable journey."
—*Seattle Post-Intelligencer*

"Nobody writes about food with Reichl's gusto and grace. . . . Wherever she goes, she describes every morsel she eats and every drop she drinks in precise and sensuous detail. The recipes she throws in for good measure will send you straight to the kitchen. . . . Fortunately, she seems to be a compulsive writer, so she'll surely carry on with her memoirs, and keep us up to date on gustatory matters, as well."
—Trenton *Times*

"In this memoir, Reichl becomes a restaurant critic. So if you think there could be no better job in the world, please take time to read before you apply. . . . [Reichl] got off to a rocky start . . . but things improved, and it's that process that makes her book such a pleasure."
—*The Denver Post*

"[Reichl's] descriptions of food go beyond flavor and beyond reporting and connect to deeper issues of identity and loss. And here I am reminded what a good writer Reichl is, and how much I miss her reviews in the *Times*."
—*The Atlanta Journal-Constitution*

"Reichl is a warm and generous writer."
—*Chicago Tribune*

"You not only like Reichl, but see in her life the full realization of a simple truth, easily lost in fast-food times, that eating is more than a biological necessity; it is an essential part of our psychological well-being, too."
—*Biography*

"This delightful memoir . . . picks up where [Reichl's] first bestselling work, *Tender at the Bone,* left off. Readers and fans who hankered to learn the details of her coveted career now get them—and then some. This book reads like a well-edited—and quite romantic—film, full of hard work, good luck, love, joy, pain, travel, celebrity chefs, and always fine cuisine. The recipes (for the most part quite replicable) are reminiscent of flashbacks in a movie, loaded with visual memory. Elegant description captures the imagination, tempts the palate, and illustrates Reichl's well-deserved reputation as a food writer."
—*Library Journal*

"Reichl's passion, humor, abandon, intelligence, whimsy and vital sense of food as culture have revolutionized a nation raised on Betty Crocker cookbooks and school cafeterias. . . . This second volume of memoirs . . . is both bittersweet and almost hilariously indulgent. For Reichl, all passions are connected. In fact, her sensory reactions are so synesthetic you wonder how she survives."
—*Bookpage*

"Reichl knows that to be a good judge of food, 'you need to know a lot about life.' There's an abundance of it in her book, with recipes on the side."
—*The Arizona Republic*

"[A] delightful new memoir . . . The book reads like a novel, a real page-turner that I hated to put down."
—*Pittsburgh Post-Gazette*

"The descriptions of the meals are often downright sensuous, which seems appropriate from the woman who has become one of the most influential voices in American food. . . . But dining alone can't propel a memoir to the bestseller list. . . . [*Comfort Me with Apples*] is as rich, colorful, and entertaining as a nine-course dinner. I'm ready for thirds."
   —*The San Diego Union-Tribune*

"When Ruth Reichl gave up writing restaurant reviews for the *New York Times* . . . I had mixed emotions. Sure, I was happy for her—new job, new challenges—but I knew I would miss her. Is she a friend of mine? No, But her writing made me feel that way. . . . If you haven't read Ruth Reichl's reviews, *Comfort Me with Apples* is a perfect introduction. If you have, pick it up to get to know her a little better. . . . It is in itself the stuff of which great meals are made: good food, yes, but also charming atmosphere, intelligent conversation, camaraderie."
   —*The Providence Sunday Journal*

"Lord, if there aren't a lot of books that focus on some aspect of love or eating! But how many are there that cover both, and do it very, very well? I don't think there are many as engrossing, as well-written, and as captivating as *Comfort Me with Apples,* by Ruth Reichl."
   —Fredericksburg *Free Lance–Star*

"A good book is comfort food, and you finish Reichl's as you finish a good meal, satisfied, content, hopeful. With a sense that we need to cook for one another more, pay attention to the everyday, realize that the everyday is momentous."
   —Greensboro *News & Record*

"A book that defies putting down . . . Reichl's work is as compelling as any writer could wish. Insightful, humorous, sensual, sometimes scandalous, but always as mesmerizing as the reviews with which she once ruled the New York restaurant scene, Reichl's book is a must-read."
   —Charleston *Post & Courier*

RUTH REICHL, former restaurant critic of *New West* magazine, *California* magazine, the *Los Angeles Times,* and *The New York Times,* is now editor in chief of *Gourmet* magazine. She lives in Manhattan with her husband, her son, and two cats.

COMFORT ME
WITH APPLES

More Adventures at the Table

RUTH REICHL

RANDOM HOUSE

TRADE PAPERBACKS

NEW YORK

2002 Random House Trade Paperback Edition

Copyright © 2001 by Ruth Reichl
Reader's guide copyright © 2002 by Random House, Inc.

All rights reserved under International and Pan-American
Copyright Conventions. Published in the United States by Random House Trade
Paperbacks, an imprint of The Random House Publishing Group, a division of
Random House, Inc., New York, and simultaneously in Canada
by Random House of Canada Limited, Toronto.

RANDOM HOUSE TRADE PAPERBACKS and colophon
are trademarks of Random House, Inc.

This work was originally published in hardcover by Random House, an imprint of The
Random House Publishing Group, a division of Random House, Inc., in 2001.

Library of Congress Cataloging-in-Publication Data
Reichl, Ruth.
Comfort me with apples : more adventures at the table / Ruth Reichl.
        p.   cm.
ISBN 0-375-75873-9
1. Reichl, Ruth.   2. Women food writers—United States—Biography.
3. Cookery.   I. Title.
TX649.R45   A3   2001
641.5092—dc21   [B]   00-053355

Random House website address: www.atrandom.com
Printed in the United States of America
8 9

Book design by J. K. Lambert

This one's for Nick

CONTENTS

COMFORT ME
WITH APPLES

THE OTHER SIDE
OF THE BRIDGE

*The primary requisite for writing well
about food is a good appetite.*

A. J. LIEBLING

■ Easy for him to say: He was independently wealthy. Personally, I found the primary requisite for writing about food to be a credit card.

And that was a problem. I pictured myself sweeping into fabulous restaurants to dine upon caviar and champagne. Maître d's would cower before the great Restaurant Critic. Chefs would stand behind the kitchen door, trembling. "What is she saying?" they would whisper to my waiter. "Does she like it?" I would not betray, by word or gesture, my opinion of the meal. And when it was all over, I would throw down my card and cry "Charge it please!," then gather my retinue and float regally out the door.

Unfortunately, the first time I tried this I hit a few snags.

In 1978, San Francisco's fanciest French restaurant belonged to a chef who had cooked for the Kennedys. The valet stared at my beat-up Volvo and shook his head. He could not, he insisted, accept a car that used a screwdriver in place of a key. The maître d'hôtel was equally overjoyed by my arrival; he looked me up and down, took in my thrift-store clothing, and led me straight to the worst table, the one that shook each time a waiter came out the kitchen door. The sommelier appeared worried when I ordered the '61 Lascombes. He had, he was sorry to inform me, sold the last bottle. He was certain that a nice little Beaujolais would make me very happy. And when the captain announced that the special of the evening was freshly made terrine de foie gras, he pointedly told me the price.

The biggest humiliation, however, was yet to come. "Your credit card, madam," said the maître d'hôtel frostily, "has been rejected." He stood over me looking more smug than sorrowful; clearly he had been expecting this all along.

"It couldn't be!" I insisted. "I just got it yesterday."

"It says, madam," the maître d'hôtel went on, "that you are over your limit." He leaned down and hissed menacingly. "Do you know what your limit is?"

Unfortunately, I did. After years of righteous poverty I was prepared to sacrifice my principles and leap back into middle-class life. The middle class, however, had its doubts about me. Although I was now a bona fide restaurant critic, the banks were not impressed. Where, they wanted to know, were my debts? How had I managed to live thirty years without owing anything to anyone? Were there no college loans, no car payments, no mortgages, no revolving lines of credit? How could I possibly be trusted with a credit card?

In desperation I had put on my very best dress and arranged for an appointment with the bank manager. After making me wait a suitable length of time, he graciously permitted me to show him the masthead of *New West* magazine. I was hoping that my association with *New York* magazine's West Coast sibling would impress this man, that he would recognize it as Northern California's most important regional publication. But the manager merely looked bored. As he unhurriedly put on his half-glasses, I wished that I had tamed my hair out of its usual wildness. I patted, vainly, at it and tried pulling the most excitable curls behind my ears. They popped willfully forward. He snorted.

He scanned the list of contributing editors. He noted my name. He grunted. "Meaningless," he said at last. "What we are looking for is something to show that you will pay your bills. Can you show me a pay stub?"

"I'm freelance," I stammered. "I don't get a paycheck. They pay me by the article."

He drew visibly back from me. He looked sorrowful. "Unreliable," he sighed at last, staring at my ringless fingers. "It says here," he said, peering skeptically at the papers in his hand, "that you are married? To a Mr. Douglas Hollis?" The tone of his voice implied that he wondered what someone who looked like me might be doing with someone who sounded like that.

"Yes," I replied. "I am."

"And what does Mr. Hollis do for a living?" he inquired. "His income does not seem to be represented here." I considered giving him my feminist line, but one look at his sour face decided me against it.

"He's an artist," I said. "He does site sculpture. He actually hasn't had much income in the past couple of years, but that's about to change—"

"I understand," he said firmly, and made a mark on the paper. Despite his name, Mr. Hollis was clearly no more trustworthy than myself.

After months of pleading, the bank was finally persuaded to part with a Visa card. If I proved conscientious and faithful in my payments, the manager suggested, I might, in due time, be permitted a bit more credit. We would have to see. In the meantime, he was prepared to go out on a $250 limb.

It was not enough. I was not surprised. I had known from the start that this job would be trouble. I had been writing short magazine articles for a couple of years, but nobody I knew took them seriously. They were considered, like my restaurant job, just a side-line to support my real work as a novelist. Fixing the money part turned out to be easy; I wrote the fancy French restaurant a check and asked my editor for an advance. The rest would be more complicated.

On the day I became a restaurant critic, my primary emotion was fear. As I drove home from the magazine, I practiced breaking the news to the people I loved best. I found the prospect so terrifying that I forgot to be frightened of the bridge and I reached the far side of the Bay before realizing that I had crossed the entire span without my usual panic. I turned off the freeway, and as my ancient car bumped through the Berkeley flatlands, past the small old cottages with their softly fading paint, I tried to find the perfect way to put it.

"I've just gotten the best job in the world!" As I heard myself say the words, I knew they wouldn't do. They would be fine in San Francisco or New York, but this was the People's Republic of Berkeley. This was the heart of the counterculture. Every single person I knew was going to disapprove.

I walked into the hallway of the peeling Victorian house I shared with my husband and five other people and waited for their reactions.

Nick, our household patriarch, was sitting in the shabby, crowded living room. He stroked the bushy beard that gave him the air of a prophet and said, "Let me get this straight." He plunked himself into one of the tattered armchairs we had found at the flea market and began pushing the stuffing back into the arm. "You're going to spend your life telling spoiled, rich people where to eat too much obscene food?"

"Something like that," I murmured, too embarrassed to defend myself.

He shook his head in disappointment. A devotee of millet and Dr. Bronner's balanced mineral bouillon, Nick had done his Berkeley best to turn our household into a model of politically correct consumption. We had, at various times, been ovolactovegetarians and vegans, and we were, at all times, vigilant about the excesses of agribusiness. For a long while we grew our own food, and we even, for a short while, depended upon dumpsters for our raw ingredients. Nick had valiantly tried to overlook my forays into the world of fancy food, but this was going too far. For the first time in the many years I had known him, he became speechless.

Jules, the most sympathetic member of our household, tried to be optimistic. He poured himself a glass of wine from the gallon jug on the table and said, "Free meals!" He turned to Nick and said, "Think how our food bills will go down."

Nick shook his head. "Not mine," he said. "You couldn't pay me to set foot in one of those decadent, bourgeois institutions. Have you told Doug?"

"Not yet," I admitted, going out to the garage, where my husband was working on the band saw. He had sawdust in his straight brown hair, and he smiled when he saw me, as if just the sight of me had improved his day. He turned off the saw, leaned against it, shook a Camel out of the pack that was always in his shirt pocket and lit it.

"The magazine's asked me to be their restaurant critic," I blurted out.

"Of course they have," he said, putting his arms around me. Doug was my biggest fan and greatest supporter. I buried my head in his faded blue work shirt and inhaled his scent, a mixture of clean laundry, cut wood, and tobacco. "Why wouldn't they? You're a great cook and a great writer. But you don't have to say yes."

I stood back so I could see him. He has one of those handsome, all-American faces that get better as they age, and in our ten years together his cheeks had slimmed down, become angular. His youthful rosiness had disappeared, leaving him looking chiseled, intelligent, and kind. Now he said earnestly, "Why don't you stop working? I'm making enough money now. You could quit the restaurant, give up magazine work, and stay home and write."

"That would be great," I hedged. "But you don't understand. I really *want* to do this."

"Why?" he asked. "You're wasting your talent."

"I don't have to do it forever," I replied. "But I think it will be good experience."

"You'll be stuck here!" he said with such vehemence that I understood there was something more on his mind. "Look, I'm getting commissions all over the country, and I thought you'd bring your typewriter and come with me. We'd be together."

"I was never very good at playing the great artist's wife, remember?" I reminded him. "After the third art patron chucks me under the chin and says condescendingly, 'And what do you do, dear?' I always get mad. Even if I didn't have this new job, I probably wouldn't come with you that often."

"So don't come," he said in his soft, reasonable voice. "Stay here if you want. But you should be writing your novel, doing something important."

"But don't you see," I said, surprising myself with my own passion, "writing about restaurants doesn't have to be different from writing a novel. It can be important. The point is just to do it really well. I have this idea that I could write reviews that were like short stories—mysteries, romances, even science fiction."

Doug did not seem convinced; in those days we all considered art and commerce to be in opposition, and Doug thought I was willfully choosing the wrong one.

"Just think about it before you say yes," said Doug, turning on the band saw. I left the shop, got into my car, and went to see what my colleagues at The Swallow, the collectively owned restaurant where I cooked, would think about this new development. The reaction there was almost violent. "You're giving up good honest work to be a parasite" was how one of my fellow workers put it. "I'll be embarrassed to have known you." He turned his back on me and said, "In fact, I'm embarrassed now."

I had counted on my parents, at least, for a little support. But when I called New York to break the news, expecting jubilation over the fact that I was about to make more than the minimum wage, they were unenthusiastic.

"A restaurant critic?" said my father, repeating the words as if I had said "undertaker" or "garbage collector." I imagined him standing by the cluttered table in the hall of their Greenwich Village apartment, folding his tall frame down until he could see himself in the mirror hanging above it, patting the long strand of hair over the bald spot at the top of his head. His German accent became stronger when he was upset, and now, as he said, "You're going to spend your time writing about food? When are you going to do something worthwhile with your life?" all the *w*'s turned into *v*'s.

"And what about children?" cried my mother. She was probably sitting on the bed, newspapers and books scattered around her as she ran chipped red fingernails through her short gray hair. "Now that Doug is finally making some money, you could move out of that ridiculous commune, settle down, and have a family."

At any other time of my life I would have bowed to this pressure. To be honest, I was astonished that I did not. I had always been the ultimate good girl. I was thirty years old and I had spent my whole life pleasing other people. Although I lived in a commune, I was married to a man my parents loved, called my mother every day, and spent most of my time cooking the meals and cleaning the house. At The Swallow, I worked hard and never showed up late. I had never before faced universal disapproval.

But I had finally found my true calling, and I was not prepared to turn it down. "You were born to be a restaurant critic," said the editor who gave me the job, and I felt that she was right. Food was my major passion; I had been feeding people since I was small. I had been a cook, a waitress, a kitchen manager; I had even written a cookbook. Now I understood that all along I had been training myself to be a restaurant critic.

But Liebling was wrong. Appetite is not enough. And knowledge is not sufficient. You can be a decent critic if you know about food, but to be a really good one you need to know about life. It took the next few years to teach me that.

You'll see.

2

THE SUCCESS MACHINE

■ Autumn in Berkeley. The thin evening sun was creeping into the tiny attic bedroom I shared with Doug. The dresser was built into the dormer window, and the closet was a cupboard tucked below the eaves. The room was white, with sloping walls and a pointed ceiling that made it feel so much like a ship's cabin that you found yourself bracing for the roll. The only way two people could possibly occupy the room at the same time was if one of them was sitting on the single piece of furniture, a handmade bed covered with a star quilt in primary colors.

At this moment Doug was the seated one. His suitcase lay open on the bed in front of him. He was folding clothes and listening to me rage as I paced the scrap of floor and dressed for dinner.

"Don't they trust me?" I complained. "I've had the job almost a year. They say I'm the best restaurant critic they've ever had. Why did the magazine have to go and hire a food editor?"

My husband zipped up my vintage velvet dress and made appropriately soothing sounds.

"I don't want a new boss!" I fumed. "Especially some paunchy middle-aged guy from Los Angeles. I can just imagine what he's going to be like!"

"He may not be so bad," said Doug, folding another shirt and putting it in his suitcase. "Maybe you'll like him."

"Easy for you to say," I answered irritably, "now that you've gotten so successful. That museum in Omaha will put you up in some splendid hotel, wine you and dine you for an entire week while everyone tells you what a great artist you are. You'll build a wonderful sound structure that catches the wind, makes beautiful music, and mesmerizes the entire city. Meanwhile I have to go to the city's dreariest restaurant and have dinner with some fat creep from Los Angeles. Is this fair? Did I mention that the magazine's wine writer is coming along? Do you have any idea how boring wine writers are?"

Doug watched as I went into the bathroom, which was even tinier than the bedroom, and stood on the toilet to get a full-length look at myself. The only big mirror in the house was in Nick's bedroom, but his door was closed; Ravi Shankar ragas were drifting beneath it, and God knew what he was up to in there. In the year since his girlfriend Martha had moved out, a series of women had gone parading through the house.

"You look fine," said Doug. "I wish you were coming with me. I wish I had time to come with you." He refrained from adding that I had chosen this life, that he continually offered to support me any time I wanted to quit. He just wasn't an I-told-you-so kind of guy. Now he snapped the suitcase shut and added, "If I don't leave right now I'll miss my plane."

We went down the narrow rear stairs and I stood at the door watching him back his van out of the driveway, which was so littered with Nick's collection of derelict vehicles that Doug just missed the old Harley-Davidson rusting by the side of the house. I watched his taillights turn the corner before climbing into my

1960 humpbacked Volvo and negotiating the obstacle course myself. When I hit the motorcycle I didn't stop; another dent would be barely noticeable on either vehicle.

I was in a terrible mood. I told myself this was because the editors I was about to meet would be tiresome bores, but deep down I knew that that wasn't really what was troubling me.

Doug's continual traveling was the problem. It marked a milestone in our marriage. We had met in college when Doug came knocking on my door in search of another woman. I invited him in, cooked him dinner, and we spent the whole night talking. We were amazed at our luck in finding each other; he moved in the next day. Until recently we had rarely spent more than a few hours apart at a time. After eleven years, we completed each other's sentences. Our friends called us Duth and Rug.

Doug wanted to make art, I wanted to write, and we moved to Berkeley so we could live cheaply and not become part of what we called the success machine. We steered clear of the stuff of ordinary existence, the clothes and cars and furniture that other people spent their money on. We chose a communal household on Channing Way because the rent was forty-five dollars a month and we could support ourselves with part-time jobs. I cooked in a restaurant; Doug did carpentry. We bought our clothes in thrift stores, borrowed our books from the library, and thought of a night at the movies as a major treat.

We had only two extravagances: Doug spent money on art supplies, and once a year we went out for a really great dinner.

It was always at the same restaurant: Chez Panisse. This tradition went back to our first weeks in Berkeley, when my parents came to inspect our commune. They were not thrilled to find themselves sleeping in a bedroom with a curtain in place of a door, but it was the food that finally drove them away. They endured three nights of brown rice, tofu, and lentils with a side order of anti-agribusiness theory, and then insisted on going out to eat. There was, it seemed, a new local restaurant Mom was eager to try. "It sounds so cute," she said. "They serve just one meal every day."

"What if you don't like it?" I asked. This was not an opportunity I was prepared to squander.

"I wondered about that too," said my mother. "You have nothing to worry about. If you don't like the meal of the evening, you can ask for steak!"

When we got to Chez Panisse, Mom looked around the attractively rustic room and said, her voice dripping with disappointment, "This looks more like a house than a restaurant." She surveyed the bare wood and burnished copper. She glared at the tangle of wildflowers in the middle of the dining room, daring it to turn into tulips or roses, or at the very least some respectable hothouse plant. She scrutinized the menu. "Wild mushrooms on toast," she read. "Blanquette de veau. A salad of baby lettuces. Lemon tart." She was calculating the cost. "I'll have the steak," she announced when she had finished.

Our waiter, a thin young man with an intellectual air, looked doubtful as he wrote the order down. Sure enough, the kitchen door had no sooner closed behind him than it reopened to allow the owner to come marching out.

Alice Waters was Berkeley's latest claim to fame. She was a petite, pretty woman who swept through town trailing disappointed men in her wake. She had chestnut hair and a generous mouth that turned up at the corners. Her hazel eyes were framed by bangs, and when I saw her in the markets she was always wearing eccentric clothes that made me want to reach out and softly caress them.

I was awed by her—and a little jealous of her reputation. She seemed so formidable that I was taken aback by the sound of her whispery little voice. "I was afraid people would be worried about eating veal," she said. We had to lean in to hear her. "But you see, these are not commercial animals." Alice began telling my mother about the humane manner in which the calves had been raised. When she realized that wasn't working, she tried a different tack.

"Have you been to France?" she asked.

"Yes," my mother said. I winced, knowing exactly what was coming next. Mom could never resist an opportunity to say, "I got my Ph.D. at the Sorbonne."

Alice beamed. "Wonderful!" she said. "Then you know how much better food tastes over there!" She smiled at my mother and said winningly, "Our vegetables taste the way they do in France. All the little carrots and onions in the blanquette were cultivated by people I know. They don't use pesticides at all. I've adapted this recipe from Richard Olney. Do you know his book?"

Mom didn't.

Alice warmed to her subject, going on about the people who grew the grapes that made the wine that went into the sauce. "We only use good wine for cooking," she assured my mother. "I wouldn't cook with a wine I wouldn't drink."

My mother remained unconvinced. Alice remained adamant. "The steak just isn't as good as the blanquette," she said. There was steel behind that sweet whispery voice. "I don't want you to be disappointed with your meal."

"I won't be," said Mom, whose voice also had a metallic ring. She was certain that the steak offered better value. She was determined to have it. In the end, Alice relinquished the duel, gave a defeated little shrug, and retreated to the kitchen. This, I would learn later, was completely uncharacteristic.

Mom did not regret her decision, even when my father held out a forkful of silken veal in a sauce made of thick, sweet cream. "Try this, darling," he said. "It tastes like my childhood." Lost in some nostalgic German reverie, he recited a line from Goethe under his breath.

"My steak is delicious too!" cried Mom. It wasn't; I understood why Alice had not wanted to serve this mediocre meat, which must have come straight from the freezer. My mother didn't care; filet mignon cost more than stewing veal and she was getting her money's worth. A few months later, when Chez Panisse was reviewed in a national magazine, Mom's triumph was complete. "I discovered it!" she bragged to her friends, and as the restaurant grew more famous Mom embellished Alice's steak protest until it had turned into a meaningful conversation.

But although it pleased my mother, the national success of Chez Panisse did not impress the people of Berkeley. Sweet suckling pigs cooked over wood fires, ragouts of red wine and squid, and the best bread ever served in America might astonish others, but they were not what we loved best about Chez Panisse. The restaurant stood for pure products, small farms, and sustainable agriculture, and we went there because it was a place where you could eat fabulously without feeling apologetic. Their food was grown by people who cared for the earth and served by people who cared for one another. Even the dishwashers were well paid. In Berkeley, these things counted.

Over the years, Alice turned into a Berkeley icon. She became so famous that when my editor asked me to interview her, right after I became a critic, it took me days to work up the courage to call. I expected her to say no. Instead, she invited me to her house.

I was surprised to find that she lived in a small Victorian in the flatlands of Berkeley, within walking distance of Channing Way. The house seemed so modest, so unassuming, so ordinary.

And Alice seemed so friendly. "Oh," she said when I knocked on the door, "it's you." She smiled winningly and I instantly understood her charm. "You worked at The Swallow. I know you." Her arms were filled with fuzzy branches covered with the tiniest blue flowers. "Aren't they beautiful?" she said. "Do you know borage? You eat the flowers. Here, taste." She stuffed a blossom into my mouth. I chewed on it as I followed her through the dark living room and into the kitchen, thinking how very blue the flower tasted.

Alice's kitchen was spotless, but it was far from fancy. The stove was an antique and the refrigerator looked like a relic from the Ice Age; it didn't even have a freezer. "I saw it in the window of a junk shop," she said, proudly patting the door. "It cost two hundred and twenty-five dollars." She did not own a single modern appliance.

"Did you always know you wanted to run a restaurant?" I asked, looking around.

"Oh no," she said. "I was a Montessori teacher. But I hated teaching because I didn't have any patience. I found myself sort of biting the children."

"You couldn't have," I said.

"No, really," she said, "I did. There was this little kid who was biting everybody and I couldn't figure out what to do, and it was just an impulsive thing and I bit him." She still seemed shocked at her action, all these years later. "I hurt him," she admitted. "And then I thought, I've got to get out of here."

"And so you opened a restaurant? Just like that?"

"Well, I love feeding people. I need to have that kind of communion. When I was working at the *Express Times,* people came over every night, and I would put out food."

"Sounds like my house," I said.

As we chatted she washed lettuces, crushed garlic, and talked to her mother on the telephone. People kept showing up—before the afternoon was over, dinner for four had grown to dinner for a dozen. "What I always wanted in a restaurant," she said, "was something like this. Just a place where my friends would come and hang out for hours."

As Alice said that, her friend Pat put down her rolling pin and commented, "And look what you ended up with. A restaurant that none of your friends can afford." There was a definite edge to her words.

"I know," said Alice wistfully. "But the trouble is, once you're successful at something, it just sort of follows you around and haunts you."

■ ■ ■

Why was I remembering all that as I drove across the Bay Bridge? The sky was reflected in the dark water, and I looked down and watched an airplane pick its way delicately among the stars. And then I understood the connection: Success was following us around, haunting us. For the past year, Doug had been moving all around the country while I stayed home and reviewed restaurants. Our relationship seemed the same, but I had a prickly sense of change. Doug was going east while I went west, heading to a restaurant none of my friends could afford. I was suspended between Berkeley and San Francisco, and success was riding shotgun as I catapulted across the bridge.

Trader Vic's turned out to be exactly what I had expected. I looked at the people milling expensively about the waiting room, angling for tables, and thought of the word Nick had used: "obscene." He had a point. But there was one surprise: The wine writer was shy, earnest, and about my age. In his rumpled clothes and dirty sneakers, Phil Reich would have fit right into our Berkeley household. The maître d'hôtel seemed to think so too. He examined us both briefly and announced that there would be a wait. A long wait.

"He obviously hopes we'll leave," said Phil, introducing himself. "Wait until he sees who's taking us to dinner. He'll change his tune."

"So you've met this food editor?" I asked.

"A few times," he replied.

"What's he like?" I asked.

Phil looked me up and down appraisingly, as if trying to decide how honest he could be. He took in my frizzy brown hair and worn velvet dress. "I don't think he's your sort of person," he said finally. He looked over my shoulder and added, "See for yourself."

A substantial man with thick black hair was bearing down on us, wearing a suit, a tie, and an air of extreme self-satisfaction. How old was he? I couldn't tell, but he seemed very grown up—forty, at least—and he was so tall, so large, that the crowd seemed to part before him. As he got closer I could hear the maître d'hôtel gushing, "Oh, Mr. Andrews, how nice to have you with us again." I squirmed resentfully; just by walking in the door he had taken control, and I was afraid that he would see right through me.

"See?" whispered Phil as the maître d'hôtel led us past the throng to our table; those with Colman Andrews did not wait. The food editor immediately summoned a wine list. It appeared, and the two men began speaking in tongues.

"Mayacamas Chard?" asked the food editor, raising his eyebrows as he peered down at the list.

"Hasn't been through malolactic," Phil replied.

"Francophile myself," said the editor. "Preferably bone."

"Caymus?" asked Phil.

"Malolactic?" the editor replied.

"Of course," said Phil, nodding.

I listened, baffled, as the words rolled off their tongues. I had a moment of triumph when I translated "bone" to "Beaune," but by then the men had moved on to a discussion of barrels. As they tossed facts about new oak and old redwood into the air, the sommelier hovered unhappily in the distance. Our glasses were still empty. When the men lurched into an argument about which year Hanzell stopped using white foil around the neck of the bottle, I knew I had to do something.

"I'm hungry," I announced.

The food editor had very good manners. "Sorry," he said, summoning the waiter. "Let's start with the '66 Krug," he said. "It's my favorite."

"Mine too," I said before I could stop myself. And then, what the hell, I threw myself into it and added, "Such a wonderful year for champagne." Phil shot me an odd look, and I wondered if I had gotten it wrong. Wasn't Krug champagne? Were there good years, or were they all the same? I could feel my cheeks getting hot.

Apparently I had not made a fool of myself because the editor said, "Too bad they don't have any triple-zero beluga. It's perfect with the Krug."

Suddenly I heard myself saying, "If I can't have triple-zero, I'd rather not eat caviar at all." Phil looked rather stunned by this, but the editor smiled so warmly that I was soon disdaining black truffles. I had never actually eaten them, but I had once read an article by M. F. K. Fisher, who felt that they were vastly overrated. This stolen opinion earned me such a look of respect that I offered another: It was just a tragedy, I said, that the government kept all the real cheese from coming into the country. I waxed eloquent about the great cheeses made with the unpasteurized milk upon which the FDA frowned.

"But even in France," said the editor, "the quality of cheese is starting to decline. I'm going to Paris next month, and my expectations are very low."

"You have to get outside of Paris," I said, grateful, finally, to be on solid ground. "You have to go into the countryside." I told him about the cheese maker I had met when I had a summer job on the Île d'Oléron.

"You've eaten Oléron?" he asked. "I thought they weren't making that anymore." I wondered how he could possibly know such an obscure fact, but I did not let on. Acting utterly world-weary, I told him about my friend Marie, the last living creator of Oléron cheese. He was very impressed, and for a moment I almost liked him.

The food editor ordered for all of us. He ordered a lot. There were appetizers and a fish course. There was lamb from the Indonesian ovens. ("My father always ordered the lamb when he came to the Trader's," he said in a voice hinting at ancestral mansions and generations of family retainers. Under the table, Phil gave me a kick. Over the table, he raised his eyebrows. I giggled.)

Dinner went on for hours. Once we got past the competitive part, somewhere between the salad and the cheese course, it all got easier; and as we started on the third bottle of wine, it actually began to be fun.

Afterward we sipped cognac from big snifters that the sommelier warmed over candles. Wrapping my hands around the cozy chunk of glass, I watched the food editor push an unruly lock of curly black hair out of his eyes and realized that he wasn't as old as he'd seemed. I began to wonder if the early pompousness had been an act too. Maybe he thought that was how food editors were supposed to behave.

"When was the last time you were in France?" he asked suddenly.

"It's been years," I said sadly. "I haven't been able to afford a trip."

"You should make an effort," he said. "You're a restaurant critic; you don't want to seem provincial. Have you spent time in L.A.?"

"Almost none," I replied like a true citizen of Berkeley. "I can't stand the place."

"You have to rise above that," he said. "It's not Paris, of course, but you ought to know what's going on in the other part of the state. Los Angeles is starting to be a good restaurant town."

"Are you offering to pay for a trip?" I asked, looking up at him.

"Why not?" he replied. "After all, I *am* your editor."

▪ ▪ ▪

When I went down to breakfast the next morning, the sour smell of spilled wine rose up and hit me like a fist. The kitchen table was littered with peanut shells and crumpled napkins; dirty plates were piled high in the sink. Used coffee grounds, looking horrifyingly like ants, spilled crazily across the counter. I was cleaning up the mess, still jabbing angrily at the dishes, when Nick bounced cheerfully into the room asking, "So how was dinner?"

"Fine," I growled, muttering imprecations under my breath. Nick peered into the pan in which I was about to scramble eggs and said, "You aren't planning to cook those in butter are you?"

"Yes," I said.

"Didn't you read that article I left out for you yesterday?"

Actually, I had. Nick was constantly leaving me articles from worthy publications detailing all the reasons why I should not eat one or the other of my favorite foods. Butter was his most recent target; he was currently very big on soy.

"I won't eat tofu on my toast!" I was protesting when the phone rang. I picked it up and shouted, "Yes?"

"How was dinner?" It was Doug's calm voice.

I tried to visualize him as he spoke, to see the clean curve of his body, his earnest good looks. I imagined him with the prairie behind him, his toolbox at his feet, leaning into the phone. I thought of my behavior of the night before, all that bluffing about food, and a wave of embarrassment swept over me.

"Fine," I said. "How's Omaha?"

"Great!" he replied. "They love my work. The people here are really terrific."

He sounded so pleased with himself, so happy to be there, that I had a sudden thought that one of those terrific people might be a woman. But instead of posing that question, I asked for reassurance. "I'm really lonely without you," I said. "I hope you'll be home soon."

Doug missed his cue. "This won't be a short trip," he said. "Probably have to stay here longer than I expected. We've started testing a structure that's an ethereal tent. The strings stretch from a central pole so that they snatch music from the breeze. But it's got to be in the right site, and it'll take a while to find it."

"I really miss you," I said hopefully. Maybe I'd go out there for a few days. Maybe he'd ask me to.

"It's good to be in a completely different environment," he replied, bypassing yet another cue. "Omaha is surprisingly beautiful. I'm getting all kinds of new ideas."

"Doug!" I suddenly felt like a pathetic little kid, jumping up and down for attention. But instead of simply saying that I wanted to go to Omaha, I said, "I think we need to talk about whether all this traveling is a good idea."

"It's probably not," he said reasonably, "but as long as you're doing that job and I'm doing this one, I don't see that we have any choice."

I persisted. "But we're thirty-one years old and it's time we started thinking about having a family." Why couldn't he understand what I was saying?

"We do need to talk about it," he said, "but I think we should wait till we're together."

I knew I was being impossible, but I couldn't help myself. "You *do* want to have children, don't you?" I continued, knowing the answer. Having a family had always been part of our plan. All I really wanted Doug to say was that he missed me. But I had finally gotten his attention.

"I always assumed we would," he said reluctantly. "And I'm not against the idea. But now I'm not sure. I'm really excited about the way my work's been going, and I don't want to do anything to jeopardize that."

I gasped, feeling like a woman who has steamed open a letter addressed to someone else and uncovered a secret she did not want to know. By silently asking Doug to tell me that everything was the same, I had discovered that it was not. "So you might not want children at all?"

"Oh no," he gasped. And then, on an ascending note, "No, no, no!"

"What's the matter?" I asked, alarmed.

"All the strings just snapped. There's too much wind. I really have to go." Behind him I heard an urgent voice shouting, "Doug! Come quickly." The voice was female.

"You better go," I said, but my feelings were hurt. I felt shamed and, for the first time in eleven years, very alone. To reclaim my dignity I made a sudden decision. "I'm going to L.A.," I said. "This new food editor thinks I need to know the restaurants down there."

"That's a good idea," said Doug, his mind on the wind.

"Doug?" I said. "I love you." But it was too late; he had already hung up.

CRAB CAKES

I put down the phone and did what I always do when I'm upset: I cooked.

But this time I was making more than a meal. I was cooking in shorthand, sending a message to myself. Just look at this list of ingredients! Crabmeat, a true luxury, was definitely not on the Channing Way list of approved foods. For that very reason I found the sizzle each time a crab cake hit the butter in the pan profoundly satisfying.

I will say this: Everybody loved these crab cakes. Even Nick overcame his butter aversion long enough to say, "It's too bad Doug's not here to taste these. He would really have enjoyed them."

1 pound lump crabmeat
½ stick (¼ cup) unsalted
  butter
½ small onion, chopped
1 teaspoon coarse kosher salt
2 large eggs
1½ teaspoons Worcestershire
  sauce
1 teaspoon paprika
½ teaspoon freshly ground
  black pepper
2 tablespoons prepared tartar
  sauce
2 slices firm white sandwich
  bread torn into small
  pieces
6 tablespoons fresh bread
  crumbs

Pick over the crabmeat to remove any bits of shell and cartilage, being careful not to break up the lumps of crab.

Cook the onion and ½ of the teaspoon of salt in 1 tablespoon butter in a small skillet, over moderate heat, until the onion is softened. Let the mixture cool.

Whisk together the eggs, Worcestershire sauce, remaining salt, paprika, pepper, tartar sauce, and onion mixture. Gently fold in the crabmeat and torn bread (the mixture will be very wet). Gently form the mixture into six cakes, each about 3½ inches across and ¾ inch thick. Line a tray with a piece of wax paper just large enough to hold the cakes and sprinkle it with half of the bread crumbs. Set the crab cakes in one layer on top of the paper and sprinkle the tops with the remaining bread crumbs, patting them gently to adhere. Cover the crab cakes loosely with another sheet of wax paper and chill for 1 hour.

Melt the remaining 3 tablespoons of butter in a large nonstick skillet over moderately high heat until the foam subsides. Cook the crab cakes until golden brown, about 3 minutes on each side.

Makes 6 crab cakes.

3

PARIS

■ The Rent-A-Wreck I picked up at LAX was in better shape than my Volvo. The horn worked, the turn signals operated automatically, and the radio got both AM and FM; I hit a blues station and sang along with Willie Dixon as I turned onto the Santa Monica Freeway. The magazine was putting me up at the Beverly Wilshire hotel, and I loved the cool, opulent privacy of my room. L.A., I thought, as I drove to meet the food editor for dinner, might not be so bad.

The feeling lasted until I arrived at Ma Maison and saw the Jaguars, Rolls-Royces, and Mercedeses parked in front. How could I possibly hand my Rent-A-Wreck to the valet? I couldn't. I drove right past the restaurant and parked on the street. As I struggled to lock the door I was conscious that the damp night air was frizzing my hair. By the time I got to the restaurant I was excruciatingly aware that my dress was hemmed with Scotch tape and my shoes were in need of a shine.

But the restaurant's covered patio with its AstroTurf and white lawn furniture restored my confidence; Ma Maison was oddly tacky. The big red and blue beach umbrellas with the word RICARD splashed across them were meant to be raffish, but they were slightly pathetic. When the restaurant's owner looked me up and down in the appraising manner of aging Frenchmen who think women are good for only one thing, I straightened my back and stuck out my chin.

Patrick Terrail led me through the patio to the dim interior of the restaurant. He escorted me to a table, but it was so dark that all I could see was the outline of the food editor seated across from a massive man, a small mountain, planted at the far side. As we got closer I thought he looked vaguely familiar, but I couldn't remember his name.

"Colman," said Patrick in a sort of lewd Rod Stewart rasp, "your guest is here." The food editor leapt from his seat and introduced me to the mountain: It was Orson Welles! The actor surveyed me with intelligent eyes that seemed trapped in the flesh of his face. I shook the great man's hand, and then Colman and I followed Patrick out of the darkness to the twilight of the patio. Colman, I realized, reminded me of the natty young Welles of *Citizen Kane*, the ne'er-do-well who was thrown out of every elite American college. He held my chair as I sat down; a few hours earlier I would have found this hopelessly hokey.

We began with '66 Krug and a pot of caviar.

"Triple-zero?" I asked.

"Of course," he replied. "Let's just eat it with spoons."

The caviar was gray and glistened. When I put some on my tongue it was not salty, the way other caviar was, but seductively fruity with a taste that went on and on. I swallowed and the flavor resonated down my throat. Then I took a sip of champagne, and instead of washing the taste down it brought it back to life, sharper now and more intense. I closed my eyes.

I was somewhere else when a voice just above my head said,

"Colman!" I jumped and opened my eyes. A man in a tall white toque was standing at the table. He had a round face and a snub nose he kept rubbing with his finger, like a little boy. "Colman," he repeated in a thick Austrian accent, "shall I make a menu for you? I have a few dishes I would like you to try."

So this is how real restaurant critics live, I thought. Movie stars. Caviar. Special menus.

"Shall we let Wolfgang impress us?" Colman asked, cocking his head to one side.

The chef turned and looked at me imploringly, as if my opinion were the only thing in the world that mattered. "I've been doing something with oysters that I think you will like," he urged.

Unsure of what Colman wanted, ever so slightly I nodded my head.

"Good!" said the chef. "I go cook now." As he walked away Colman said, "Wolfgang Puck is the most talented young chef in Los Angeles. I think he's going to be important. I hope you like his food."

There were baked oysters wrapped in lettuce, sprinkled with caviar and bathed in beurre blanc. There was terrine de foie gras with warm toast. The flavors danced and the soft substances slid down my throat. We drank Corton-Charlemagne and talked about New York and Paris and Rome. It all felt unreal, as if our dialogue had been lifted from one of those 1930s movies where mink coats go flying out of windows and there are only happy endings. He was Cary Grant. I was Katharine Hepburn.

With the duck ("Just like Tour d'Argent") we drank a '75 Petit-Village (Colman had no use for old wine). And then we had a chunk of Roquefort and a wedge of Brie. As we ate the cheese, so ripe, so rich, Patrick passed the table and said, under his breath, "I smuggled it past customs in my underwear." I believed him.

Colman didn't like sweets, so I ate his dacquoise and then I ate mine. We had cognac. He smoked a cigar. Suddenly it was five hours later and the movie stars were all going home. By the time we were the only people in the restaurant, Patrick Terrail and Wolfgang Puck were sitting with us. We drank more cognac and talked about food. I felt beautiful and charming. I felt a million miles from Berkeley. Then Colman waved his hand and said, "Just put it on my account." I had never known anyone with a house account in a fancy restaurant before.

Colman pulled out my chair, put his arm around me, and asked where my car was. "Perfect," he said when I told him I had parked on the street, "we'll just come back for your car in the morning." He held the door for me.

"Yes," I said, walking through. The valet opened the car door. I climbed in.

▪ ▪ ▪

I woke up crying, stunned by my recklessness, wishing I could replay the night and give it a different ending. Overnight I had turned into some other person, become a stranger to myself. What had come over me? I was the least promiscuous person I knew. I had never even considered having an affair. In college my virginity had been a standing joke; guys whose names I did not know would sidle up and ask, "Still a virgin?" as if the very notion were ridiculous. Even now the number of men with whom I had slept would not fill the fingers of one hand.

I lay there, next to this man I barely knew, consumed with self-loathing. I berated myself for a while and then tried making it Doug's fault: If he didn't travel so much, none of this would have happened. That made me feel better, but not for long.

As daylight filtered into the room I weepily attempted to turn the situation into a soap opera. What would become of me when Doug discovered what I'd done? The two men dueled in the dusky room, leaping on chairs and making noble speeches, before the sheer ridiculousness of all that caught up with me. Doug would be hurt, but it would not be the end of the world, or even the end of the marriage. He knew that I loved him. Besides, it was not impossible that Doug was, at this very minute, in the arms of someone in Omaha. There was that female voice . . .

But I could not fool myself into believing that what Doug was up to had any bearing on why I had woken up in bed with a stranger. And that was what I had to figure out.

Colman was suave and handsome. He was wonderful company. But I had met other attractive men and never before been tempted to sleep with them. What was it that I found so irresistible about this man? I replayed the night in my head—the caviar, the oysters, the foie gras, the cigars. It had been like a wonderful dream, all my fantasies made real. Colman was like a character from some book I had read, like a man from another time, a bon vivant who had unabashedly devoted himself to food. He knew more about the subject than anyone I had ever met, and it suddenly occurred to me that if I had set out to invent the perfect man for this moment in my life, I could not possibly have done better.

Knowing this did not make me less fearful. I still wanted to get up, get dressed, and run home to the safety of Berkeley. But I resisted the impulse, and when Colman woke up, when he turned and said, "I know just where I'm going to take you for lunch," I smiled and said, "Can't wait."

■ ■ ■

"Are you still in Los Angeles?" my mother asked every day. "This is a very long trip."

"There are a lot of restaurants here," I said. "Besides, Doug's still in Omaha."

"How old is that new food editor of yours?" she asked suspiciously.

"Old, Mom," I said, stretching three years, "a lot older than me." I was grateful that Doug's radar was not as good as my mother's.

He called often, but each time it was only to say that he had to stay a little longer. The wind was with him, and in Omaha they really, really liked him.

▪ ▪ ▪

Colman had his own table at every restaurant in Los Angeles, and there was nothing he did not know about food.

"You've never tasted real mozzarella made with buffalo milk?" he asked one afternoon, sweeping me out the door. "I know just where to go." We drove to an industrial section of Santa Monica and went into a shabby-looking bar. "This is an Italian restaurant?" I asked, peering dubiously around a modest establishment.

"Wait," he said. A trim, handsome man appeared and began dancing happily around us. "Oh, Colman," he said in one of those absurdly romantic Italian accents, "you've come at the perfect moment. I have just returned from the airport. Look what I picked up!" He held out crumbling chunks of Parmesan cheese and glistening green bottles of olive oil.

"This is Piero Selvaggio," said Colman. "He can't get great Italian products here, so he's been importing what he needs."

"Wait until you taste these!" Piero exulted. "What a meal you will have!"

The two men huddled for a moment, deciding on a menu. Words like *focaccia, Amarone, vero olio* showered down on me and I snuggled into them in happy anticipation.

"Close your eyes," said Colman. He held out a glass, and I took a sip. The wine was sweet and bitter at the same time, with an enormous flavor. It tasted like cherries and almonds mixed over a smoky fire. "Mmmm," I said.

"Now taste this." He put the softest little ball of sweet, buttery cheese in my mouth. I swallowed, and it was like sunshine and green fields.

Then Piero bustled up with six bottles of extra-virgin olive oil and good bread and demanded we taste them all, one by one, and decide which we liked best. One was green and spicy, another heavy and slightly sweet. The differences were astounding.

We had come for lunch; we stayed through dinner.

■ ■ ■

When I told my mother that I was planning a trip to France, she was immediately suspicious. "Is that food editor of yours going to be there?" she demanded.

"He has nothing to do with it," I replied with as much dignity as I could muster. "He doesn't even know I'm going."

"But he will be there," she said.

"Yes," I replied in a very small voice. "He will."

"PussyCat," she said, "you're asking for trouble."

I certainly did not need her to tell me that. But ten minutes after Doug had called to say that his wind tent was progressing more slowly than he had anticipated and he would be in Omaha at least two more weeks, my friend Béatrice called from Paris. Her apartment in the Sixth Arrondissement was empty, and it was mine if I wanted it. I took this to be a sign from heaven. Within minutes I had found a student charter flight to London and invented an assignment.

■ ■ ■

I took the boat train from London to Paris, sitting up all night with the scruffy kids with knapsacks and high hopes. It all felt comfortingly familiar—the dim light, the furtive departure from Dover, the French douaniers at Calais stamping their feet in the early-morning cold. And then I was on a train speeding through the gray countryside and everyone around me was speaking French. For a moment I remembered the terrible homesickness I had felt in my first years at French boarding school, and a great wave of loneliness swept over me. What did I think I was doing? My mother's voice was in my ear, suddenly very loud. "People don't behave this way," she said disapprovingly. Before I could stop her, she went on. "It will serve you right if that food editor won't even see you. And then what will you do, Miss Smarty Pants, all by yourself in Paris?"

I didn't have an answer. So I drew the shabby silver-wolf coat from Value Village around my shoulders and stared out the window, wishing I were in Berkeley, where it was sunny and I was not alone.

It was a cold, misty day, and as I stepped onto the platform at the Gare du Nord the train coughed up clouds of vapor, which enveloped me in a man-made fog. I looked up, and the black train hunched its back like a malevolent cat and hissed angrily at me. It was such an unfriendly sound that it suddenly hit me that I had only an address and Béatrice's assurance that she had written a note to the concierge. A sudden vision materialized: the concierge, looking me up and down and dismissing me with a curt, "Je n'en sais rien. On ne m'avait rien dit. Au revoir, mademoiselle." I looked down at my shoes and wished, once again, that I had thought to polish them.

The Métro was filled with people looking very purposeful, on their way to work. Watching them reading their papers and scurrying off to their jobs made me feel foreign, aimless, and alone; by the time I reached my stop I was so homesick I could barely drag myself from the train. I tried to shake myself out of the mood; I knew it was ridiculous. And then I climbed out into the air and started searching for the rue Auguste Comte, a bit startled by the elegance of the neighborhood.

Béatrice lived in a pale Beaux-Arts beauty of a building, with baroque curves and graceful wrought-iron balconies. I patted my hair, wishing it looked less like a rat's nest, and bit my lips to give them color before pushing open the huge wooden door into the entryway.

"Vous désirez?" the concierge inquired. Her voice was like ice. She was exactly what I had expected: a small, officious woman with short, sensible black hair and shapeless, colorless clothes. My French deserted me completely, and I stammered in English, "I am the friend of Béatrice du Croix. I will be staying in her apartment?"

She fumbled for her glasses and peered at me. "Je ne parle pas anglais," she said shortly, and turned to go.

"Je m'excuse," I said quickly, a flood of French coming to my rescue. "Le voyage était si fatigant. Je suis l'amie de Béatrice du Croix. Nous nous connaissions à l'école. Elle m'avait gracieusement offert son appartement."

"Elle parle!" said the concierge sarcastically. She did not encourage me to continue.

"On ne vous a rien dit sur moi?" I continued, a bit desperately. Already I saw myself on the street.

"Oui, mademoiselle," she finally conceded. She went to a desk, pulled out a large iron key, and handed it to me. She sniffed. "Troisième étage. Vous avez deux semaines. Au revoir." And she shut the door, leaving me in the blackness of the hall.

"Welcome to France," I muttered as I pressed the light for the landing. It sputtered reluctantly on, and I started the climb.

But once I had shut the door behind me, none of that mattered. It was a wonderful apartment, filled with light even on this gray day. I went to the window and looked out over the Luxembourg Gardens. And then I put my clothes into the beautiful eighteenth-century carved wooden armoire, climbed into the enormous sleigh bed covered with embroidered linen sheets, and fell fast asleep.

I woke up ravenous and went to explore the tiny Parisian kitchen. The refrigerator was a little box beneath a marble counter, but when I opened it I found bottled water, a few gnarled apples that looked like windfalls, a package of butter, a wedge of Chaource, and three bottles of Pouilly-Fumé. Two cracked blue bowls held brown eggs and walnuts, still in the shell. An ancient heel of bread sat on the counter, surrounded by bowls of spices, olive oil, vinegar, and a couple of bottles of vin ordinaire. This would certainly do.

I sliced the bread as thinly as I could and toasted it to make crackers. I put the cheese on a plate, surrounded it with sliced apples, and made myself an omelette. Then I poured myself a glass of wine and sat eating my good French omelette and my cheese and crackers, thinking that I was being a guest to myself and feeling very much like M. F. K. Fisher.

I piled the dishes into the sink and went to draw a bath in the enormous clawfoot tub. I found some crystals in a big glass, and when I sprinkled them into the water the tub began to fill with mounds of white bubbles. I poured myself another glass of wine and stepped into the bath. For a long time I lay there in the clean steam, feeling my body relax in the warmth. I would spend the afternoon at the Louvre.

Wrapped in towels, I wandered back into the bedroom and noticed the phone. It was an enameled white antique, perfect for calling your lover. I stared at it as I considered what to say to Colman. I lay back on the lacy sheets and downy pillows. Somewhere out in the Gardens someone was playing a flute, and I followed the thread of music. There was plenty of time; lulled by Mozart and the featherbed, I drifted off to sleep.

It was dark when I woke up, and I was momentarily disoriented. What time was it? Without stopping to consider what I was doing, I reached for the phone and called Colman's hotel.

Waiting for the desk to connect me with his room, I panicked and hung up. My heart was thumping loudly in my chest. What if he was not alone? What if he wouldn't see me? I felt vulnerable and foolish and frightened, and by the time I got the courage to call back my hands were shaking.

Then his deep voice was in my ear and it went through me like a shock. "Where are you?" he asked.

"In Paris," I said.

"What are you doing here?" he demanded. He sounded irritated.

"Visiting friends," I answered.

"Is Doug with you?"

"No, I'm alone."

"Well," he said, considering, "we should get together sometime. But I was just on my way out to meet someone for dinner. Why don't you give me your number, and I'll call you in the next few days?"

I gave him my number, and he hung up. I wished I could snatch the call back. The days stretched out, empty, before me. Ten days was a long time. Why had I come? Maybe I could find an earlier plane home.

I burrowed into the pillows, ready to escape back into sleep. In the morning I would make a program, keep myself busy. I'd go to Beaubourg, spend a day at the Louvre, wander through the market on the rue du Cherche-Midi. If Colman called, I'd have lots to tell him . . .

But what if he called tomorrow? I had never had a fancy meal by myself. I wasn't even hungry. But Colman would not waste his time in Paris making omelettes. What would he do? He would probably go to Taillevent or Tour d'Argent and eat a ten-course meal capped off with cognac and a fat cigar. Well, if he could do it, so could I; I was not going to tell him I had fasted on my first night in Paris.

Taillevent and Tour d'Argent were booked, but Guy Savoy was happy to provide a table for a single cover. How soon could I be there?

On the Métro I eavesdropped on my neighbors, trying to fix the sound of French in my ear. I did not want to seem like a tourist in the restaurant. When I arrived I said my name as carefully as possible, hoping that they would not know I was American. The maître d'hôtel seated me at a small table near the bar and asked if I would like an aperitif.

"Une coupe de champagne," I heard myself saying, to my surprise. He went to get it, returning with a little dish of salted, buttered nuts, tiny puffs of warm cheese gougères, and the menu.

I asked for the wine list as well, and the captain looked pleased with me. He returned, and we gravely discussed the possibilities for the evening. It took us fifteen minutes to arrive at a decision, but when we were done he assured me that I would be very content with my meal.

Though uninvited, my mother appeared with the first course. "Is this how you will spend the next ten days?" she inquired. "Eating absurdly expensive food all by yourself? Trying to impress waiters? Where will the money come from?"

"Be quiet, please," I said. "I'm busy. I want to remember every detail of this soup." I described it for myself, the cream, the truffles, the faintly nutty flavor that could only be sherry.

"He won't call anyway," she said, meanly I thought. I ordered a half bottle of Chassagne-Montrachet to go with the terrine de poisson and tried to describe the captain's demeanor as he served it. "When I came in," I told my phantom mother, "he thought to himself, Oh, a woman, she'll have the salad and some plain fish, and he was sorry he had taken the reservation. But I have turned out to be someone who likes to eat, and now he is a happy man."

"You're not going to order more wine, are you?" she asked with some alarm.

"Try me," I said, ordering a half bottle of '70 Palmer. Mom looked at the price and was scandalized, but the captain looked at me with serious interest and leaned in to ask how I liked it. I took one sip and thought how there is nothing, really nothing, like great wine. Mom just faded, like the Cheshire cat, as I began to describe the taste of the special lamb raised on the salt marshes of the Landes to myself. And to Colman. I was not lonely.

I had dacquoise for dessert, thinking of Los Angeles, and then, just because it seemed sporting, I ordered cognac with my coffee.

The room was practically empty now, but my captain urged me to have another glass of cognac as he set down the petits fours and macaroons and chocolates. I was sated and sleepy, however, and wanted nothing so much as to be in bed. "Our driver will take you home," said the captain as I paid the (enormous) bill. I added another hundred francs to the tip; it was still cheaper than a taxi.

I barely remember walking up the stairs, and I don't remember taking off my clothes or getting into bed. But when the phone's irritating beeping began to sound, that is where I was. I groped for the receiver, knocking the phone off the stand as I did so.

"Bonjour!" said Colman's voice in my ear. "Tu dormais?"

"Yes," I said, "I *was* asleep."

"Well, you're wasting your time in Paris. Get up. Get out. Come meet me for coffee."

"What time is it?" I asked.

"Time to get up," he said. "It's nine. Meet me in half an hour at the café at the foot of the boulevard Saint-Michel, just before the bridge. It's called Le Départ. I'll be there at nine-thirty."

I thought you were busy.

I can't possibly be there in half an hour.

You can't just snap your fingers.

I contemplated saying all those things, but what I really said was "Okay."

As soon as I hung up, I began to worry. Why had he called now? I knew that he was going to tell me that I should not have come, that he did not want to see me. It was like him to do it in person instead of on the phone. And to get it out of the way.

Well, I wasn't going to make it easy for him. I took my time, changed my clothes three times, wanting to make him regret what he was about to lose. I put on my green velvet skirt and a purple silk blouse, and then I changed it for a pair of plain black pants and then went back to velvet. Was this best? I didn't know, but now I was so late that I threw on the silver wolf and left.

▪ ▪ ▪

Colman was sitting at a table by himself, tapping his paper irritably against the table. He stopped in mid-tap when he saw me and just looked up, without saying anything. I had planned to shake his hand, but instead I just sat down across from him and stared.

He looked wonderful in Paris. His hair was very black, and in his good clothes he looked like neither a Frenchman nor a tourist but some prosperous cosmopolitan who was at home in the world.

"Café?" he asked. I nodded. "Un crème," he said to the waiter; his accent wasn't bad, but it was clear he was not French. For the first time in my life I was glad my mother had sent me off to that French school. Just to show off, I said to the waiter, "Je voudrais aussi une tartine," because the words are hard for an American to pronounce correctly.

"Why is everybody ordering bread and butter this morning?" the waiter wondered in French. "I haven't sold a croissant."

"Oh," I replied, "it's the weather. Some days are just bread-and-butter days."

Colman seemed impressed by the exchange.

The coffee was just bitter enough. The bread, a skinny ficelle, crackled when I bit into the crust. The crumb was white and soft, and the butter was cold and sweet against it. "This is why I came," I said to Colman, and for that moment I meant it. "It's like having France in my mouth. If I stay away too long I forget the flavor."

Colman leaned across the table and took both my hands in his. "I'm so glad you're here," he said. "How long are you staying?"

"Ten days," I said.

"Well, we have to make them count."

I had clearly said the right thing.

■ ■ ■

My Paris was uncomfortable pensions on the outskirts of town, cheap meals that started with watery soup and ended with watery flan. It was always being cold. It was hours peering through the gloom of the badly lighted Louvre.

Colman's Paris was not mine.

He liked to start the day by strolling through the flower market and listening to the birds. Every morning he woke me with fresh flowers. Then he took me to Ladurée for coffee and croissants and we sat there, beneath the ancient paintings of nymphs and angels, bantering with the waitresses in their black dresses and white aprons. After three days we were regulars, and they didn't even ask what we wanted, but simply put out the pots of coffee and hot milk, and the plates of croissants.

He showed me streets I had never seen before and small, out-of-the-way museums. He took me to the cemetery and we danced around Proust's tomb, and afterward we went to Le Petit Zinc and ate platters of claires and spéciales washed down with a cold, crisp Sancerre. We walked along the Seine in the damp November air, and when my feet got cold he insisted on taking me to the nearest shop to buy me a pair of boots.

"But I've never spent two hundred dollars on a pair of boots," I protested, looking at the soft maroon leather he'd picked out.

"And you aren't now," he said.

"It's so extravagant," I protested.

"But do you like them?" he wanted to know. And of course I did.

Colman never considered the price. Of anything. He bought first-class tickets for the Métro and front-row seats for the Opéra. At night, walking along Saint-Michel, we went in and out of jazz clubs and he introduced me to the joys of La Vieille Prune. I loved the way it tasted, like gentle cognac.

"That first day," I said one night, after my third Prune, "you were going to tell me to go away. Weren't you?"

Colman looked down at me. "Was I?" he asked. "I don't remember." It wasn't like him to be clumsy, and I had a fleeting thought that there might have been another woman. If there was, I didn't want to know about it. "Besides," he said, catching himself, "that was a different time. It was before we had Paris."

■ ■ ■

"You think these things happen," I wrote one night in my journal as Colman lay in the other room, sleeping. He, no surprise, had not just a room but a suite. "And of course they do—sometimes—but never to you. Or you think that when they do you'll be too dumb to recognize it. But there it is, it's actually happening, and even I'm not so stupid that I don't enjoy every second. Both of us keep pinching ourselves. Is this really taking place?"

I watched us as if we were strangers, kissing and laughing on the Métro, incapable of keeping our hands off each other. I envied us, even as I lived it. We were the people everyone smiles at. It wouldn't last. This was the least sensible thing I had ever done in my life.

■ ■ ■

"Wear your best dress tonight," said Colman.

"Where are we going?"

"You'll see."

He took me the long way round, to get me lost, and then he made me close my eyes for the last few blocks. When I opened them we were standing in front of Tour d'Argent. "This is where we are dining."

"My first three-star restaurant," I said. And for a moment I thought what it would be like to go to a three-star restaurant with Doug. I was a restaurant critic, but I was still green enough that fancy places made me nervous. If I were with Doug we would both be embarrassed, and we'd get the worst table in the house and spend the whole night worrying about how much money we were spending.

But Colman had no shame. He gave his name at the front and the owner rushed up to shake his hand and lead us to a table by the window. "My nephew told me to take very good care of you," he said as he pulled out the chair. "Is that chef he has at Ma Maison really as good as he says?"

Colman nodded. "Better," he said.

"Well," said Monsieur Terrail, "we'll have to see if we can't impress you even more than he does." He opened a bottle of Krug '66 and poured us each a glass. Then he disappeared. Colman raised his glass and suddenly I saw, through the bubbles, Notre Dame flooded with silvery light just across the Seine.

Dinner was a dance. Colman and Monsieur Terrail were moving in perfect time to the music, and I floated along between them as they dipped and swayed. What would we drink with the foie gras frais? Colman thought perhaps a Meursault, an older one. Ah yes, Monsieur Terrail was in perfect agreement; it was a fine thing, he thought, to have such a sympathetic guest. The wine would be very nice, did he not agree, with the brouillade aux truffes?

The foie gras was molten velvet in my mouth, and when I took a sip of wine the flavor became even more intense, richer and rounder than it already was. Colman looked at me, and I felt the thrill all the way down to my fingertips. I understood, for the first time ever, why those turn-of-the-century restaurants had private rooms with velvet couches. I would have liked a couch.

The scrambled eggs with truffles were even better than the foie gras. Minutes earlier I would not have thought it possible. Each forkful was like biting off a piece of the sun. It was like musk and light, all at once, and suddenly I burst out, "This is what I always imagined sex would taste like."

Colman put back his head and roared. "Being with you," he said, "is just like being by myself. Only better." And he picked up my hand, across the table, and kissed it.

Monsieur Terrail was back now, lighting a candle. He crooned a little as he decanted the wine, and I knew it must be very, very good.

"What is it?" I whispered.

"Oh," said Colman. "A Petit-Village from my birth year." He looked a bit smug and said, "You know, '45 was a very good year."

"And '48?" I asked.

"Not as good," he said. And then, quickly, "But a very good year for women."

I thought, briefly, of what the world was like when the wine was put into the bottle. Paris was being liberated; there was dancing in the streets. I imagined I could taste all that. Afterward there was sorbet and framboises Chantilly and an ancient cognac. "This is probably costing more than I make in a year," I said to Colman.

"Probably," he said. "You know, I was thinking that tomorrow we could take the train to Boyer for lunch. It's only got two stars, but it will probably get its third this year. I want you to taste la fameuse truffe en croûte."

We were very drunk walking back to his hotel, and I put my head on his chest as we walked, listening to his deep, wonderful voice resonating through his coat. I wanted the night to never end.

We did go to Boyer the next day, where we drank antique Roederer champagne from 1911. "I hope I'm this vibrant when I'm sixty-seven," said Colman. There was a kind of magic to champagne that old, a wine bottled before automobiles or airplanes or either of the major wars. A wine bottled before women had the vote. Watching the liquid come sparkling into my glass, I thought of all the years it had been waiting in that dark bottle, what a different world it was emerging into. I was drinking history; I liked the taste.

The whole truffle was incredible too; it looked like a lump of coal wrapped up in pastry. The crust was flaky, but once I got through I hit the truffle, which tasted the way a forest smells in autumn when the leaves are turning colors and someone, far off, is burning them.

Colman watched as I ate; I could feel my cheeks get flushed. "I always thought truffles were overrated," I said. "I had no idea. Thank you."

He took my hand, caressed it. "Tomorrow," he said, "I have another surprise." There was an odd look on his face, dreamy and wistful. "I am going to introduce you to someone very special."

I couldn't imagine who it might be.

▪ ▪ ▪

A marcassin, the hide of a young wild boar, was stretched across the door of the restaurant we were approaching. "You don't see that much anymore," said Colman. "But this is an old-fashioned bistro, the real thing."

"Chez Isadore," I read, looking at the writing above the boar's prickly speckled fur. "Is it Isadore I'm here to meet?"

"No," he said. He led me inside, where it was warm and steamy and smelled like butter, onions, wine, and meat. The room was filled with solid people, planted firmly at their tables. A man in a long white apron, platters stacked up his arms, whirled through the room, bantering as he delivered food. "Monsieur Colman!" he cried joyfully when he spotted us. He cocked his head and looked quizzically at me. "Is this . . . ?" he asked. Colman shook his head, almost imperceptibly, and then quickly said, "This is my good friend Ruth, from California."

With a puzzled look on his face, Isadore took my hand politely.

"Monsieur awaits you," he said, leading us to a large table beneath the mirror in the corner.

A short, quite stout older man with a bald, shiny head was sitting there reading a newspaper. He beckoned happily when he saw us—he had beautiful hands—and stood up, painfully, as we approached. He looked exactly the way I have always imagined A. J. Liebling, which I found oddly disconcerting.

The man embraced Colman as well as he could, given that he was half his size. He showered upon him one of those loving looks usually reserved for one's children, and I wondered if he might be Colman's father. I thought he had told me that his parents were dead.

"So this is why we have seen so little of you." The man looked me up and down, very frankly, and I was a little embarrassed by the scrutiny. "Je m'appelle Claude," he said, taking my hand. Then he turned to Colman and said—reproachfully, I thought—"Pepita has missed you."

"How is she?" asked Colman.

He sighed. "Fragile, I am afraid. But come, what am I thinking of? Let us sit down. I have taken the liberty of ordering. Do you mind?"

Even dining with him was the way I had always imagined a meal with A. J. Liebling. We were no sooner seated than Isadore arrived with trays of oysters—spéciales and claires—balanced on each arm. He set them on the table—four of them!—and poured glasses of Sancerre. "Never stint on oysters," said Claude. "It takes away the pleasure." He picked up an oyster, gave it a solid squeeze of lemon, and raised it to his mouth. "Ah," he said when he had downed it. "They are excellent! We must have more." He beckoned Isadore to bring another platter.

As he ate he asked questions. Where was I from, why was I here, what had I thought of Boyer? He asked about my family, my work, my hopes. Before the oysters were half gone he had collected an entire dossier on me. "Are you a reporter?" I asked, taken aback by the intensity of the interview.

"Bravo, ma fille!" he said. "I was, for more than fifty years, before I retired. That is how I met Colman's family. I was sent to California when he was a small boy. Pepita and I could never have children, and so I have always thought of Colman as a little bit my own. Now we will have some grilled sardines; Isadore says they are excellent today, and he has never misled me." He turned to Colman. "Tell me, shall we have a different wine?"

"I was thinking of Burgundy with the sardines," said Colman, who always sped through the whites in his rush to the reds.

"My sentiments precisely," said Claude. "I have trained you well."

Then there was a roast partridge with an enormous pile of crisp, hot frites. It tasted wild and funky, with that high, almost electric note you find only in birds that have never been caged. "The secret," said Claude, "is in hanging the birds long enough. When I was a boy every bistro in Paris knew how to hang its meat, but Isadore is one of the last of the breed. In other restaurants partridge is no better than chicken. Worse, in fact; it's dry chicken."

Colman was saying very little, just watching the interchange between this wonderfully crusty old Frenchman and me. I thought, from the expression on his face, that I was doing pretty well. Still, when Isadore arrived with a bottle of Bordeaux and began decanting it, I felt momentary panic. More?

"The marcassin, of course," said Claude. "You must try it. Marcassin is disappearing in France; in ten more years it will be gone." I took a bite and words like "morne," "farouche," and "goût de terroir" came leaping to my lips. I was a little drunk, and Colman and Claude were egging me on.

When the boar was gone there was still wine in the bottle. "A pity to waste this, don't you think?" asked Claude, summoning Isadore to the table. The room was starting to empty out of patrons and fill up with the scent of cigars. It was so much like going back sixty years to that fantasy Paris of the twenties that I was almost in tears. I wished I were wearing an ankle-length black skirt instead of pants, and a white lace blouse. "Do you have a piece of cheese hidden away, a piece of cheese that will do this Pauillac justice?" asked Claude.

Isadore considered. "Bien sûr," he said. "I think perhaps the aged Gouda would do very well. I have had it in the cellar for two years, and it has a roundness the wine will like." He rushed off to fetch it, and Colman excused himself.

"Well, ma fille," said Claude when we were alone. "How did you come to be in Paris?"

"Oh," I said flippantly, "I followed Colman here."

"He didn't invite you?" he asked gleefully. Why was he so happy about this? Did he enjoy the notion of women throwing themselves at his adopted son?

"No," I said, "he didn't invite me. But I hoped that he would spend some time with me if I came. I didn't quite imagine, though, that it would be like this."

"Like this?" he inquired.

"Love," I breathed, taking another sip of the wine. "I didn't expect to fall in love."

Claude looked alarmed. "L'amour?" he asked. "Vraiment?" He peered deeply into my eyes, as if my answer really mattered. I couldn't see why he cared so much, but once again I had the nagging thought that there might be another woman in Colman's life. "But aren't you married?"

"Yes," I said.

"And are you going to tear your life up for Colman?"

I shook my head. "No, I am not. Even if I wanted to leave my husband, which I don't, I do not think that we would make a very good married couple. This is just . . ." I searched for the right word. "Magique" is what I came up with. That seemed right. "A moment of pure magic," I repeated. "I am grateful for it. But I know it would not last."

He nodded. "I have found," he said, "that in marriage friendship is sometimes more important than passion."

"Yes," I said. "And my husband is a very good friend."

Claude looked relieved. He liked me well enough, I could see that. He liked the fact that I spoke French. He liked my appetite. But he did not think that I would suit as Colman's wife.

Colman returned, and Claude nodded reassuringly at him. Colman looked relieved, and I felt as if something important had just taken place but I did not know what it was. But then Colman took my hand and the moment passed and we had framboises with Chantilly and cognac and the two men filled the air with the smoke from their cigars. It was dark by the time we left the restaurant, and we put Claude into a taxi and walked all the way back to Colman's hotel, singing.

■ ■ ■

I was supposed to take the night train back to London, but Colman persuaded me to take the new fast hovercraft across the Channel and spend another day in Paris. When I wavered he just went and bought the ticket. And so we had one more day. And then it really was time for me to leave; I could hardly imagine a life without him anymore. "Stay," he said, laying a bunch of roses on the pillow next to me. "You could take a plane tomorrow and we could still have another day in Paris."

I shook my head. "I'm already gone. It has to end sometime."

"Okay," he said. "I'll take you to the train. We have time for coffee."

"Vous partez?" said our wonderful waitress at Ladurée. "C'est triste. I am so in the habit of seeing you two lovers." And she brought us each a hazelnut-filled croissant and would not let us pay. I bit into it, trying to memorize the taste. "A week from today I'll be sitting at the kitchen table in Berkeley," I mused, "eating a bowl of millet. And you, what will you be doing a week from this moment?"

Colman reached across the table and took my hand. "I guess the time has come," he said, taking a deep breath. "I don't quite know how to tell you this. But . . ."

"What?" I asked. He looked so stricken that I tried to make things easier. "Don't worry," I said. "We can still see each other. It just won't be the same."

He took another breath, as if to say something, and then stopped. He took my hand and said sadly, "No, it will never be the same again."

DACQUOISE

There was a time, in the late seventies, when it seemed that every French restaurant in Paris, Los Angeles, and New York served dacquoise. For me it is still more than a dessert; it is a promise that something wonderful is about to happen.

FOR THE ALMOND MERINGUE
1 1/4 cups whole blanched
  almonds
3/4 cup plus 2 tablespoons
  granulated sugar
1 tablespoon cornstarch
6 large egg whites
1/4 teaspoon cream of tartar
pinch of salt

FOR THE MOCHA BUTTERCREAM
1 cup granulated sugar
6 large egg yolks
1/2 cup heavy cream
2 tablespoons instant espresso
1/4 teaspoon salt
2 sticks (1 cup) unsalted
  butter, softened

Garnish: 1/4 cup sliced toasted almonds and confectioners' sugar for
  dusting

TO MAKE THE MERINGUE

Preheat the oven to 275°F. Line two large baking sheets with parchment paper and on each draw a 10-inch circle, using the bottom of a 10-inch springform pan as a guide. Flip the paper over (the circle will show through).

Pulse the nuts in a food processor with 2 tablespoons of the granulated sugar until ground fine. Add the cornstarch and pulse until combined. Beat the egg whites with the cream of tartar and a pinch of salt in a standing electric mixer on high speed until soft peaks form. Gradually beat in the remaining ¾ cup sugar on low speed, then beat on high speed until it forms stiff, glossy peaks. Fold in the almond mixture gently but thoroughly.

Divide the meringue mixture between the two parchment circles, spreading to fill in the circles evenly. Bake the meringues in the upper and lower thirds of the oven, switching the position of the baking sheets halfway through baking, until firm and pale golden, about 1 hour. Slide the parchment paper with the meringues from the sheets and place on racks to cool.

TO MAKE THE BUTTERCREAM

Beat the egg yolks with ½ cup sugar in a standing electric mixer on high speed until thick and pale, about 4 minutes. While the yolks are beating, whisk the heavy cream with the remaining ½ cup sugar in a small saucepan and bring to a boil, stirring, until sugar is dissolved. Gradually whisk half of the hot cream into the yolk mixture to temper the eggs; then whisk the yolk mixture into the remaining hot cream, along with the instant espresso powder and salt.

Cook the custard over moderate heat, stirring constantly, until an instant-read thermometer registers 170°F. Transfer the mixture to the clean bowl of the standing electric mixer and beat until cooled completely. Beat in butter 1 tablespoon at a time and chill, covered, for at least 30 minutes.

TO ASSEMBLE THE DACQUOISE

Carefully remove the meringues from the parchment and spread one meringue (smooth side down) evenly with the buttercream. Top the buttercream with the remaining meringue (smooth side up) and decorate the outside edges of the buttercream with toasted almonds. Chill the dacquoise, loosely covered, until firm, at least 2 hours; before serving, dust the top with confectioners' sugar.

Serves 8 to 10.

COOK'S NOTES

Meringues may be made one day ahead and kept in an airtight container at room temperature.

For a taller dacquoise, make three 7-inch meringue circles instead of two 10-inch ones (the baking time will be slightly less). Sandwich the meringues with buttercream and decorate in the same manner.

I've found that the easiest way to cut dacquoise is with a serrated bread knife, sawing rather than using pressure.

4

BLOW YOUR
SOCKS OFF

■ Home again.

I'd get up in the morning, stare at the seven huge recycling bags beneath the sink, and find myself filled with despair. I was always cold. Berkeley is not warm in winter, but at Channing Way we did not turn on the heat unless you could actually see your breath in the living room. This was not a money-saving gesture; it was a political statement, our contribution to the environment. I knew it was a noble cause, but it gave me one more reason to yearn for Paris.

I had known the trip was dangerous, understood that I was asking for grief. But I had underestimated the risks. It had not occurred to me that the fantasy of the affair would make my real life so unsatisfactory. I dreamed of truffles as I cooked dinner for the guests who turned up every night, stretching a single chicken to feed twelve. Baking the wholesome whole-wheat bread of which we approved I'd remember the delicious crackle of biting into one of Poliâne's crusty loaves. Holding my breath as I turned the compost pile with the pitchfork, I'd think of wild berries and mountain greens at the fragrant market on the rue du Cherche-Midi.

The hardest part of having an affair is hiding your emotions. Living in a commune made it more difficult; I had six people to pretend to, six people to convince that I was happy to be home.

More, really. Our house was always crowded. People sat in the kitchen having political discussions about the Shah of Iran. They sat in the frigid front room drinking wine and watching reruns of *Mary Hartman, Mary Hartman* on our blurry television set. There was always someone out in the workshop with Nick, or down in the darkroom with Jules.

They came because they were lonely and wanted company, or because they were traveling and in need of a bed. They came because they were hungry and there was always room for one more at the table on Channing Way. I had always loved this energy, thrived on the excitement, but after Paris my feelings changed.

"I'm tired of living in this mess!" I raged to Doug one morning, as we picked up the detritus from yet another late-night revel. I plunged my hands into the soapy water of the sink and handed him a wineglass. He had returned from Omaha, flushed with success, at the same time I returned from Paris. His wind tent had been ephemeral, and so lovely that a wealthy Philadelphia collector had heard about it and insisted on having one for her Main Line mansion. Doug was heading out, again. "If you charge this woman a lot of money, we could move," I said. "We could afford to have a child."

"I'm just not ready," said Doug, rubbing the glass so hard it began to sing. "Maybe in a couple of years. But right now I need to focus on my career. I don't have time to think about having children."

"You mean you don't want to spend time thinking about our relationship," I said, handing him another glass.

"Don't *you* want to focus on your career right now?" he asked, holding the glass up to the light.

"I don't see it as an either-or proposition," I said, realizing that we were finally having the long-delayed conversation. "Being a restaurant critic and being a mother are not mutually exclusive. We would both have to make adjustments, but most people manage. We've been together eleven years. We have to think about children."

Doug shook his head. "The timing's not right for me," he said. "At the moment my art comes first."

"But you'll feel different later on?" I said. "In a year or two?" It was not really a question, because despite what Doug had said when he was in Omaha, I thought I knew the answer.

Doug surprised me. He set the glass on the counter and put his hand down into the soapy water so he could take mine. "I've been thinking about this a lot," he said, stroking my soap-slicked palm, "and I want to be honest with you. I'm not sure."

The room got colder. "You mean there's a possibility you might not want children at all?" I asked.

"Yes," he said. "There is that possibility."

It was the first time he had actually uttered those words, and I went silent with shock. At last I managed to say, "I wish you'd told me earlier." Then I walked out the back door to my little studio on the porch.

"I didn't know," he said, starting to follow me. At the stairs he changed his mind and turned back.

I walked into my workroom feeling dizzy. I had never seriously considered the possibility that Doug and I might have different plans for the future. What else was there that I did not know about him? In a moment of defiance I turned on the electric heater I had sneaked into my studio; at least I would be warm.

My little workroom, with its sagging floor and cracked windows, felt exactly like a tree house. It was filled with crippled flea market furniture I had accumulated over the years; the desk was a legless library table propped on two-by-fours, and the chair was a swivel affair from the forties missing most of its springs. Piles of colorful threadbare rugs covered the gaps in the floor, the windowsills were filled with toys, and drawings were tacked to all the walls. Plants were everywhere, stretching for the light. It was the one room in the house that was completely my own.

I looked around at the bright colors and thought of Doug's spare studio. Our differences had seemed so superficial; it had never occurred to me that they might run deep. Perhaps he was not the person I thought I knew. If he really didn't want children, maybe I had never known him at all.

What now? With uncanny timing, Colman chose that precise moment to call. "I miss you," he said. "Come to L.A. for the day."

It was one answer. This time it was an escape.

■ ■ ■

Other men would have been carrying flowers. Not Colman. When my plane landed in Burbank he was standing at the gate with his hands behind his back. He kissed me and said, "Close your eyes and open your mouth." I sniffed the air; it smelled like a cross between violets and berries, with just a touch of citrus. My mouth closed around something very small and quite soft, the size of a little grape but with a scratchy surface. "Do you like it?" he asked anxiously.

I tasted spring.

"They're fraises des bois, from France!" He slipped another in my mouth.

"We have six hours," I said, savoring the flavor, back in the fantasy of romance. "I have to be on the four forty-five plane to Oakland. If I miss it there's no way I can explain what I'm doing in L.A."

"Six hours," Colman replied, "is almost forever."

■ ■ ■

Sometimes he flew north and we drove to Napa in my beat-up Volvo. Once we went as far as Mendocino, trying to recapture the romance of Paris. But time and distance were taking their toll on this relationship as well, and I could feel Colman drifting away. A couple of months after we got back from Paris he came north to take me to a dinner in Sacramento, and when I picked him up at the airport I had the distinct feeling that he wished he were going alone.

Although he was edgy, he could not ruin my mood. I had told Doug that I was going to Sacramento with some colleagues, and it was such a relief not to be sneaking around that my mood was buoyant. If I got home late, it wouldn't matter. I tried teasing Colman as we drove, but he seemed so distant that by the time we reached Sacramento I finally asked, "Did something happen this week?"

"No, why?" he said, directing me into a residential neighborhood filled with low ranch houses. "Turn right here."

"I don't see any restaurants," I said.

"I never said we were going to a restaurant," he snapped. Something *had* happened. "Here's the house." It looked like all the others on the street, but for one thing: the Alfa Romeo in the driveway. Its plates read OINOS.

"Latin?" I asked.

"Greek," he said, in a tone implying that any idiot would know that fact. "It means wine. It belongs to Darrell Corti, who knows more about food and wine than anyone else in America."

"Even you?" I teased.

He didn't even smile. "We call him the walking encyclopedia," he said curtly, ringing the doorbell.

Without waiting for an answer Colman opened the door and walked into the living room. Moving through, I had a vague impression of overstuffed furniture, rugs, and paintings. It looks like one of my mother's friends' houses, I thought. And then we were in the kitchen, and that didn't look like anything I'd ever seen. It was large and astonishingly well equipped. A smallish man wearing a V-neck cashmere sweater and a tie was leaning against an enormous refrigerator, holding a phone and gesticulating wildly as he carried on a conversation in Italian. Something simmered deliciously on a commercial stove, and a table held a heap of caviar, set on ice. The man's voice got louder. He ran his hand, passionately, through his wavy black hair. Then he slammed down the phone.

"What was that about?" asked Colman.

"A recipe," the man replied, pouring vodka into little iced glasses and handing them to us. The phone rang. He ignored it. He pointed to the caviar. "I'm Darrell," he said. "Taste that. I made it myself."

"You made caviar?" I asked.

"Certainly," he replied. "Why not? There is a very interesting possibility that we might resurrect the caviar industry here in California."

"I didn't know you could make caviar," I said, and immediately wished I had kept quiet. Colman shot me a furious look and then, as if to cover it, piled some caviar onto a mother-of-pearl spoon, tasted it thoughtfully, and shook his head.

"I know," said Darrell ruefully, opening a jar of Russian beluga so we could compare the two. "We have some way to go."

The phone continued to ring. Darrell finally relented, picked it up, and shouted, "Basta, Biba, ch'e amici!" before slamming it down once again. I watched this performance as I tasted the two caviars, willing myself to notice the difference between them. It was mainly a matter of texture; the homemade caviar had the slightly fruited saltiness of the beluga, but it was a little mushy. "It will be better next time," muttered Darrell. "Don't fill up on it." He waved us into the dining room, where a linen-covered table was set with good china and heavy silver. Crystal wineglasses paraded down its middle.

We sat down and Darrell filled the smallest of the glasses with an amber liquid. Then he went into the kitchen and returned carrying bowls of soup; as he set one before me the steam wafted up, bathing my face in warm fragrance. I leaned into it, liking the feeling, and saw pale cubes of foie gras floating languidly in the broth. I fished one out. As my mouth closed over it a small explosion occurred: The foie gras had dissolved, leaving only its melted center. The richness flooded down my throat and I thought what an astonishing sensation it was, to see solid and sense liquid. Colman looked startled too, and Darrell watched us, a small smile playing on his face. He picked up his glass and tasted the wine. "Try it," he urged. "It's sherry from 1950." The wine was complicated, so rich, nutty, and concentrated that each tiny sip sent little ripples of feeling down my back.

"Wow!" I said. Colman looked pained. Darrell merely collected the plates and went into the kitchen, and I wondered if he too thought me an idiot. When he returned he was carrying a regal duck lacquered to a glisten. "Canard à l'orange!" he announced.

My heart sank; I had expected more from this great food person. The restaurants I reviewed all served some variation on stringy gray duck in melted marmalade, and I hated the stuff. Disappointed, I took a bite. And then another.

My mouth was filled with a powerfully bittersweet impression. Separating the flavors, I picked out the mellow richness of the meat folded into the piquant sharpness of the oranges. There was nothing sweet or cloying about this dish. Darrell watched my face. "The secret is Seville oranges," he said, pouring wine into our glasses. "They grow right here in Sacramento. I wanted to see how these Chiantis matched with duck."

"This duck is . . . magnificent!" I blurted out. Colman shot me a worried look, and I knew that I had embarrassed him again. Trying to recover I said, "This '52 Antinori is so soft and woody."

Colman glared at me. "Soft" was obviously not the operative word. "It's amazing," he said, "that a wine this old has so much tannin."

After that I decided to keep quiet. Colman noted that the '62 had a lot more bite. And then Darrell weighed in on the '69, which was very hearty. Taking a large swallow, he pronounced it perfect for duck.

He got up to get the next course and returned carrying a majolica dish piled high with asparagus. He passed the platter and as I took some of the bright green spears I realized that there was no cutlery on the table.

"Fingers are the best utensils for eating asparagus," said Darrell, "but first dip them in this."

He handed me a little dish filled with something resembling molasses. I didn't know what it was but said nothing as I dipped a spear into the pruney brown liquid. It was thick enough to cling, and when I put it in my mouth I found the asparagus had acquired a sweet-sour, resiny taste.

"Mmmmm," I sighed before I had the sense to stop. I peeked at Colman, who had a quizzical look on his face. He doesn't know what it is either, I thought happily.

"Have you never had aceto balsamico?" asked Darrell. I kept still, but Colman shook his head. Darrell leaned back. "It is produced in only one town in Italy," he said, "Modena. The process is similar to sherry: As the vinegar ages it is moved from one barrel to another. Each barrel is made of a different variety of wood, and each imparts a different flavor. For great balsamico, the process takes an entire lifetime, the vinegar becoming more concentrated as it progresses through subsequent barrels of red oak, chestnut, mulberry, and juniper. Every true Modenese family has barrels in the basement, and it is said that when the Americans arrived at the end of the war, each family fled with its barrel of finished balsamic. They simply could not imagine life without it."

"No wonder," I said, plunging another spear into the vinegar. "Where can I get some?"

"Oh, you can't," said Darrell. "It is not a commercial product. This was a gift from a friend; his grandmother made it."

"In that case," I said, picking up another spear, "I'll have to have some more."

Darrell served a pale soufflé decorated with sugared violet petals for dessert. Then he handed out tiny glasses of a very sweet wine. "Eiswein," he said, "made of Scheurebe grapes."

"I love this," I said before I had time to think. "It tastes like grapefruit." Why couldn't I keep my opinions to myself? But Darrell only nodded solemnly and said, "That's exactly what I've always thought!" Looking at Colman he added, "This one you should keep. Such enthusiasm!"

Colman looked at me speculatively; I couldn't imagine what he was thinking. After a moment he said, "You don't think enthusiasm clouds the critical faculties?"

"Not at all," Darrell replied. "What's the point of knowing a lot about food if all you get is disappointment?"

It was very late when we finally left, and neither of us knew our way around Sacramento. In the dark, somehow, we got lost, and the only map I had was something I had picked up at a thrift store. We followed it anyway, and got more lost. "The road on this map probably disappeared fifty years ago," said Colman with genuine irritation. It was three in the morning; we were miles from home. "You're so, so . . . Berkeley!" he cried and then lapsed into an aggrieved silence.

It's over, I thought. The dream has died. By the time I dropped Colman at his hotel it was almost four, and the interior of the car was electric with his unspoken ire. He got out, taking the angry air with him, and stalked off. The car was comfortable again as I drove through the dark streets of Berkeley. Doug was asleep in our warm, cozy room. I sniffed; the air smelled familiar and welcoming. When I climbed into bed Doug put his arms around me, nuzzled my hair, and sighed. I was very happy to be home.

▪ ▪ ▪

But that feeling didn't last. Doug was so busy that he seemed oblivious of my mood, and I found myself mooning over Colman, diving hopefully for the phone each time it rang. But it was always just another gallery, museum, or architect eager to talk to the artist of the moment. Doug was particularly excited about the call from the Olympic Committee. "They want me to create a sound sculpture for the winter games at Lake Placid next year!" he exulted.

Only one person seemed to take notice of my misery. One morning Jules sat down at the kitchen table and said, "You'd better say something to him."

"Who?" I asked, taking another sip of coffee.

"Doug," he said. "He thinks that once he bought into the marriage program he would never have to work at the relationship again. But I'm sure he doesn't want to lose you."

"What do you suggest?" I asked.

Jules shook his head. I was tempted to tell him everything—about kids, about Colman, about Paris—but I couldn't. It seemed so disloyal to Doug. So I picked up the paper and hid behind it.

As the days went on I became more and more morose. But Colman never called. And when he finally did, it was only to summon me to a staff luncheon in Los Angeles.

"Do you want me to spend the night?" I asked.

"It's up to you," he replied. After a small silence he added, in a carefully neutral tone, "You're welcome to stay here." Not even the world's greatest optimist could consider that an invitation.

"I think I'll just come for the day," I said.

"Suit yourself," he replied. I thought he sounded relieved. "The meeting will be at Ma Maison, and Wolfgang is cooking something very special. I've asked everyone to bring a bottle of wine." With a sinking feeling I listened as he told me that he planned to bring a '68 Heitz Martha's Vineyard from his cellar and that Charlie Perry, one of the Los Angeles critics, was bringing two bottles of '66 Ducru-Beaucaillou. Phil Reich had some rare Zinfandels from Joseph Swan.

"Are we being graded on this test?" I asked.

"You're being absurd," he said. But I knew better.

I didn't want to carry wine on the plane, but I had plenty of time to buy something in Los Angeles. The lunch wasn't until one, so I'd have the entire morning to dig up an impressive bottle.

But the plane was late, and the only Los Angeles wine store I knew turned out to be closed for renovations. I climbed into my Rent-A-Wreck and started searching. To my dismay, Los Angeles was not exactly rich in wine emporiums. At noon I was still empty-handed. There must be something, I thought, pounding the steering wheel in frustration.

I drove around in circles, looking for a wine store. Any wine store. I found nothing. At 12:30 I lowered my standards and cruised desperately down Sunset Boulevard, twisting my head from side to side, looking for a wine store, a liquor store, anything. At 12:45 I was still driving down Sunset. I passed La Cienega and kept going. At 12:50, in a panic, I pulled into the parking lot of a dingy little deli and liquor store. I turned off the engine and weighed my options: I could say I had broken the bottle on the way over (I could not imagine Colman believing that) or I could walk into the store and pray.

I prayed. I ran in, inhaling the odor of age, cheap scotch, and gin and said, "What's your most expensive wine?"

The old man at the counter turned and began peering at the dusty bottles behind him. He wiped off a few labels with his shirtsleeve. "This one's fifteen dollars," he said. He wiped a couple more bottles. "No, wait, this one's eighteen." He swept at a couple more with his arm and then said triumphantly, "Look at this! Been here a long time. It's thirty bucks!"

"You got anything more expensive?" I asked.

He put his hand on one hip and spoke very slowly. "Ma'am," he said, trying to explain this to a person of obviously limited intelligence, "we don't have a lot of call for thirty-dollar wine here."

"I'll take it," I said.

"You want to know what it is?" he asked.

"Oh no," I said. "I like surprises."

▪ ▪ ▪

Wolfgang started with his famous oyster feuilleté with beurre blanc. With that we drank champagne. With the pâté de foie gras he offered us Sauternes, swaddling the rich meat in the plump, honeyed wine. Not until charred slices of very rare duck breast appeared did Colman begin to unwrap the bottles we had brought.

There were aahs when Charlie's old Bordeaux were unveiled. Phil's rare Swan was suitably impressive. Colman's wine was vigorous and fine. Then it was time to unwrap my bottle. I closed my eyes and held my breath. There was a gasp of excitement. I opened my eyes and saw eager hands reaching for my bottle. I had, apparently, been lucky.

Afterward, we drank Château d'Yquem with the dacquoise, and then the guests began collecting their belongings and drifting away. Before long Colman, Phil, and I were the only ones left at the table. I started to rise, but Colman pulled me down. "Stay," he said, "please stay." He poured more wine into my glass.

Phil had said very little during lunch, but now he poked at what was left of the dacquoise and asked, "Aren't you tired of all this French food?"

I was startled out of my reverie. "Are you?" I asked.

"Yes," he said, "I think it's time Americans started paying attention to what we have here. We're making great wine; we should be cooking great food." He said it with passion, as if there was more than food on his mind. "This probably isn't the greatest time to tell you," he suddenly blurted out, looking straight at Colman, "but I quit. I'm moving down here to help open a restaurant."

"A restaurant?" I asked. "Why?"

"Because," said Phil, his eyes shining, "I've met someone who is trying to do something new, and I want to be part of it."

"Who is he?" I asked.

Phil leaned back, struggling for words. "He's not like anyone you've ever met," he said slowly. "He's a guy with a vision. He has this idea that he can create an entirely new kind of restaurant using all local products. He's lived in France, he's cooked in France, he's rich, and he loves food."

"Sort of like James Beard or something?" I asked. Phil burst out laughing.

"Oh no," he said. "He's only twenty-four. And thin. But he has big plans. Art. And silver. Special plates he's importing from France. But the main thing is that he's going to find great products. He says if he can't, he'll grow them himself. You see, he's not like the rest of us. He's a rich kid, and he thinks he can do anything."

"How much will you be making?" Colman asked.

Phil shrugged. "I don't know," he said, as if it were the most banal question. "But Michael gave me twelve grand to buy wine."

"He's not paying you?"

"Well, he's giving me a place to live."

"Where?" I asked.

Phil looked sheepish. "His living room."

"And what are you living on?"

Phil practically blushed. "I sold some of my wine cellar," he mumbled. "But you don't understand. Michael's is going to be something entirely new and American. It's history in the making. I just have to be a part of it!"

"If this restaurant is anything like it sounds, it will be a great story," said Colman, giving me a significant look.

"The opening of a new kind of restaurant," I agreed. "Sounds interesting."

"Of course you'd have to come back to Los Angeles for a few weeks to work on it," he said, his eyes still on mine. "I know a place where you can stay. Do you think you could do that?"

"Yes," I said happily. "Oh yes, I can do that." For the first time in weeks life seemed fine.

"Good," Colman said. "That's settled. We're losing a wine writer and gaining a story." Looking at me he added, "And speaking of wine . . . How on earth did you ever come up with a '61 Cheval Blanc?"

"Oh," I said airily, "just luck."

▪ ▪ ▪

Doug and I drove to the airport together. He was off to Lake Placid, to select a spot for his sculpture. "Everything's okay, isn't it?" he asked. I wondered if Jules had said something to him. But this time I was the one who didn't want to talk.

"Of course," I replied. "You're going to be famous."

"Maybe you are too," he said.

He parked in the long-term lot and we carried our luggage into the terminal. He put his arms around me and I inhaled his familiar scent. He gave me a kiss, and as he walked away I stood watching his lean body move gracefully through the crowd; from the back he could have been the Marlboro Man. He looked over his shoulder just before he turned the corner, and raised his hand in a wave. I waved back. Then he disappeared from sight as we went to get our separate planes.

■ ■ ■

"Look at the car I got you," said the agent at Rent-A-Wreck, open-ing the door. "I thought you'd like this." He thumped the hood of the yellow Cadillac affectionately. The car was the size of a small yacht, with tan leather seats as soft as butter.

"What did I do to deserve this?" I asked, climbing in.

"We take care of our good customers," he said, loading my lug-gage into the trunk. "We thought it was time you got an upgrade."

The Cadillac was a smooth ride. There was no smog, and the sky sparkled, very blue against the snowcapped mountains that encir-cled the city. The entire East Coast, according to the radio, was blanketed in snow. I rolled down the window and felt the sun on my arms.

■ ■ ■

Michael's pink stucco building would have been hard to miss even if it were not on a residential street. Dumpsters were lined up on the lawn, and a board was nailed across the front door. I pushed it aside and went into a room so dark it took me a few seconds to realize that Phil's famous restaurant did not yet exist.

Through the gloom I spotted a group of young construction workers leaning against a sink on the far side of the room. I care-fully picked my way through the debris, past sawhorses and spilled nails. They were standing in what would one day be a kitchen, and they were deep in conversation.

"I don't know what's going to happen now," the tallest one was saying when I got close enough to hear. "Michael just got turned down for a loan." He looked like a string bean with a Prince Valiant haircut. "The finance company was not amused by his corporate name: Acid Enterprises."

Phil had said that his visionary was young, but now I began to understand just what that might mean. He was a kid, the same age as these cute workmen now discussing cars with such concentration they had not even noticed my entrance. "I can drive my Lotus into a parking lot at fifty miles an hour," the string bean bragged. "I don't even have to stop; it slides right under the bars. It really pisses them off."

I didn't know much about cars, but I knew construction workers didn't drive fancy sports cars. Could these be the chefs? I cleared my throat. They all glanced in my direction, and one of them said, "We're not hiring waitresses yet." He had a humorous face framed by a curly brown beard, and when I did not reply he added helpfully, "I'll take your name if you want."

"I don't want to be a waitress," I said. "I'm looking for Michael."

"Oh, sweetie," he said, "he's not going to do you any good. He's got a girlfriend. Better stick with me."

"But he's expecting me."

"Oh shit," he replied. "You're not that reporter from *New West*, are you?"

"Yes," I said, "I am."

There was an awkward moment of silence. And then he shrugged and accused, "But you don't look like a reporter."

"You're not exactly my idea of a chef either," I shot back.

He laughed and said, "We were supposed to give you some espresso and tell you that Michael would be back soon. But he forgot that we don't have an espresso machine yet. He tends to overlook inconvenient details." He pointed to a box. "I'm Jonathan Waxman. Have a seat."

I did. Jonathan nodded to his right and said, "This is Mark Peel." He nodded left, to the string bean. "This is Ken Frank. He's head chef. You may have heard of him." With a smile he added, "They call him the 'enfant terrible of Los Angeles.' "

"Don't tell her that," said Ken, grimacing as I shook his hand.

"I've heard it before," I said. "You're twenty-four and you've already had your own restaurant. What was your training?"

"I didn't have any," he said, waving a hand. "I just worked my way up from being a dishwasher. That, of course, was in France. In six months in France you can learn to be a chef in L.A."

"So why did you come here?" I asked, taken aback by his arrogance.

"Because," he said, less flippant now, "it's time that changed. We need to stop copying France. I'm a third-generation Californian and I want to create a California restaurant with California produce, California wines, and California employees. Michael's philosophy is a lot like mine."

A grin broke across his face, making him look even younger. "Anyway," he added, "the day I went to talk to Michael the owner of the restaurant I was working in tried to beat me up. It seemed like time to leave."

"Somebody try to beat you up too?" I asked, turning to Jonathan.

"Oh no," he replied, "they don't do things like that in Berkeley. I've been working with Alice Waters at Chez Panisse, and I've learned a lot from her. But I'm bored with Berkeley. And I like Michael's philosophy."

"So you just picked up and moved down here?" I said. "This guy must be something!"

He nodded. "He is. And he's letting me stay with him out in Malibu."

"It must be getting pretty crowded," I murmured. I couldn't help myself.

■ ■ ■

An hour later Michael had not appeared. "When do you think he'll be back?" I asked hopefully.

"There's no saying," said Jonathan. "Let's make lunch." He threw me an apron. "You can peel these tomatoes." He set a cutting board on an overturned box and handed me a knife.

After I had slipped all the tomatoes out of their skins I asked if he wanted the seeds removed. "Of course," he said and I blushed, thinking what an amateur question it was. I tried to make up for it by removing every seed, but they were slippery little things, and a few resisted my attempts to get at them.

"Sloppy," said Jonathan when he came to inspect my work, "but I can hardly yell at you. You're not getting paid."

"Neither are you, if I remember correctly," I replied.

"Just try not to cut your fingers off when you chop those tomatoes, okay?" he said curtly. I focused on keeping my fingers tucked and ostentatiously looked around the kitchen so everyone could see that I was not watching my hands. I tried to chop very fast and very fine. Still, I was not impressing even myself.

Jonathan threw me a pan. "Now cook that down into a coulis," he said.

"I need something to stir it with," I said.

"We don't have anything," he replied in a tone that implied that only sissies would use an implement to stir a pot. "Use your fingers."

I was still dipping my fingers gingerly in and out of the blisteringly hot sauté pan when a pretty woman with pink cheeks and short brown hair ran into the kitchen waving a copy of the *Los Angeles Times*. " 'Talented young chef Mark Peel says that chefs should be well educated,' " she read in an elegant English accent, " 'and go to college so that they're not dull.' "

"Oh no," said Mark, looking extremely embarrassed. "I didn't say that. Or at least I didn't say it in that context. I just meant it about me."

The woman came over to the stove, looked at me, and asked, "Are you going to work here?"

"Meet Sally Clarke," said Jonathan. "No, sweetheart, she's not working here. She's that reporter from *New West*."

"Oh, pleased to meet you," said Sally, with what seemed like relief.

"How come the *Times* was writing about you?" Ken asked querulously.

And suddenly I heard myself saying this: "Don't worry—after my article comes out you'll all be famous."

This statement was greeted by a momentary silence, and my cheeks went scarlet. What on earth had made me blurt that out? And then I realized the silence had nothing to do with me; Michael McCarty had arrived.

He was not as tall as Ken or as handsome as Mark, and he lacked Jonathan's sweetness. But he carried himself like a movie star. Within seconds he was the center of a vortex of sound.

"Look at this beef!" Ken was saying to him, holding out a filet. "We've been to every meat supplier in town, and they all insist this is the best they've got."

"This cream is awful," Jonathan moaned. "It's manufacturer's cream. We need something better."

A workman was shouting at him in Spanish and Sally was saying something about the damn computer system. Michael appeared to be answering them all simultaneously.

"Don't worry about the meat and the cream," he told the chefs. "I'll get the boys to come and take a look at the restaurant. When they see the type of place we're running, they'll come up with something better." He might have been holding a cigar for all his bravado, and when all three chefs looked skeptical he said, "Remember, I've already gotten someone to bring fresh pork loin from Chicago, even though everyone said that couldn't be done. And we're setting up a computer system to keep inventory, though everyone said that couldn't be done either." He turned to me and flashed an enormous smile. "You must be Ruth. I hope I didn't keep you waiting. Let's go up to my office."

As I pulled off the apron and started to follow him, Ken suddenly said, "Oh yeah, I forgot to tell you. Your banker was here."

Michael winced. All the air seemed to evaporate from his body, leaving him looking small, young, and vulnerable. "Did you talk to him?"

"No," said Ken.

Michael's swagger came back as suddenly as it had deserted him; he expanded before my eyes, puffing up with confidence. "Good. He doesn't know I'm over budget again."

As we walked up a rickety flight of stairs he said earnestly, "You have to understand, Ruth, I'm a wheeler-dealer. It's all a matter of juggling time and money. Ninety-eight percent of the time it works, but it doesn't always. Sometimes everyone wants their money at the same time. Like now. But that's the way it goes. Most people get their paycheck and immediately eliminate the cash. They just don't know how to use it."

As we walked into the office he turned and punched me lightly in the stomach. "Got five thousand dollars you can lend me?"

▪ ▪ ▪

"I don't think he was kidding," I told Colman later. We were sitting on his bed drinking wine out of the Steuben glasses he stored in a box beneath it. "He really needs the money. He even asked Jonathan if his father would buy one of the paintings he bought for the restaurant."

"Is it good art?" asked Colman.

"Oh, yeah," I said. "He's got great taste. He's got Hockneys and Johnses and Diebenkorns. I don't think any restaurant has ever had such terrific art before. And he's not just borrowing it, he's buying it. He says that a nice meal is not enough—the place has to be an event. No wonder he's over budget. He thought the restaurant was going to cost three hundred thousand dollars, but it's already up to half a million. He's just refinanced his house to get more money."

"You can't lend him money," said Colman with some alarm. "You're reporting on the place, for Christ's sake."

"Do I look like I have five grand?" I asked.

"Well," he said with a grin, "appearances can be deceiving."

Looking around the room, I realized he might be talking about himself. I was seeing him more clearly now. Colman was a natty dresser, he wore Armani aftershave, and he had house accounts in every restaurant in Los Angeles. But his tiny Hollywood apartment had piles of unpaid bills stacked in every corner. The Mercedes he drove off in every morning was highly buffed and very smooth; only inside did you discover that the seats were torn, the radio gone, and the odometer stuck, unable to turn over anymore. For all his flash, Colman moved precariously from week to week.

But although he didn't have much money, he lived like a rich man. Every chef in Los Angeles was his friend, and red carpets unrolled beneath his feet. He got up early every morning to go off at six A.M. in his tennis whites. Whom did he play with? He only smiled when I asked. Just as he smiled when he said he had to work late and came home after midnight, complaining of deadlines but smelling of wine. Strange women smiled coyly from across every dining room, and when I answered the phone it was often a female voice. "Soon, in a week or so," I'd hear him whispering into the phone.

I whispered too. Sometimes in the middle of the night I'd get out of bed and call Doug in Lake Placid, pretending I had just gotten in.

"The restaurant's almost finished," I said.

"I think I found a site today," he replied.

"Phil was sick today. Michael seems to have forgotten I'm not on his payroll, so he had me unload the wine delivery."

"The committee is planning a big party next week. We're supposed to announce what we're doing. I have nightmares about not having an idea in time."

The conversations never went anywhere, but I found his voice reassuringly familiar. Talking to Doug made me feel that although I was playing a role, I still had a real life to return to.

▪ ▪ ▪

Meanwhile I spent my days hanging around the restaurant, trying to be both helpful and invisible. Ken was not particularly friendly, but Mark and Jonathan were easy to talk to, and day by day we could see Michael's fantasy coming to life. "It looks different than any restaurant I've ever seen," I told Colman, describing the cool modern dining room. "It's a sort of a desert Bauhaus look with a bit of Moorish thrown in. And no matter where you sit, you see the garden. I feel as if he's taken the whole idea of a restaurant and thrown the windows open. It feels expensive but not stuffy. You'll like it."

"Yeah, but what about the food?" he wanted to know.

"Michael keeps saying that the food is not the most important thing," I replied. "But they spend an awful lot of time trying to find ingredients and arguing about techniques. Yesterday they had a big fight about beurre blanc. Ken said that if you don't put a whisk in, it doesn't get gray. Jonathan said it wasn't true. They argued about it all afternoon."

"Why do you think guys like that have given up jobs in the best restaurants in California to go work there?" he asked.

"I asked Michael that very question," I replied. "You'll like his answer. I just transcribed the tape; I'll read it to you." I flipped through my notes, looking for the quote. "Here it is: 'You see, Ruth, they will all one day probably have their own little restaurant somewhere. And they're all here for two reasons. One, because they like to work with me. And two, because I'm not a fifty-year-old Frenchman who owns the restaurant and is mean. They've all been working with these crusty old bastards who treat 'em like assholes, you see what I mean? If you were a second or third chef in Bertranou's kitchen at L'Ermitage and you wanted to do something, do you think he'd let you? Never. We're doing something different here. I'm allowing it to happen. There's tons of room for creativity. I want to do the weirdest things.' "

"That's great," he said. "You've got to use it."

"Don't worry," I replied. "I will. He said something else I really loved. Let me find it." I scanned the notes. "Here. Listen. 'What I want to do is the best possible ingredients cooked in the simplest way. Sure, it's not the world's most interesting menu, but my specials are the things that are supposed to blow your socks off.' "

" 'Blow your socks off!' " he repeated. "That's great. It's going to be a good story. If he ever opens the damn restaurant."

"It must be close," I said. "Michael's been wandering around moaning about money and saying he needs cash."

"How close?" asked Colman. I had another one of those worried moments when I wondered if he was trying to get rid of me.

"Mark says we'll know we're close when Michael calls the first waiters' meeting," I said. "Until then it's just talk."

■ ■ ■

But things did seem to be coming together. The kitchen slowly filled up with equipment, and helpers arrived to peel vegetables and do dishes. And then, one morning, a man came through the door staggering beneath the weight of a big box and saying, "I have the fish order?" as if he could not believe he had come to the right place.

He set the box down on a makeshift counter, and the chefs gathered around to scrutinize his wares. Ken peeled a shrimp and popped it into his mouth. "Two days old?" he inquired. The man nodded. Ken slit open a salmon trout and sniffed it suspiciously. "They're real nice," said the fish man, shifting his weight from one foot to the other. Ken said nothing. He poked at the whitefish. "Canadian all you have?" he said disparagingly. The fish man mumbled something about next week. "This Canadian stuff's too fatty to make decent terrine," said Ken.

"I brought you a nice box of bones," said the fish man hopefully. Jonathan peered into the box and frowned. "Grouper," he sniffed. "It makes terrible fumet. The bones are too gelatinous, and the fish lacks flavor. Anyway, this one was past its prime."

"Fresh salmon next week," the fish man said, retreating.

"The first order is always good," said Ken when the fish guy had gone.

"Good?" I said. "But you were so negative about everything he brought."

"You can't let them get too sure of themselves," he replied. "We'll have to see what he comes up with in a couple of weeks, when it counts."

"Not a couple of weeks," said Michael, "a couple of days."

The chefs turned to stare at him. "Oh," he said casually, "didn't I tell you we're having a waiters' meeting this afternoon?"

▪ ▪ ▪

"You're going to have to be agile," Michael said, looking out at the sea of surfers. "I don't want anyone who can't roller-skate stumbling around my dining room."

When Michael explained that all the tips would be pooled, with 10 percent going to the kitchen, 10 percent to the busboys, and 10 percent to the bar, a groan went up. "Does that mean that we'll have to report all our tips?" someone asked, and Michael said yes. Another groan. "The kind of place I run, you'll be audited. You might as well be prepared for that. My buddy over at L'Ermitage, his waiters get audited every year."

The waiters were even less enthusiastic about the next part of the speech. Michael held up the heavy Christofle silver he had purchased in Paris. "Keep your eyes on the silver. Please, if you don't do anything else, just do this one thing. Do it as a favor to me. Everybody in town is waiting for me to trip on this one. Everyone said, 'Michael, you can't use Christofle. You won't have any by the end of the first month.' I've got to prove that they're wrong."

He looked around to see if anybody was leaving. Nobody was. "Any questions?"

There was just one. A guy with long blond hair held up his hand. "So when are we opening?" he wanted to know.

"Day after tomorrow," said Michael, "but it all depends on the inspectors. They will all be here today."

"They will?" said Phil, with some astonishment. "Don't you think you might have mentioned this little detail?"

■ ■ ■

A day later Michael was strolling through the dining room balancing a telephone on each shoulder. "We open tomorrow," he said into one. "J'ai besoin de vraies morilles," he said into the other.

He turned back to the first phone. "We'll do dinner just for friends," he said. "Maybe forty, fifty people. Then we'll do the real thing the following night." Into the second he said, "Vous les trouverez." And he hung them both up.

"Who are you going to ask?" said Mark. "And how are you going to convey the impression that you expect them to pay?"

"Easy," said Michael, with characteristic confidence. "I'll just call up and say that we're open for business and would they like to come for dinner. Don't worry. They'll come. They'll pay."

He and Phil went off to the garden to draw up the list. "No, not him," I kept hearing, "I don't want any industry types."

Phil nodded at me and said, very softly, so as not to hurt my feelings, "You gonna let her come?"

"Sure," said Michael. "She has an expense account. Seven o'clock. She can bring one person."

▪ ▪ ▪

Colman beat me to the restaurant. At 6:30 Michael realized he had forgotten flowers, handed me a wad of money, and ordered, "Find a florist." By the time I had arranged the lilies and tea roses in the largest water glasses, it was 7:15.

"Problems?" murmured Colman as I slid breathlessly into my seat.

"Opening-night jitters," I replied.

"Some of these dishes sound awful," he said, surveying the menu with a certain skepticism. "Raw scallops with beets? Give me a break!"

He was even less impressed when a shocking mash of pink topped with two translucent rounds of scallop was set before him. "Is this safe?" he asked, poking it with a fork. "It looks like melted lipstick topped with plastic beads."

"Try it," I urged. "Michael copied it from the man he modestly calls 'my pal Pierre Vedel in Paris,' but he insists that Maine scallops are better than anything in France. He gets them from some woman named Ingrid who has her own boat."

"It's good," Colman conceded, somewhat reluctantly. "The sweetness of the beets works with the scallops."

"Now try the hot goat cheese salad," I said. "Michael's taking these old dried-out petits chèvres and putting them in the oven. When they come out they're moist and runny, like really good Brie. And wait until you see the frisée! You won't believe how beautiful it is. Locally grown, from some place down in Rancho Santa Fe."

"Appetizers are easy," said Colman, reserving judgment. "We'll see how they do on the main courses."

But when he tasted the squab, he put his head to one side and nodded, which is what he did when he liked a dish. He took a second bite and considered it. The bird had simply been boned, rubbed with herbs, and quickly charred on the grill. The meat was rare and rosy, the skin crisp and almost black.

"Even the French chefs are saying these Santa Barbara squabs are better than anything in France," I said.

He shook his head. He took another bite. And then another. "What's the sauce?" he asked.

"Raspberry vinegar, reduced," I said. "The vinegar was a problem. The bottle said 'raspberry' in English, but 'strawberry' in French. It was just white vinegar with a squirt of fruit syrup. So Ken made his own, with fresh fruit."

"Okay," Colman conceded at the end of the meal, "these guys are onto something."

"Yeah," I said. "Michael's arrogant as hell, and you have to take everything he says with a grain of salt. But there's a real idea here. The food they're doing is fresh and local, but it's different than what my friends are doing up in Berkeley. It's less earthy. It's got attitude."

Colman cocked his head and said, "Don't waste this speech on me."

"I know, I know," I said. "The article."

"You're going to have to work fast," he said. "You should probably go right home and start writing."

"Can't wait to get rid of me?" I teased.

He looked embarrassed and said nothing, not even a polite response. I noticed that his forehead was dotted with sweat. He seemed so acutely uncomfortable that I suddenly remembered the early-morning tennis and the midnight deadlines. "There's another woman?" I asked.

He nodded solemnly.

The pain didn't register at once. It was as if I had hit my thumb with a hammer and was waiting for the throbbing to start.

He kept his eyes on mine and took a deep breath. "I don't think there's an easy way to tell you this," he went on. He stopped for a moment and then blurted out, "We're going to get married."

"Does Claude know?" I asked.

"Yes," he said. "I called to ask his permission. We're going to Paris for the wedding."

That hurt more than anything. I lifted my chin, trying to keep the tears from spilling onto my cheeks. I croaked a bit, speaking over the lump that was in my throat. "I'm married," I managed to choke out. "Why shouldn't you be?"

ASPARAGUS WITH BALSAMIC VINEGAR

This is the simplest recipe: All it requires is fat asparagus, excellent balsamic vinegar, and a few fingers.

Because you want this to be lavish, count on a pound of asparagus per person. Buy the fattest stalks you can, and choose ones that are closed at the tip end. (Asparagus open up as they get older, and they don't taste as good.)

Trim the bottom of the stalks with a vegetable peeler. Unless you have an asparagus pot, trim the asparagus so that they will fit into your largest skillet.

Fill the skillet halfway with water, bring the water to a boil, and add salt to taste; then add the asparagus. Cover and cook 5 to 10 minutes, depending on the thickness of the asparagus, or until the spears are still firm but soft enough to pierce easily with a skewer or fork. Don't overcook; they become mushy.

Drain well. Set them on two plates, arranging them attractively. Sprinkle with sea salt.

Serve with a small dish of balsamic vinegar to dip them into. Insist that your guests use their fingers.

MICHAEL'S PASTA
AND SCALLOPS

I took notes on this dish one afternoon while Jonathan was noodling around in the kitchen. The notes were pretty sketchy, so Lori Powell, who tested the recipes for this book, completely revised the directions. But I like the result; this dish has the freshness, the simplicity, and the luxurious quality that characterized the food Michael served when he first opened his restaurant. The dish later turned into pasta with scallops and chardonnay-cream sauce, one of Michael's signature recipes.

1 cup fish stock
1 cup heavy cream
½ pound sea scallops, tough
   muscles removed
salt and pepper

½ pound fresh linguine
1 tablespoon fresh lemon
   juice, or to taste
3 ounces golden caviar

Garnish: 12 fresh tarragon leaves and 12 small fresh basil leaves

Boil the fish stock in a large saucepan until reduced to ¼ cup (about 4 minutes). Add the cream and, being careful not to let cream boil over, simmer until reduced to ½ cup (about 6 minutes).

Prepare the grill for cooking.

Pat the scallops dry and season them with salt and pepper. Grill the scallops on a lightly oiled rack until just cooked through (1–2 minutes per side). Transfer scallops, as cooked, to a covered plate and keep them warm.

Cook the linguine in a 6- to 8-quart pot of boiling salted water until al dente. Reserve ½ cup of the cooking water and drain the pasta in a colander. Return the pasta to the pot and toss it with the cream sauce, ¼ cup of the pasta cooking liquid, and the lemon juice; add salt and pepper to taste over moderate heat until hot (adding more liquid if necessary, a tablespoon at a time).

Serve the pasta mounded on plates. Top with scallops and caviar. Garnish with tarragon and basil.

Serves 4.

5

GARLIC
IS GOOD

■ When I woke up the next morning I was stretched across the couch in the large, empty living room of Michael's Malibu house. I opened my eyes and found Jonathan sitting on a big chair, peering fearfully at me. "You okay?" he asked.

I moaned. "You were in no shape to drive last night," he said, "and we didn't know where to take you. In the end I just drove your car here."

My lips were cracked and my head felt like an enormous watermelon. When I tried to stand up, I fell down. I was finally able to stand long enough to negotiate the steps to the car, and I sat there for a moment, breathing hard and waiting for the nausea to pass.

The trip up the curving coast road was excruciating; the sun was very bright, its rays piercing my forehead and stabbing into my eyes. My stomach had become a separate and alien creature whose sole mission in life was attack.

I barely remember the flight back to Berkeley, and the drive from the airport has been mercifully erased from my memory. I hauled myself up the stairs, my head pounding with each step, and sank, gratefully, into my own bed.

Maybe it was pneumonia, I said. At the very least it was the flu. It was not a complete lie; for days I felt hot and queasy, as if I were burning up with fever. Swallowing anything, even water, was impossible. I lay in bed with my face to the wall, feeling as if my world had ended.

Doug came home to care for me; his solicitude broke my heart. He brought me cold compresses and glasses of ice water, and when I could no longer pretend that my ailment was physical he spoke wisely about the depression that often follows a fever.

If he only knew, I thought to myself, and was horrified, all over again, by the way I had betrayed him. I listened to him working in his studio, comforted by the familiar sounds, thinking that maybe I could resign myself to a life without children.

I would have liked to stay in bed forever, liked to forget that I had ever embarked on this sorry episode. The phone kept ringing, but I refused to answer it. I knew what the calls were about: Colman was marrying another editor at the magazine and everybody wanted to discuss it. The one person I was foolish enough to talk with informed me that Colman and his fiancée had been seeing each other for months. "But they had to keep it hidden," the woman confided, "because he was living with someone else. Nobody knows who."

After that I avoided the phone altogether, but I still had a deadline to meet. Three days before the piece was due I dragged myself out of bed and walked down to my workroom.

I stared at the blank paper for a moment and then, from out of nowhere, the first line arrived. "In the kit that they sent to the press," I typed, "they look more like rock stars in a group called 'The Chefs' than people who actually cook." The words came pouring out. Writing the article saved me. If, in fact, I could be said to have written it; the article seemed to write itself. It was finished in three days, and afterward I found that I was, once again, able to eat.

When Colman called to discuss what I had written, the sound of his voice brought it all back, and I shook so hard I could barely hold the phone. The conversation was quick; he was like ice and he stuck to business. He got married, and for weeks afterward I tortured myself by calling his apartment, but his wife always answered, and each time I heard her voice I banged the phone back into its cradle.

"Stop doing that," said Colman the first time I reached him at the office. Almost a month had passed, and the sound of his voice had become a little less painful.

"Doing what?" I replied as innocently as I could.

"You know," he said. "It makes my wife crazy."

"I don't know what you're talking about," I said with as much dignity as I could muster. "I need to discuss something with you. I want to write a story about garlic."

"Garlic?" he asked. "Who cares about garlic?"

"Berkeley cares about garlic," I said, launching into my pitch. My plan was to exorcise Paris by going back to my roots. What did I care about champagne and caviar? I was a Berkeley girl, and I was going to write about something earthy, something elemental, something that really mattered.

I told Colman about Les Blank, a Berkeley filmmaker who was making a movie about garlic. Colman was not responsive; the Museum of Modern Art was presenting a retrospective of Les Blank's work, but no one in Hollywood had ever heard of his cult classic *Spend It All*. I explained about *The Garlic Book*, a big best-seller in Berkeley, but since it was not a must-read in Tinseltown, Colman didn't care. Trying to interest him in Berkeley's obsession with garlic sausages seemed hopeless, and I suspected that a restaurant in the High Sierra with a menu dedicated entirely to garlic would hold little fascination for him. But I knew that there was one thing in Berkeley that could attract Colman's attention.

"Alice Waters . . ." I began, and I was rewarded with a quick intake of breath, ". . . has an annual garlic festival."

"She does?" he asked.

I knew that would get him. "I'm surprised you didn't know," I said smugly.

There was a silence. Then, very slowly, he relented. "You might be onto something," he admitted. "Will she talk to you?"

"Of course," I said with a certain degree of pride, "she'll talk to me. We're both from Berkeley."

■ ■ ■

I found Alice standing in front of the open fireplace in the Chez Panisse kitchen, slicing garlic into slivers and then stuffing them beneath the skin of several plump ducks. A big spray of apple blossoms framed her head; Chez Panisse was the only professional kitchen I had ever seen that was decorated with flowers.

She put down her knife when she saw me. "An article on garlic?" she asked, wiping her hands on her apron. "That would be perfect. The next garlic dinner is going to be a benefit to raise money so Les can finish his film. A little article would help. What can I do?"

"Give me the menus from the past few festivals," I replied. "I need to persuade a skeptical editor that this is a good idea. He lives in L.A. and he doesn't think anyone is interested in garlic."

Alice gave a little sigh and cast me a sympathetic glance. "Of course," she said. She wiped her hands again and added, "Let me find you some good-looking copies." As she walked into her office she called over her shoulder, already a co-conspirator, "And if that doesn't work, maybe we can think of something else."

"Don't worry," I said when she came back with the menus. "These will do the trick."

▪ ▪ ▪

Colman called as soon as he got the menus. "Grilled tripe with garlic, herbs, and bread crumbs sounds wonderful," he said, perusing the menu from the first garlic festival. "So does poached fish with tomato and aioli whisked into the fish broth. And I love the idea of fresh figs, white cheese, and garlic honey." He began reading the dishes from the second year, stopping when he got to the Troisgros recipe for roasted pigeons stuffed with whole garlic. "We should have gone to Troisgros when we were in France," he said wistfully. For a moment it was as if the past few weeks had never happened. Then he remembered and hurried on. "Just imagine how good Japanese buckwheat noodles with seaweed in a soy, garlic, and chive sauce must taste."

"Which festival was that?" I asked, hoping to get the good feeling back.

"The third," he said. "She served it after the garlic baked under ashes. And before the roasted suckling pigs from garlic-fed sows." He stopped for a moment and asked, "Do you think that the piglets really tasted like garlic just because their mothers were fed garlic?"

"Alice assured me that they were very potent," I replied huskily. My voice was sticking in my throat; talking to Colman had suddenly become so painful I would have said anything to get him off the phone. But our conversation had come to an end. The menus had the desired effect, and Colman was converted to the garlic cause.

Before long Colman seemed convinced that the idea had been his in the first place. Or maybe it was just an act; maybe he only wanted to reinforce the notion that our relationship was strictly business now. Whatever the reason, he kept throwing statistics at me. Did I know that garlic consumption had gone up 200 percent in ten years? Was I aware that California grew 90 percent of the garlic consumed in America? He wanted me to visit a garlic farm.

He wanted me to spend time with Les Blank. He wanted me to interview Alice Waters. And wasn't there some restaurant up in the mountains that made a specialty of garlic?

I had no desire to keep him on the phone, so I refrained from reminding Colman that a few weeks earlier this restaurant had bored him to tears. I merely replied that Les was going to Truckee that weekend to film the restaurant's owners, and that he was taking some sausage maker along.

"You have to go too!" said Colman, "You could build the whole story around the trip!"

▪ ▪ ▪

Doug drove me to the station. "I'm glad you're feeling better," he said, stroking my hand. "You've got color in your cheeks again. This trip sounds like it's going to be fun."

"Why don't you come along?" I asked. "You love garlic, you love Les Blank's movies, and you love the mountains."

"I wish I could," he said. I thought I detected a wistful note in his voice. "But I've got too much work to do here."

"It's only a weekend," I pleaded, but he shook his head.

Les was at the station, standing next to the sausage maker, a huge man with a shaggy beard. Next to them was a small mountain of movie equipment.

"I'll hand the stuff up to you," said Doug as the train came chugging into the station. We leapt on board while Doug stood on the platform handing lights, tripods, and cameras through the window. As the last camera came aboard, the train lurched off. I looked out, watching Doug become smaller and smaller in the distance.

The seat suddenly sagged away from me and the sausage maker's wild head was reflected on the landscape in the window, like a big buffalo obscuring the scenery. He heaved himself into the seat, and I turned to ask, "Why did you come on this trip?"

"I've always wanted to visit La Vieille Maison," he said. "Robert

Charles is a pretty interesting guy. He was too weird to stay in France. Did you know he once had a restaurant in San Francisco that only served lamb?"

"You're kidding, right?" I said.

"No," he said earnestly. "He really did. The funny thing is, he actually made a go of it; you couldn't get into the place. Now he's into garlic. I like the guy's spirit—I want to see what he's up to."

I pointed to the box of sausages next to his seat. "Is your interest professional?" I asked.

He grinned, which made him look even more like a wild man. "Sort of," he admitted. "I've been considering quitting my day job and selling sausages instead. I want to see what Robert thinks of my garlic sausage."

"What do you do now?" I asked and was surprised to learn that this large, furry man had a Ph.D. in biology. "But I'd really rather be in the food business," he said. "It's so much more fun. I want to see if I can make a living selling sausages. Do you think it could work?"

I didn't want to be discouraging, but it seemed like a long shot to me. So I mumbled something polite and suggested that we go to the dining car. How was I to know that Bruce Aidells would one day be the sausage king of America?

■ ■ ■

The day had faded into darkness when we finally pulled through the mountains into the Truckee station. The air was like crystal as we got off the train, and our breath became visible. For a group in search of the holy garlic grail, this seemed prophetic.

It was instantly clear that we would have no trouble locating La Vieille Maison: We could smell the restaurant from the station. The scent became stronger as we walked down the main street of Truckee, past dilapidated wooden buildings that gave the entire town the air of a hokey Western movie set.

The garlic trail ended in front of what would have been the saloon. "Charlie Chaplin stayed here when he was filming *The Gold Rush*," said Les, seeming pleased. A man stood in the doorway; with his trim beard, black shirt, and pure silver hair he himself might have stepped out of a Chaplin film. Around his neck, on a heavy chain, was a silver head of garlic. "Robert Charles," he said, bowing theatrically and waving us through the door.

The dining room was lit only by candles, which sent shadows racing up the walls. A rustic bar occupied one wall of the room; the entire center was taken up by a long wooden table laden with bottles of wine and loaves of bread. We set the equipment down and gathered around the table as Robert poured the wine. Suddenly the garlic aroma increased, becoming so strong, so powerful that it was as if an enormous tangible creature had come crowding into the room. But it was only a woman wearing a small, tight shirt and carrying two big bowls. She set them on the table, swept her long black hair out of her eyes, and announced, "Aioli!"

"My wife, Amora," said Robert, sitting down.

Amora brought long baguettes to dip into the garlic mayonnaise, which was soft, airy, rich, delicious. Eating that aioli was like biting into savory clouds. As we ate, Robert told stories of his native Provence, where women sit in the sun with mortars squeezed between their fat thighs, furiously pounding garlic into aioli. As I listened my eyes grew heavy and I began to sink into an odd, sleepy euphoria.

"Ah," said Robert, "she is feeling the garlic effect." He patted my shoulder. "Now you know why we love garlic so much."

Wrapped in this haze of garlic we ate dinner: garlic soup and garlic tart and brains cooked in brown butter with garlic and sage. There was boursin, the garlic-laced cheese, for dessert. We had been eating for six hours—not counting the French toast we had consumed on the train—and somehow I was not full.

"Yes, yes," said Robert sagely, "this too is the garlic effect. You do not even feel uncomfortable after the meal, but full of energy, non?" He motioned to Les. "Monsieur Les, I think now is the time to begin the filming."

"You're filming now?" I asked. It seemed very late.

"It is never," said Robert, "too late for the garlic massage."

"Garlic massage?" I asked. "What garlic massage?"

"The one that we do in the south of France," said Robert. "There is nothing like it."

I looked around to see who the intended recipient of this massage might be. "There is nothing better for the skin than aioli," said Robert ingratiatingly. "The Arlesiennes massage it into their skin to repel insects and promote suntan. And what a heavenly smell they have—oh là là!" He kissed his fingers in my direction.

I was just thinking that it might be fun to give my body up to olive oil, eggs, and garlic when he looked at Les and added, "Your film is too serious, Monsieur Les. Think how nice it will be for the film."

Monsieur Les looked wistful, and I came to my senses and emerged from the haze. Even a Berkeley girl has her limits. And being naked on film was beyond mine.

"Not me," I said firmly. "I am a reporter." I picked up my notebook and held it like a shield. "I am here as an objective observer. My job is to keep notes about all of this. Why not massage Bruce?"

Robert eyed the large man at my side. He shuddered visibly. "Monsieur Bruce?" he squeaked. "Non, non, c'est impossible!" Before I could say another word, he turned and surveyed the room. As he made his way toward a buxom blonde with very long hair, he was almost running.

We watched him lean persuasively toward her. He gestured to Les, to the camera, to me sitting there with my notebook. She smiled, considered, licked her lips. And then she gave a small nod, strolled to the bar, and removed her clothes. She stretched herself languidly across the wood. Robert flexed his fingers. The cameras rolled. Working around the naked woman, Robert began to make the aioli.

"You begin with four cloves of peeled garlic," he said, smiling into the lights. "First you pound them in the mortar for half an hour." He pounded assiduously and added, "It is not how much garlic you use that is important; it is how well you pound it. When you can turn the mortar upside down without anything falling out, then it is enough." He turned the mortar over to demonstrate.

"Then you add the yolk of an egg and a bit of salt. And then a soupspoon of good mustard. And now, slowly, slowly, you pour in a pint of olive oil. When it is a thick mayonnaise you add the juice of one lemon. Voilà!" Robert dipped some bread into his creation and ate. An ecstatic expression crossed his face; standing there, with the lights shining on his silver hair, he looked almost saintly.

He turned to the woman draped across the bar and began to massage aioli into her shoulders. As he slowly worked his way down her body she began to sigh. "Do they really do this in southern France?" she moaned as he started on her inner thighs. Robert, intent on the work of his fingers, assured her that they did. She fell silent, intent on finding her own ecstasy.

▪ ▪ ▪

Les had gotten everything he needed, so we went home the next day. Was it my imagination, or did the train really empty out when we got on board? Were people fleeing into the next car, gasping for breath? They seemed to be. "And now we know another reason why garlic is good," said Bruce. "Look at how we've cleared the car!" He stretched luxuriously across an entire seat. I stretched out too and, wrapped in fumes of garlic, slept most of the way home. I was eager to see Doug; for the first time in weeks I felt almost normal.

▪ ▪ ▪

Doug was gone. "He said to tell you he went to Seattle," Nick told me. "He said he'd be back in a few days."

"But he was too busy to even come to Truckee!" I exclaimed.

Nick shook his head. "All I know is that some woman called to say there was a project up there he might be interested in."

"A woman?" I asked.

"Yes," he replied.

"Do you find anything suspicious in the suddenness of this trip?" I asked. Nick studied me silently for a minute. "Would you care if there was?" he asked at last.

▪ ▪ ▪

The few days stretched to a week. The week turned into a second. "What are you doing?" I asked. He was studying the wind patterns for a wind harp; he had an idea for a rain piano, but he needed to test the wire; he might do something at the Space Needle. The answers were too specific, as if he had written them down before dialing. As the days went on, I found it increasingly difficult to persuade myself that his trip was strictly business. It served me right, I thought, and I asked no questions.

But now that Colman was out of my life, I could not ignore what was happening with Doug. We had once spent every minute together, but we now led separate lives. I suddenly missed him very much. I wished he would call. I sat staring at the phone, willing it to ring. When it did I grabbed it, sure it would be him.

"Hi, honey," I said happily.

The deep voice was not Doug's. "It's Les," it said. "I want you to come for dinner."

Trying not to sound too disappointed I asked, "When?"

"Now," he said. "Right this minute. This guy I met at a film festival in upstate New York is preparing a banquet at my house. He's an incredible Chinese cook. I think you'll be amazed."

I had work to do. My article wasn't finished. I was wearing overalls, and my hair wasn't combed. I didn't feel like seeing anyone.

"Come," urged Les. "This guy cooks food you've never tasted before. You won't be sorry." I hesitated some more, and I heard murmuring in the background. "Alice says to tell you that Chinese food requires a lot of garlic and I might have to film it."

"Is she going to be there?" I asked.

"Of course," he said, as if it were impossible to imagine any food event in Berkeley that did not include Alice.

▪ ▪ ▪

"Where's the cook?" I asked when Les led me into the kitchen. He indicated the stove with his chin, and I saw a tall man with a mop of curly brown hair pouring oil into an enormous wok. "This is Bruce Cost," he said.

The man smiled wanly down at me, and I was disappointed to discover that he was not Chinese. He seemed harried and distracted, and I was sorry I had come. It hardly seemed worth missing a deadline to eat Chinese food cooked by some white guy from upstate New York. I was glad that I hadn't bothered to change for the event.

"Can't you get any more heat out of this stove?" the cook asked. Les leaned over and peered at the burner. He fiddled with the dial. "You've got it all the way up," he said. "It doesn't go any higher."

"You need a bigger flame for Chinese food," insisted the tall cook, looking miserably into the wok. "I don't know if this is going to work . . ."

Oh no, I thought, he's already making excuses. I was trying to think of a graceful way to make my exit when the guy went to the refrigerator, pulled out a platter covered with light amber-colored squiggles, and handed it to me. I recoiled; whatever it was looked horribly like rubber noodles. "Why don't you take that into the living room and pass it around," he said. It was not a question.

I glared at him, but I took the platter. "What is it?" I asked.

"Jellyfish salad," he said. "I was planning to serve it with shrimp toasts, but this puny flame is going to take a long time to get the oil hot enough for the shrimp. I think I'd better serve those people something now. Chop up some of that cilantro and put it on top before you take it in. It will look nicer. See if you can find some little plates, too."

I didn't know how I had become the designated helper, but I was in no mood to fight. I opened the nearest cupboard and found some plates. "How many people are you feeding?"

"I told Les to invite a dozen."

"Do you have chopsticks or something?"

"In the bag over there," he said, pointing to a table cluttered with groceries. "There's a cleaver too."

The table was a mess—the whole kitchen was—and I found myself trying to clear a space large enough to chop on. As I did, it occurred to me that I had not even seen who else was at the party, and I put down the cleaver and wiped my hands. "I'll just go say hello," I told him. "I'll be right back."

"No," he said imperiously. "Get the cilantro chopped and those plates out there. I have to feed them something. There's some journalist Les invited, someone he thought might help me find work. He said she didn't want to come, and I don't want her to go hungry. So just get the stuff out there and say hello while you pass the platter."

"Okay," I said resentfully. Lost in my own thoughts, I barely listened to what he said, but I'd heard enough to understand that I was trapped. I chopped cilantro, liking the astringent scent of the delicate leaves, and sprinkled the cool greens over the squiggles. Then I picked up the tray and took it into the next room.

Most of the guests were people I knew from the Pacific Film Archive, which was right next door to The Swallow. Bruce Aidells was there too, and I was glad to see him. Alice came up, gave me a quick squeeze, and lifted the platter from my arms. "I'll pass this," she said. "It's jellyfish, isn't it? Here, try some."

The salad was very fine, clean and vaguely crunchy, with a sesame tang. As I took a second bite Alice gave me a little push toward the kitchen. "I'll take care of this," she said. "Why don't you go back and get to know Bruce."

"I've already had that pleasure," I muttered, but I was on my way. I found him, looking more harried than before, dropping shrimp toast into the wok.

"I loved that salad," I said, trying to be nice. "It was really, really good." He gave me a cool look and said, "Of course it was," as he plunked another pale square into the hot oil. "These will be good too." He watched impassively as the little raft submerged and then floated to the surface. He stared at the surface, waiting for the toast to turn golden before snatching it from the oil.

"I see you got the fire hot enough," I said.

"Not really," he said with a trace of bitterness. "Virginia Lee, who taught me to cook, would not approve. But we have to make do with what we have. Go find a plate or something to put these on."

When I returned with the plate he handed me the slotted spoon and said, "Take them out when they turn golden. Pass them while they're still hot. I'm glad you're here; I have so much to do."

"What else are we having?" I asked.

He lifted the lid off a big wok, and an intoxicating aroma came drifting up to us. "Pork belly," he said, displaying a rectangle of meat simmering in a dark liquid studded with ginger, scallions, and star anise. "I've stuffed it with a mixture of its own meat chopped with pine nuts, and I'm cooking it in soy and rock sugar. Then we'll have a simple roast chicken. Steamed flounder with ginger and scallions. Baby bok choy with mushrooms. Nothing fancy. But the pork belly is so rich you can't serve anything elaborate."

"It sounds great," I said, wondering how much of this feast I was expected to cook.

"I'll show you what to do with the mushrooms when you've finished that," he said. "I'm grateful for your help."

He obviously thought I had come to assist him, and it seemed rude to tell him I was only a guest. Besides, he needed the help. I decided to consider it an opportunity. "How did you become a Chinese cook?" I asked.

"I read an article about Virginia Lee in *The New York Times* and decided to take a class with her. I was working for a big corporation, living in upstate New York, but something made me drive into the city that first time," he said. "And then, I don't know, it just felt right."

"Love at first sight?" I meant to be ironic, but he did not laugh.

"Exactly! I felt that I had finally found what I was meant to do in life." As he talked I could imagine his teacher's regal presence and understand his growing obsession with the classes. "And so," he finished up, "I began to do some catering. That's how I met Les. I catered the food for a film festival in Rhinebeck, where I live." He corrected himself. "I mean, where I used to live. I've just moved out here."

"You moved out here, just like that?" I asked.

"Yes," he said simply. "I quit my job. It seemed to me that if there was anyplace in America for someone who wanted to devote himself to food, Berkeley would be it."

"I guess so," I said.

"But it's true!" he said. "Look at this. Les invited me over because he thought this journalist might somehow help me. And he introduced me to Alice Waters; he wants her to give me a job."

"Are you that good?" I asked.

"Yes," he said, as if it were a simple statement of fact, not boasting. A shrimp toast came bubbling to the surface and I turned it over, watching the oil foam around its edges.

When there were enough he piled the hot, sesame-studded tidbits onto a tray and shooed me out the door. "You have to make them eat them while they're hot," he said. "But come back quickly, because I want to show you what to do with the pork kidneys."

"I hate kidneys," I couldn't help saying.

"Not these you won't," he said confidently. "You've never had them like this. With the Chinese method, if they're done right, they're pure texture. But you have to soak them and soak them and soak them, changing the water constantly, until all the blood and flavor have been leached out. You'll see."

I was dubious, but I said nothing, and when I came back to the kitchen he showed me how to roast Szechuan peppercorns for the salad. I'd never seen them before, and I marveled at the little red pods and the deep, spicy scent that got more intense as they cooked, rising up to prickle at my nose. "When the peppercorns are so fragrant you almost can't bear how good they smell," he said, "they're done. Then you scatter them across the top of the kidneys. They'll be the first course."

"And then?"

"Then we'll have the fish, because it cooks the fastest. Come look at the flounder I bought." He opened the refrigerator and held out a big, flat, clear-eyed fish.

"How did you know where to buy fish in a town you had only just arrived in?" I asked.

"Oh," he said blithely, "I just went to Chinatown."

"And how did you know which fish to buy?"

"Buying fish is easy in Chinatown. Any Chinatown. You just get the most expensive thing they've got. The Chinese figure their customers know what they're doing. And the chickens there were fabulous. Look at this!" He held out a chicken with a very brown skin.

"How did you find one with brown skin?"

He laughed. "It doesn't have brown skin. I rubbed it with soy sauce. It makes it more flavorful. We'll put the chicken in when we take the kidneys out to the table. It cooks very quickly too, or it will if I can get the oven hot enough." He opened the oven door and stuck his hand in. "It'll do, I think."

Bruce's infatuation with cooking was so infectious that I felt my mood improve. I liked watching him work; he was too tall for this kitchen, but he had an economy of motion that made him seem fluid, like a musician. He moved as if he were meant to be here, as if each of these tools fit comfortably into his hand. His imperious manner was irritating, but in spite of that I found myself liking him. "Isn't it scary, just giving up your old life and making a new one?" I asked.

"Yes," he said simply. "But I got married young and had children young. It's now or never. If I don't do what I really want to now, I never will."

It sounded familiar. I wished him luck. After a while I asked, "Do you want a job with Alice?" I asked.

"You like working with her, don't you?" he inquired. He leaned back and added magnanimously, "By the way, I'll put in a good word for you. She promised to find me someone good to help me out, and I'll be happy to tell her how well you've done."

"Thanks," I said, suddenly understanding who I had to thank for this. "Have you met the journalist yet?"

"Oh no," he replied, "I don't like to meet people like that when I'm cooking. I'd much rather hang out in the kitchen with you."

■ ■ ■

I waited until after dinner to tell Bruce that he had been hanging out with a journalist. The timing was right. His food had been so extraordinary that Alice asked him to cook a special dinner at Chez

Panisse. The publisher of *The Garlic Book* asked him to write a book on ginger. All I asked him to do was cook another meal for me, but I really didn't have to ask. By then we were friends. One meal in Berkeley had already changed his life.

■ ■ ■

"Chinese food?" asked Colman the next day, when I told him about the meal. "Now you want to write about Chinese food? Could you please just finish the garlic article before we discuss that?"

"It's almost done," I promised. "The dinner's tonight."

"I wish I could be there," said Colman.

"I wish you could too," I replied. But as I said it, I realized I was only being polite. Garlic had worked its magic, and it was not Colman I wanted next to me at Alice's big-deal dinner.

But Doug was still in Seattle. He didn't think he was going to make it back in time. Not even for a spectacular meal at Chez Panisse.

■ ■ ■

The wine was strong. The garlic was pungent. A great flamenco singer named Anzonini Del Puerto, another citizen of Berkeley, sang his wild, lonely songs as the familiar garlic haze descended upon the table. Before long the entire room was giddy with garlic euphoria.

Wrapped up in fumes of garlic, we ate galantines of pigeon, duck, and quail with garlic mosaics. We consumed more wine as several whole baked fish, gorgeously wrapped in puffs of garlic pastry and drizzled with lobster butter, were paraded around the dining room. Platters of spring lamb were brought out, surrounded by three garlic-infused purées. We washed the meat down with oceans of deep, dark Zinfandel. Then there was an arugula salad laced with goose fat and garlic-rubbed croutons, followed by poached figs in more red wine, with garlic meringues. And more wine. By the time Les set up his camera and filmed each of us talking about why we loved garlic, I was slurring my words.

But I stood before the big fireplace at Chez Panisse, stuck a flower behind my ear, and looked earnestly into the camera. I had no idea of what I would say.

And then it came to me. The article was going to be good, and I felt at peace with myself. I did not miss Colman and I did not miss Doug. "If everyone ate more garlic, the world would be a happier place," I said.

At that moment, I believed every word.

LA VIEILLE MAISON SOUP

Robert Charles was very proud of this recipe. No wonder. Once you've tried his variation on the classic French onion soup, you'll never go back to the original.

½ stick (¼ cup) unsalted
   butter
6 large onions (about 3½
   pounds), chopped
4 large garlic cloves, chopped
salt and pepper
1 teaspoon all-purpose flour
2 cups dry white wine

4 cups chicken broth
1 teaspoon dried thyme,
   crumbled
4 large eggs
¼ pound Gruyère cheese,
   grated
¼ cup heavy cream

Preheat the oven to 325°F.

Melt the butter over moderately high heat in a heavy, ovenproof 8-quart pot until the foam subsides. Cook the onion and garlic in the butter, adding salt and pepper to taste and stirring, until the onion is softened. Stir in the flour and cook, stirring, for 1 minute. Add the wine, broth, and thyme and cook the soup at a low boil, uncovered, stirring occasionally, for 15 minutes. Cover the pot and bake in the middle of the oven for 2 hours.

Ladle the soup into 4 individual earthenware crocks or oven-proof bowls (about 1½-cup capacity) and whisk an egg into each. Sprinkle the tops with cheese and bake in the middle of the oven until the cheese is melted, about 10 minutes. Remove the crocks from the oven and spoon 1 tablespoon cream over each serving.

Serves 4.

DOTTIE'S SPINACH

When I asked Les for his favorite garlic recipe, he gave me this one. I don't even know who Dottie is. I do know, however, that her recipe will make your house smell like garlic for days, and that the fumes will precede the casserole to the table.

> *2 pounds (about 3 10-ounce bags) fresh spinach, coarse stems removed*
> *1 stick (½ cup) unsalted butter*
> *2 onions, chopped*
> *salt and pepper*
> *1 head garlic, peeled and chopped*
> *½ teaspoon cayenne pepper*
> *12 ounces cheddar cheese, grated*
> *2 cups fresh bread crumbs*

Wash the spinach well and drain it in a colander. Put half of the spinach, with water clinging to its leaves, in a heavy 6- to 8-quart pot and cook over moderate heat, covered, stirring occasionally, until slightly wilted, about 1 minute. Add the remaining spinach and continue to cook over moderate heat, covered, stirring occasionally, until wilted but still bright green, about 1 minute more. Drain the spinach in a colander. When the spinach is cool enough to handle, squeeze it dry in small handfuls and chop finely.

Preheat the oven to 350°F.

Melt the butter in a large, deep, heavy skillet over moderate heat until the foam subsides. Cook the onion in the butter, with salt and pepper to taste, stirring, until softened, about 8 minutes. Stir in the garlic and cayenne and cook, stirring, until the garlic is softened. Add the spinach and cook, stirring, for 2 minutes. Add the cheese and cook over moderately low heat, stirring, until the cheese is melted and all the ingredients are combined well. Season the mixture with salt and pepper and spread in a well-buttered heavy 1½- to 2-quart shallow baking dish. Sprinkle the top evenly with bread crumbs and bake in the middle of the oven until golden brown on top and bubbling, 20 to 25 minutes.

Serves 6 as a side dish.

6

ARMADILLOS
IN CHINA

"The two most important things in life," my ailing father said, "are imagination and laughter. They make anything interesting. Even this."

He gestured at the tray before him, on which was arrayed an extremely dry piece of a substance reputed to be fish, some plain strands of unadorned spaghetti, and the soggiest bits of squash I have ever seen. He shook his head in mock agony. "It's a disgrace to be reduced to this spiceless, saltless, flavorless food at my age." My father is, however, the most polite man who ever lived, and he always polished off his plate for fear of offending whomever it was in the hospital's labyrinthine kitchens who had prepared it.

"How can you eat that stuff?" his visitors all asked, but Dad only shrugged. "It's a matter of will. I just pretend that it's something delicious. Sometimes I can even taste what my daughter describes." He turned to me. "Where are we eating tonight?" he inquired.

—*New West* magazine, November 1980

■ ■ ■

When Mom called about my father's stroke Doug and I stared at each other in confusion. We knew he was eighty, but he had never seemed old. He still went into his office to design books every day, even on weekends, and he was extremely proud that twelve new publishers had recently offered him work. He was a man who laughed at pain and had never been in the hospital; born in a time when babies were delivered at home, he had never needed an operation. Watching Doug, I knew that the same thought was going through both of our minds: If Dad was ill, anything was possible.

Then we swung into action. Doug canceled his next trip. I grabbed the menus from the two San Francisco restaurants I was reviewing, stuffed them into my suitcase between the skirts and sweaters, and dashed down the stairs. Ten hours later we were in New York, walking into Beth Israel Hospital.

My father was propped up in a big metal bed with mysterious tubes snaking beneath the covers. His eyes were dull and he looked frail, but he smiled broadly when he saw us, and the light leapt into his eyes. Then he recalled his surroundings and bit off the smile, which turned into a frown of embarrassment. "I'm so sorry to trouble you like this," he said. Still, he didn't miss a beat before turning to Doug and asking, "Can you go to the office? There are three jobs I promised for yesterday."

They both seemed relieved to turn the sickroom into a workplace, and I had a moment of intense jealousy as I watched their heads bent together, going over the details of Dad's designs for books. They understood each other so well that they barely needed language; as Dad began to draw a title page Doug, silently, finished it.

"You could not have married a better man," said Dad when Doug had left for the office. "You have no idea how relieved I am that he's here."

Yearning to communicate with my father the way Doug did, I pulled the menus out of my suitcase. "Would you help me with my work now?" I asked.

Dad looked delighted. "Of course!" he said. I handed him the menus. "See if you can guess, just from looking at the type, what these two restaurants are like," I said.

Dad took the menus and ran his fingers over the type, just as he did with books. He loved type; it spoke to him. I simply transcribed what he said. Talking to my father had never been easy for me, and our encounters had often left us both at a loss for words. But I had hit the right note, and the next few hours were the most comfortable that Dad and I had ever spent together.

Dad decoded the restaurants amazingly well, and when he was done we were both so enthralled with the exercise that we continued by pretending to eat together. The nurse came in just as we were finishing "dessert" and stood in amazement, watching us eat nothing. "Delicious cheesecake," said Dad, grinning at her.

It was, perhaps, the strangest restaurant review ever written, but it made my father happy. He had never been very interested in my work, but writing that review changed everything. Now he said, "My daughter's going to China," to every person who approached his bed. And then, as if this were a special badge of honor, he added proudly, "She's going to a city that has been closed to Caucasians for more than thirty years. She's being sent there by a magazine."

Metropolitan Home had actually wanted Colman for this assignment, but he suggested that I take his place. "You're interested in Chinese food," he'd said when he'd called to tell me about it. "I thought you'd like to go."

"Feeling guilty?" I'd asked.

"Do you want the assignment?" he'd replied.

Of course I did. Nine years after Nixon's first trip, China still seemed remote, mysterious, and unexplored. My father loved poring over the brochures, with their misty pictures of dancing children dressed in red. "You'll be seeing things no American has ever seen," Dad said. When I protested that it was not all that exotic, he quoted the flowery words of the brochure. " 'You have the opportunity to leave the pressures of the twentieth century behind,' " he intoned solemnly. " 'Experience,' " he said, " 'a brief journey into another time.' " He read on, mentioning the fact that my access to the village of Taishan would be unrestricted and that I would witness "a more natural way of life." But to my father, this was the clincher: " 'Few people,' " he read, " 'have toured rural China and come away unchanged.' "

"But I don't want to change," I protested.

"Nonsense," said my father, "everybody changes." And then he said what he always said just before the nurse arrived with the tray of dreary, unsalted glop that the doctors were convinced would make him well: "Promise me you'll go. Even if I am not better. Even if I die. You may never get this chance again."

■ ■ ■

"He'll get better," I said to Doug as we left the hospital. I swung my arms in the gray, humid air, conscious of how effortlessly my legs were moving across the sidewalk. My own good health felt like a reproach, and as I kicked crumpled paper cups and old Popsicle sticks out of my path I felt light enough to fly.

Doug touched my arm, bringing me back to earth. "I doubt it," he said flatly. "He'll die before he turns into one of those pathetic old men hanging around the house. He won't live if he can't work."

"He's eighty years old," I said. "He doesn't have to work."

"Ruth, think," said Doug, "Do you really think he wants to spend all his time alone with your mother?"

"No," I answered, seeing his point. "When I was little I envied the way he could escape to the office, while I had to stay home with her. I remember once when I was very young, years before we knew she was manic-depressive, and she was giving one of those out-of-control parties. She was wearing red pedal-pushers, and she'd decided to clean the closets. The hallway was filled with piles of sheets, stacks of napkins, and mountains of blankets. In the living room silver trays, ramekins, teapots, and spoons swirled across the coffee table and bookcases, covering every surface. And heaps of sticks were stacked on the floor, looking like bonfires waiting to be ignited."

"Sticks?" said Doug.

"Yes. She used to make us go to the country in the middle of winter and cut forsythia so that back in the city we could force it to bloom. You had to get the heat up really high to make it happen. I remember Dad standing there, sweat pouring down his face, as he picked up his briefcase. I wanted a briefcase too."

"No wonder," said Doug dryly.

"Then Mom walked into the kitchen, dragging a tablecloth that had attached itself to her shoe. When I giggled Dad put his fingers to his lips. You know how Mom hates to be laughed at. Then he followed her into the kitchen."

"She was cooking?" he asked, rolling his eyes.

"Trying," I said. "She had *Life's Picture Cook Book* open on the counter, surrounded by piles of rabbit bones, bunches of celery, heaps of onions and unpeeled carrots. She'd decided to tackle the Forum of the Twelve Caesars alpine snow hare, oblivious to the fact that the recipe required four days and the party was tomorrow."

"What did your dad do?" asked Doug.

"What do you think?" I asked. "Kissed her good-bye and said, 'I have to work late tonight. Don't wait up for me.' I went to the door to stand with him until the elevator came, and I remember watching the way his whole body relaxed as he stepped in, on his way out of the house and off to the world of work."

"So imagine his life with no work," said Doug.

The light changed. I put my hand on Doug's arm. "Are you sure he won't get better?" I asked. We crossed the street, walking down Second Avenue to Saint Marks Place.

"Maybe he'll recover from the stroke," said Doug, "but I don't think he'll be able to go back to work." He swung the briefcase he was carrying and indicated it with his head. "I've had to redo every job. His hands are getting too shaky to continue designing books. I didn't say anything, but I'm sure he knows."

"What do you think he'll do?" I asked.

"Die," said Doug simply. "Just die."

We slowed down as we neared my parents' apartment, reluctant to face my mother. She was not taking Dad's illness very well. At her best with a doctor to harass or a bureaucracy to fight, she was temperamentally unsuited to the long, slow pace of recovery. She pounced on us when we opened the door, as if she had been lying in wait, listening for the sound of the elevator. "What will I do if he dies?" she raged. "I'll just be another sad old lady without a man. How can he do this to me?"

"We just stopped in to see if you want to come to Chinatown with us," I said. "I promised Dad I'd find someone to tell me about that village I'll be visiting in China."

"You and your trip!" she spat. "How can you even think of going to China at a time like this?"

"Mom," I said wearily, "we've been through all this before."

▪ ▪ ▪

"At least you made the effort," Doug said when my mother locked herself in her bedroom. "Miriam," he shouted through the door, "we're leaving now. Are you sure you don't want to come with us?"

There was no reply.

"Do you want us to bring you back something to eat?"

"Oh, don't worry about me," she said weakly. "I'll find some old crust of bread to eat while you're off enjoying yourselves."

I started to reply, but Doug put his hand on my arm. "Don't get hooked," he said. As we walked out the door I thought for a moment how much I had learned from my father. My marriage had always been a refuge.

It was still late afternoon as we walked south, through the arch of Washington Square Park and past the art galleries of SoHo. "How are you going to find people to ask about Taishan?" Doug asked.

"Easy," I said. "Most of the Chinese people who emigrated to America in the 1800s were from Taishan. There was a huge flood, followed by famine, and people came to this country to work on the railroads."

"Oh, right," said Doug. "You'll walk into the first restaurant you come to and shout, 'Anyone here have relatives in Taishan?' "

"I haven't quite worked out how to do it," I said sheepishly. "But if I can get some real details about the place it will make Dad so happy. It's the only thing that seems to cheer him up. Maybe we could just go into a few little shops and see what happens? You'll come with me, won't you?"

"Sure," said Doug gamely. He grimaced, and I was reminded of how much he loved my father. "If you really think it will make him happy."

We walked down Mulberry Street; the neighborhood was changing as, one by one, the Italian stores became Chinese. "Look," said Doug when we passed Mr. Bergamini's butcher shop. The door was closed, and taped to the dusty window was a hand-lettered sign that said, WE HAVE MOVED TO LONG ISLAND. COME VISIT US!

"Too bad!" I said. "He'll be miserable out in the suburbs. Who's going to listen to his political spiel out there?" I thought I heard his voice as I passed the shop. "The bastards," he was saying. "The manufacturers pay them off. They're poisoning the air because they're too cheap to spend the money to do things right."

I glanced at the window and saw a gesticulating shadow. Going back, I got up close, pressed my nose against the glass, and looked in: The shop was cleared out, empty, but there was Mr. Bergamini, still in fine form, still talking about the perfidy of the politicians to some hapless visitor.

"Where ya been?" he asked casually, as if it had not been seven years since I'd last stopped in for breast of veal. He touched my shoulder and clasped Doug's hand in a firm shake. "Nice to see ya."

"It's nice to see you too," I said. The shop looked forlorn, its gleaming refrigerator cases filled with nothing. The smell of bleach and floor polish hung in the air. "But I'm sorry to see that you're moving."

"Oh," he said, shrugging, "things change. The neighborhood's not what it used to be. The dairy guys still do good business. The pastry shops too. But it's mostly tourists now. You can't sell no meat to tourists, and the Chinese buy from their own. I feel like the last guinea on Mulberry Street. I should have moved years ago." He smiled painfully. "I'll be okay. I'm going to work with my brother-in-law out on the Island. He's got a fancy place out there. He calls it a meat boutique, says it sounds better than 'butcher.' It won't be my own, but what can you do?"

With an obvious effort he turned and asked politely, "And you? What are you doing these days?"

I told him about my father, and he said all the right things. And then I told him about the trip to China. "You have to meet Mr. Chan!" he said. "Come on, I'll take you!"

The mere thought of being useful to someone seemed to cheer him up; he practically skipped along the sidewalk, dodging old ladies sitting on upended crates as they peeled vegetables, and fishmongers weighing wriggling creatures on rusty scales. The air smelled like ginger, like garlic, like fermented tofu, and I wondered if Taishan would smell the same.

"Who is Mr. Chan?" I asked as Doug and I scurried behind him.

"You'll see," he said, slowing down before a trio of dingy shops. On the right was a wooden door that said PRIVATE SOCIAL CLUB in small letters. The left had a window filled with dusty pizza equipment. Between them was a small place with FLUFF AND FOLD LAUNDRY written across the door in black letters. A bell tinkled when we went in. The tired smell of dust rose up from the uneven wooden floor. Mr. Bergamini called, "Chan!" and energetically began poking at the bags of laundry piled on the counter, pushing them aside. When he had cleared enough space, a small, wrinkled face emerged from behind the white mountain, blinking in the sudden rush of light.

"Yes?" he said, as if he could not quite focus. And then, "Oh, it's you, Bergamini."

"I have a friend I want you to meet," said Mr. Bergamini. "She is going to China, and she needs your advice."

"Where you going?" asked Mr. Chan. When I told him he nodded solemnly and intoned, "Toy San."

"No," I said, "Taishan."

"Toy San," he repeated indignantly. "That is what we call our village."

"You are from Taishan?" I asked. "I mean," I corrected myself hastily, "Toy San."

"We will have lunch," announced Mr. Chan. Locking the store behind him, he led us down Mulberry and across Canal to a small storefront. The kitchen was in the window, a single wok and a steaming cauldron of boiling water. The cook looked ancient, but he moved nimbly between wok and cauldron, wreathed in clouds of vapor. Above his head slabs of bright red barbecued pork dangled between shiny brown ducks and chickens impaled on hooks. Trays nearby were heaped with cut vegetables, noodles in different shapes, and odd tangles of meat. We sat down at a grimy, plastic-covered table. At tables all around us men held bowls beneath their chins as they quickly shoveled food, with chopsticks, into their open mouths. Inhaling the funky aroma of chicken feet, pork fat, and ginger, I was suddenly very hungry.

Mr. Chan got up and said something to the cook in rapid Cantonese and the old man smiled at me with a kindly air. "Good," he grunted, scooping some broth into a bowl and handing it to Mr. Chan. Mr. Chan brought it to the table and set it in front of me.

I stared down into the clear soup. In its depths were noodles and dumplings and little twists of white and gray that I tried hard not to identify. But the steam coming off it was intoxicatingly fragrant, and I picked up the bowl between my two hands and sipped at it. It was wonderful stuff, and I took another sip, and another.

Mr. Chan showed me how to pull the dumplings out of the soup with my spoon and then pick them up with my chopsticks. He ate one himself and sighed. "It is almost like being at home," he said, his eyes nearly closed.

"Home," he repeated. "Home. Why are you going to Toy San?" And then his tone changed and he said, almost angrily, "It is no place for tourists. There is no hotel."

"Oh no," I said, "you're wrong. I will be staying at the Stone Mountain Flower Inn. It's new."

"No," he said, "you will certainly not be staying there." He waved to the waiter, who put down a plate of sliced suckling pig, the skin crisp and crackling over the milky soft flesh of the animal. He picked up a piece, delicately, with his chopsticks and sucked at the meat.

"I am too," I said. "I'll show you my itinerary."

"Show me anything you want," he said. "But you won't be staying there."

"Why?" I asked.

"Because," he sighed, speaking slowly as if to a very small and obstinate child, "it has not been built. You will find yourself in the Toy San Overseas Travelers' Hotel. And you won't like it."

"Why not?" I asked.

"No air-conditioning. No hot water. No elevator."

"No problem," I said, convinced that he was wrong. I had seen pictures of the Stone Mountain Flower Inn. *Metropolitan Home* had asked me to write about Taishan as the great new tourist destination for Americans. The hotel was one of the focal points; local food was the other.

"I hear the food in Toy San is very good," I said brightly.

Mr. Chan laughed in a manner that I considered slightly ominous. "You like Chinese food?" he asked.

"Oh yes," I said. "This is delicious."

"No," he said contemptuously, "real Chinese food. Frog. Jellyfish. Pigeon. Dog. In Toy San we eat everything."

He was not going to frighten me! I thought of Bruce's kidneys and jellyfish as I answered, "I eat those things all the time." And then, wanting to be entirely truthful, I offered a correction. "Not dog," I admitted. "But I practically live on jellyfish."

"You must be rich," he said, but he was smiling. He turned to Mr. Bergamini. "Okay," he said. "I will introduce this young lady to a friend in Toy San. This is very convenient; I have been wanting to send a letter to Chen. Privately, if you understand me."

"Privately?" I asked.

"Everyone is watched," he said mysteriously.

"Who is this Chen?" I asked a little dubiously; I wasn't sure I liked the sound of this.

"A chef," said Mr. Chan. "Before the revolution he worked for one of the most powerful families in China, and afterward he was allowed to continue cooking." A cloud passed over his face. "But that was before the Gang of Four and the so-called Cultural Revolution. They hated smart people. So they sent him back to our village to dig."

"Dig?" I said.

"Dig," he repeated. "He built the lake in the middle of Toy San. You will see it. He was already an old man, and they made him dig. Will you take a letter to him?"

■ ■ ■

"Oh, this sounds very good," said my father gleefully. "You are going to have an adventure!" He sounded healthier than he had in weeks.

"I'm glad I'm not going," Doug said. "I'm not sure I could deal with eating dog."

"It would be an improvement on this," replied my father, pointing to his dinner tray. "A big improvement. Why, I'd love to have some tasty dog right now. Maybe Chef Chen will give you some good recipes." He grinned wickedly as he poked a spoon into the glutinous tapioca. "And I certainly hope that your new friend is right about the hotel. It will be so much more interesting to stay in a place for real people than in one of those silly luxury hotels."

■ ■ ■

Two weeks later I stood in front of the Stone Flower Mountain Inn. Mr. Chan was right: I was staring at a hole in the ground.

Dear Dad,

You will be very pleased to learn that everything is just as Mr. Chan remembered. The hotel is like something from an old movie, a ramshackle building in the middle of a town that looks like a good wind would blow it over. It is tropical here, hot, sticky and humid. Air-conditioning? Of course not; we don't even have hot water.

But cold showers are really all you need in this climate. The important thing is to run the water for a long time before you get in; if you're lucky this will chase away a few of the small creatures who reside in the shower. Many insects seem to consider my room their home. When I come in at night I hear the bugs scuttling toward the corners, and when I plug the lamp in to turn it on (there's no switch) I see them disappearing into the shadows. Fortunately, I have a mosquito net over my bed. There's no TV or radio, of course, but the early-morning tai chi classes on the island in the middle of the lake are very entertaining. I guess that's the lake Mr. Chen built, but I haven't met him yet. I'm beginning to wonder if I ever will; contact with local people is definitely discouraged.

I can't wait to tell you all about this. More soon.

The journey from Hong Kong to Taishan took hours. After the ferry to the mainland, we spent ten terrifying hours on a bus that flew down dirt roads, honking constantly as it scattered chickens, children, and bicycles before it. The driver made no concessions to the slow or the lame, and dawdlers were out of luck.

Water was the only thing that stopped our driver. At each river he stomped on the brakes and skidded to a dusty halt. This didn't do much to keep the front wheels dry, but the rear ones were spared. Then, gratefully shaking our stiff limbs, the little group of journalists with which I was traveling climbed down to wait for the ferry.

There were no bridges, just flat rafts that took anything that wanted to get to the other side: people, cars, animals. The ferries were free. We crossed three brown, muddy rivers, or maybe it was the same river we crossed three times. No antennas, electrical wires, or telephone poles could be seen anywhere on the flat horizon, and we never saw a car. The quiet was profound. Occasionally a boat would float past. Women squatted over cooking pots in the bow, and they would stand up and stare at us in amazement. "And these are the people who have the Russians scared shitless!" marveled one of my fellow travelers.

It was dusk when the bus finally arrived in Taishan, but the center of town was filled with people who had gathered to see the first foreign visitors. The streets were narrow, and so claustrophobically packed that I almost fainted as I stumbled from the bus, clutching my suitcase. Something brushed my head, and I turned to find a group of children, hands outstretched, reaching for my hair. It had swollen in the tropical humidity until it stood around my head, a frizzy dark halo. One little boy locked eyes with mine; his hand darted forward, touched my head, and then snapped back as if it had been burned. It was his first encounter with curls.

My hair was a magnet for the entire town of Taishan. As I made my way toward the hotel a hundred hands reached out. I could feel them touch me, and then they stopped. Turning, I found a small man hissing and batting irritably at the hands. He shooed me into the hotel, sounding like an angry wet hen.

The man ushered us into the lobby and, still hissing, pushed the local people out of the doorway. Clucking now, he pulled the doors shut. Then he took a deep breath, gathered his dignity, and executed a bow. "I am Mr. Lee," he said in very careful English. "I am your responsible person. You will go to your rooms now and then we will have a little talk."

His officious manner made me feel like a rebellious teenager. Go to my room indeed! The rest of the group moved to the stairway, but I held back. "There is someone I must find," I said to Mr. Lee.

"Go to your room," he said. "We will talk later."

"No," I said, "I must find Mr. Chen. I have a message for him. Do you know where I can find him?"

"Chen?" he said, his voice rising with suspicion. "Chen? How do you know this man?"

"He is a friend of a friend in New York."

"A Chinese friend?" asked Mr. Lee. He hopped from one foot to the other. He bit his nails. "A friend from Toy San?" And then, making an obvious effort to collect himself, he said, "Wouldn't you like to put your affairs in order? Afterward we will talk." Without another word he turned his back and walked away.

I picked up my suitcase and headed for the wide cement stairway. At each landing an unsmiling old lady, hands folded in her lap, sat, silently watching. They followed me with their eyes as I went up. The old lady on the third floor looked me up and down, very coolly, grunted, and pointed to a room. The door was open. There was no key. I balanced my suitcase on the hard narrow bed, which was covered with a single sheet, and went to the window. It opened onto a small cement balcony but it was very hot, and even outside there was no breeze.

The bathroom was large, with rust-covered yellow tiles on the walls and floor; although it was clean it smelled slightly of urine. When I flushed the toilet the pipes squealed loudly with the sound of faintly hysterical pigs. I splashed cold water on my face, and they squealed louder.

I was startled to come out of the bathroom and find the old lady standing by the bed staring down at my suitcase as if she had X-ray vision. I had not heard her enter, but I got the message: I was keyless in China and she had her eye on me. She watched, silently, as I walked down the stairs.

Mr. Lee was standing at the bottom; the small group of journalists was gathered around him. "Troublemakers," he began, "are everywhere. My job is to see that you come to no harm. To ensure your personal safety I must ask that you talk to no one." He repeated this so many times that the man standing next to me, a freelance travel writer named Ed, began looking at me and rolling his eyes.

"After dinner," continued Mr. Lee, "you will be given bicycles." He paused, as if he were about to confer a great honor upon us. "And then, as a very special privilege, you will be free to go anywhere you like!"

"Wonderful!" whispered Ed, his voice dripping with sarcasm.

"But I emphasize," Mr. Lee continued, "that you must talk to no one. No one!"

"What if someone speaks to us?" asked Ed.

"Do not reply," said Mr. Lee. "Troublemakers are everywhere. Speak to no one except authorized persons like myself." He stared intently around at the group, trying to impress the importance of his message upon each of us.

"Tomorrow morning," he finally continued, "we will visit the hospital. There you will witness the wonders of Chinese medicine. The following morning we will visit the weekly Toy San market. And one day next week you will spend an entire day and night at a farm commune so that you can experience the life of rural China."

"This isn't rural?" muttered Ed.

"In the afternoons," Mr. Lee continued, "you will be on your own. For your personal safety I must emphasize that you talk to no one." Once again he stared, intent and silent, at the group. Finally he pointed to the door at the end of the lobby and said, "Shall we have dinner now?"

"Can we talk to the waiter?" asked Ed.

Mr. Lee did not understand the humor. "Oh yes," he replied. "He is authorized."

"What about Mr. Chen?" I asked. "Do you know how I might find him? I promised my friend in New York that I would."

"That will not be possible," said Mr. Lee firmly. "There are so many people named Chen here, how would I know which one you wanted? And even if I knew how to find this person you speak of . . ." His voice trailed off as if he were envisioning the many sinister possibilities a meeting might entail.

Dear Dad,

So far we have had no dog. We have, however, had lots of frogs, and I don't mean just the legs. Our first meal also included smoked oysters, beef with vegetables, braised duck, squid with mushrooms, and bright green broccoli drizzled with fragrant oyster sauce. And that was just the beginning.

Our group clown is a man named Ed, a travel writer from California. Overwhelmed by the sheer amount of protein on the table, he kept asking for a little bit of rice. Mr. Lee refused.

"We don't want you to fill up too early," he said. "Rice comes at the end of the meal." And that was that. He stuffed a piece of sweet-and-sour goose into his mouth, making it impossible for him to answer further questions. Free will does not seem to be a popular concept in China.

Children gather in the doorway at every meal, staring at us as we eat. It is an odd sensation; one moment I feel like a rock star, the next like a tiger in the zoo. I'm very grateful I've been using chopsticks all my life; at least they don't laugh at me like they do at some of the others.

When the goose was gone, a platter of whole steamed fish appeared. It was the best part of the meal. Only after we had dug the sweet meat out of the cheeks did a platter of fried rice appear, signaling the end of the meal.

I'm back in my room now, writing this letter. The room was empty when I arrived, but I suspect the old lady who sits on the landing has been in here inspecting my things. It's a very strange feeling.

I'm going to have to stop writing now: Huge green bugs are dive-bombing the desk and I think the only way to make them stop is to turn out the light.

I hope you're home by now. Even Mom's cooking *has* to be an improvement over hospital food.

Much love to you both.

The absence of light did not make the impression I had hoped on the big green bugs. They hopped around in the dark until I couldn't take it anymore and fled. I went down to the lobby to see if any fellow travelers were there, but it was empty. There were, however, hundreds of people standing just outside the door, and as soon as I opened it they descended on me. When I walked, they walked. When I stopped, they did too. So we walked, my entourage and me, through the nighttime village of Taishan.

The streets were pulsating with life. Peering into the brightly lit apartments I could see why: Dozens of people were crammed into each small room. In Taishan, life was lived outdoors. Women cooked the family meal over little fires in the street and children bathed there, sticking their heads into buckets to wash their hair, pouring water across each other's chests. Old men smoked and women sewed. Taishan had many things, but privacy was not one of them.

Suddenly someone tapped my arm. I jumped and looked up. A boy of about eighteen with an acne-scarred face was standing next to me. "Come," he said. I was so startled that I simply followed him. All the others followed me.

He led me to a large shop, lit by naked lightbulbs, where men sat on stools set around tables. Each was holding a little white bowl. There were no free seats, but my new friend found two stools in a corner and squeezed them against a table. He patted the seat and I sat down. As I did he handed me one of the little white bowls and a porcelain spoon.

It contained fresh bean curd, slightly sweetened and slicked with peanut oil. It had the cool quality of custard, and it slipped easily down my throat. I could feel my audience watching each swallow. Did they expect some reaction? I gave the thumbs-up sign. They smiled.

A long, canvas-covered conveyor belt stretched along the back wall. A woman stood at one end pouring a white liquid onto the canvas; another spread the liquid with a wooden paddle, her motions graceful and constant. By the time the stuff got to the two women at the far end of the conveyor belt, it was no longer liquid, and they peeled it off in wrinkled sheets. Then they twisted the sheets and threw them into baskets.

"Dried bean curd," said my new friend, answering my unspoken question. "This is the bean-curd factory." It was also, I realized, the center of Taishan nightlife.

"I am Fu-Tung," he said quite loudly. And then suddenly he dropped his voice so that I could barely hear him. "Keep eating. Don't reply. Mr. Chen sent me. Pretend I am not talking." His English was excellent. His lips barely moved.

I looked down into my bowl and said nothing. "He knows that you have a letter for him. Tomorrow afternoon he will come to your hotel. You will know who he is. He will find a way to take the letter without making trouble."

Raising his voice he asked, in loud, jovial tones, "Might I be so presumptuous as to invite you to my home for tea?"

An adventure—and an invitation to a private home: I had hit the jackpot. My friend gallantly pulled out my stool, and with the entire group trailing behind we left the bean-curd café.

Fu-Tung lived in one room with his parents, his grandparents, his sister, his sister's husband, and their son. "My great dream," he said as his mother made tea, "is to have my own apartment." Dozens of people stood in the window, peering in, jostling for a better view. "But I think," he continued, "that this will never be possible. May I ask you for a favor?"

"Yes?" I said.

"I am very anxious to improve my English."

"Your English," I said honestly, "is very good."

"No, no," he said, "it is very poor. But if you would record some readings for me in English, I could practice. Would you be good enough to do this for me?"

"Of course," I said. He handed me a small tape recorder and a worn workbook called *Essential English*. I slid them into my pocketbook. We drank our tea out of small cups with rice embedded in the porcelain. Mr. Chen's name did not come up again. Then I walked, with my entourage, back to the hotel.

■ ■ ■

Mr. Lee was waiting for me, jumping up and down with rage. "I told you to talk to no one," he said. "And what do you do? On your very first night you deliberately disobey me and have contact with private citizens! You have entered a citizen's house! This is strictly forbidden!"

"What are you going to do," I asked, "have me arrested?" I felt as if I were about thirteen. Whistling loudly, I went up the stairs.

Someone was standing on the second-floor landing. The light was off, so I could not see his face, but he hissed at me as I passed. "Measures," he said in a heavy German accent, "vill be taken. Be careful. Trust no one."

"Oh, Ed," I said, but I did feel like a spy. I hid the workbook and tape recorder in my suitcase and then, ignoring the big green bugs, I wrote another letter to my father. I knew he would delight in this as much as I did. As for me, for the first time since Paris, I felt that I was really living in the moment. I did not know where my life was going, but right now the future did not trouble me.

■ ■ ■

When I awakened the old ones were practicing tai chi on the island in the lake. I watched them for a while and then went to breakfast. "Ah," said Ed when I sat down and surveyed the dim sum on the table, "the American operative has arrived!" He was highly amused, and I laughed with him; in the light of morning the whole thing seemed ridiculous.

Then Mr. Lee slid into the seat next to mine.

"The tape recorder," he said holding out his hand. "I must ask you for it."

I picked up one of the unsweetened coconut cakes that looked remarkably like Hostess SnoBalls. "Why?" I asked with all the insolence I could muster.

Mr. Lee pursed his lips. "Because we cannot have everyone in Toy San bothering our foreign visitors with requests for English lessons," he said. "If we permit this infraction of the rules, tomorrow there will be hundreds of people here with tape recorders." His hand waved imperiously.

"I don't have it here," I said.

"Fetch it at once," he replied. I wanted to ask where he had learned a word like "fetch," but I restrained myself. I wondered what he would do if I refused. We stared at each other, defiantly, for a moment, and then I blinked.

The watch lady was not at her post, so I was not surprised to find her in my room, calmly brushing ants off the desk. I removed my suitcase from the armoire and extracted the tape recorder. Was it my imagination, or had my suitcase really been searched?

■ ■ ■

Mr. Lee was right behind me as I boarded the bus to the hospital. When I sat down, he took the seat next to mine. "You are a troublesome girl," he said reproachfully. "How old are you?"

When I told him I was thirty-two, he seemed genuinely surprised. "But you are older than I am," he said, as if this must be some trick. "Why aren't you wearing any makeup? Don't all American women wear makeup?"

"Obviously not," I said.

"And we must talk about your clothing," he continued.

"My clothing?" I replied.

"Yes," he said. "You are not wearing anything to hold up your breasts. This is disrespectful to the doctors at the hospital." Saying this did not embarrass him in the least. "And it would be more respectful if you did not wear sleeveless tops," he went on.

"Bras and sleeves," I said. "I'll try to remember."

"Yes," he said, "please do." Turning to address the entire bus he announced, "We have arrived at the hospital. Now you will experience the wonders of Chinese medicine."

Dear Dad,

The whole time we were at the hospital I thought of you. I'm happy that you're not a patient here. We were taken to watch an operation for stomach cancer; the patient was anesthetized with nothing more than some acupuncture needles. Ten of us crowded into the operating room while the doctor reached into the open cavity of his abdomen. He cut off a tumor and held it up. Then he held something else aloft. "The liver," he said, cradling it in his hands. There was something unreal about it all. The doctor and nurses were scrubbed, gowned, and masked, but our group went entirely as we were.

"Aren't they worried about germs?" I asked Mr. Lee when we were back in the bus.

"Oh," he replied, "your germs don't count." For the patient's sake I certainly hope he's right.

Gotta go now. We're about to get our first Cantonese lesson, and I don't want to miss it. If I ever get to meet Mr. Chen, it might be useful to be able to communicate with him.

An elderly gentleman was standing in the hotel's lobby, next to a blackboard. Very thin, with wispy white hair and a short silver beard, he looked like the poet in every old Chinese painting. "This," said Mr. Lee, "is the professor. He will try to teach you a few words of Chinese. This will be helpful to you tomorrow in the market."

The professor drew a character that looked like an abstract picture of an armless person in mid-stride. "Here," he said, "is the word for person. Yun." He pronounced it "jan."

He added a stroke that looked like arms. "Now it is dai yun, a big person."

He went on, adding strokes to make a man, a woman, a husband, a wife. Handing out pieces of paper he asked us to draw along with him. Then he came around, correcting our drawings. When he got to me he looked down at my paper and said, "Good effort. But it would be better if you held your pencil properly. Let me show you." He took my hand to guide the pencil, and I watched as my hand made a few careful strokes. "Good," said the professor, "very good." He picked up my hand again, and together we made a few more strokes. When I looked down I saw that we had written English characters, and that they spelled "Chen."

I wondered how a chef had turned into a professor; I wondered what would happen next. One moment it all seemed thrilling; the next it felt unreal. I wished I understood, really understood, what was going on. As the class ended the professor asked if there was any way he could be of service to us. I saw my chance. "I am here to write about food," I said. "I would be very grateful if you could help me arrange a visit to the kitchen and translate for me."

"Certainly," he said gravely. "I would be honored. I will arrange it with your responsible person. It may take a few days. . . . But perhaps I will see you tomorrow. I will accompany your group to the market." He looked at me with a twinkle and added, "In the meantime, please do not accept any invitations to tea. You foreign devils are so much trouble!"

▪ ▪ ▪

Before I went to bed I slid the letter for Mr. Chen out of my suitcase, folded it into a small square that fit neatly into my palm, and put it into my shirt pocket. What, I wondered, did it say? I slept in the shirt; I did not want the letter to disappear during the night.

The next morning the watch lady was on the landing when I emerged from my room. She half-shut her eyes, like a big lizard in the sun, and scrutinized me as I walked down the stairs. The letter in my pocket felt very heavy.

While my fellow travelers complained about the lack of bacon and eggs, I devoured fluffy white bao filled with barbecued pork, little steamed shu mai with crinkled tops, and yeast rolls filled with a sweetened egg-yolk paste. Best of all were the shrimp dumplings in the shape of bunny rabbits.

"In his old life," explained Mr. Chen as we walked to the market, "the chef specialized in dim sum."

"His old life?" I asked. Mr. Lee was in front, leading us toward the market, and Mr. Chen and I trailed behind. It was still relatively cool, and we were walking along the edge of the lake with a few hundred local people following us.

"Before all this," he said with a wave at the little village, "China was a land of tradition. Every important kitchen in our region had two chefs. One was responsible for dim sum. One was responsible for everything else." In a softer voice he asked, "Do you have something for me?"

I nodded.

"Put it in your hand," he said even more softly. I reached into my pocket. Then, in a louder voice he said, "You will find that even your modest hotel has two kitchens. But," he laughed softly, "unfortunately only one chef." As he said this he suddenly seemed to stumble and lurch forward. I put out my hand to help him; taking it he gently extricated the paper.

"I am an old man," he said, gasping a little. "Have you a handkerchief?"

I handed him a tissue. He took it, wiped his forehead, and then crumpled it and put it in his pocket. I presumed the letter was now in the tissue, but it was so quickly done that I couldn't say for sure.

"I am so sorry to be so clumsy," he said. "But I am better now."

"Were you a dim sum chef?" I asked.

"Oh no," he replied, standing up very tall. "I was a banquet chef. I hoped, one day, to go to America."

"Is that why you speak such good English?" I asked.

"Yes," he said. "I studied very hard. I have relatives in New York. But that was a long time ago. This, you see, is my great work." He pointed sadly to the lake.

"What happened?" I asked.

Mr. Chen shrugged. "Let us just say that there was a period in our history when studying hard was not appreciated. People like me were sent off for reeducation. That lake was my university."

▪ ▪ ▪

The Taishan market was a rambling, raucous expression of capitalism that filled the entire town. Farmers bicycled in from the outskirts to fan through the streets, setting up stalls and building makeshift bamboo pens for the pigs, chickens, and ducks. They filled plastic buckets with water and added clams, octopus, squid, and frogs. There was no cut meat, although there were many sausages.

One man was doing a brisk business in rhinoceros horns. Another sat with a snake wrapped around his neck, telling fortunes. There were fruits and vegetables in vast profusion, and spices were everywhere. The scent of ginger, garlic, and fermented tofu hung over the town, just as it did in New York's Chinatown. But there was another, deeper odor too: Pigs were being slaughtered at the end of the street, and the smell of blood hung in the air.

"How do you like the food in your hotel?" asked Mr. Chen.

"Do you want the truth?" I asked. He nodded.

"It is monotonous," I said. "The meals are very big, but they are all the same. And it does not seem that different from the Cantonese food I have eaten in New York. It is not going to be easy to make an appealing travel article out of this trip."

"Peasant food!" said Mr. Chen vehemently. "You are eating the best in the village, but it is peasant food."

"I wish you could cook for me," I said, taking a wild guess at what might be in the letter. He didn't say anything, and I pressed on. "What would you cook for me if you could?"

A wistful look came over his face. "I would make you a real Beijing banquet," he said. "That is the royal cuisine, the real cuisine of China. There is a great attention to detail. In judging Beijing cooking you must look for three things: The color must be varied and beautiful. The texture is important too; all the pieces must be cut to uniform size. And then, of course, the ingredients must all be seasonal. I would make you a very simple dish. Perhaps something with shrimp, which I miss very much. You know, when I was an apprentice we had to peel the shrimp in cold water, to keep the texture correct, no matter how cold the weather, no matter how much our fingers stung. If we did not, we were beaten." He said it with deep nostalgia, the way old soldiers tell war stories.

"Will you give me a recipe?" I asked.

"Yes," he replied. "One of the old ones. I will write it down for you. I will give it to you when I give you the reply for Chan."

■ ■ ■

Had I been observed passing the letter to Mr. Chen? Mr. Lee did not allow us any more time alone together, and he was vague about my request to visit the kitchen at the Overseas Travelers' Hotel. In the meantime, we were trotted off to schools, ceramics factories, kindergartens. We went to the farm commune too, although our experience of rural life was brief. After a short tour of the rice paddies and tea in the home of the wealthiest farmer, Mr. Lee abruptly herded us back onto the bus.

"I thought we were spending the night," I protested.

"No," said Mr. Lee, "we are not."

"You are obviously too dangerous to be allowed to corrupt the farmers," said Ed as we stepped back onto the bus. "Have you been having unauthorized discussions again?"

"Honestly," I said, "this is not my fault." Still, I couldn't be certain, and I felt guilty. I felt that something mysterious was always going on just below the surface, that nothing was what it appeared to be. Even the most mundane activities seemed to have layers of hidden meaning.

Curious, I took the seat next to Mr. Lee for the trip back to Taishan. "Why did we have to leave?" I asked. "Why were we not able to spend the night in the commune?" He stared at me and said only this: "What kind of birth control do you use?"

Did he really want to know? Why? He seemed so unembarrassed that I simply told him. When I was done he said casually, "By the way, I have arranged for you and Professor Chen to visit the hotel kitchen tomorrow."

Dear Dad,

The kitchen was dark but fairly cool, with windows looking out onto the lake. Three huge woks were set over coals, with running water just above them. Big, puffy golden sheets were strung across the room. Mr. Chen said that they were fried pig skin. I asked him what they were for and he turned to the chef, who was wearing a Mao cap, and asked. Apparently we will have it tonight for dinner, cut into squares and served in sweet-and-sour sauce. Then he pointed to some other sheets hanging nearby. "See those?" he asked. "That is unfried pig skin. That will be used for poorer customers; the chef will cut it into thin, thin strips and weave it into imitation bird's nest." Only in China do pigs turn into bird's nests.

The chef showed us the tank where he kept the fresh fish. He pointed to the stuffed bitter melon, which was for our dinner, and mountains of pork ready to be cooked in different ways. As we passed a small forest of broccoli waiting to be washed, the chef said something to Mr. Chen and smiled at me, the gold tooth in the front of his mouth shining very brightly.

"He would like you to take his picture in the dim sum kitchen," said Mr. Chen. The chef led us into a smaller kitchen and very proudly showed off his array. I got out my camera and the chef picked up a dumpling, a curious yeast-bread filled with roast pork, rolled in coconut, and deep-fried. He smiled. The light flashed. Then we followed him back to the main kitchen.

The chef went back to cooking, tossing squid in a wok with celery. He added a ladle of golden liquid and with one swooping gesture scooped the food out of the wok and onto a platter. A second later it was sitting on the chopping block, the squid scored like a pinecone and gleaming white against the pale green celery.

Mr. Chen told me to taste it and then asked if I could guess the secret ingredient. I felt as if it was a test, so I tried really hard. There was an indefinable richness to the dish, and I thought of that golden liquid, and guessed chicken fat. Mr. Chen was delighted with me. I had passed! "Chicken fat," he said, "is the secret of Cantonese cooking." See how much I'm learning?

Then I spied a small, strange animal that was skinned and ready to be steamed. I didn't recognize it, so I asked Mr. Chen what it was. He said he didn't know the English word, but that it is covered with hard feathers. I couldn't imagine what hard feathers might be, so he went off and returned with a sort of armor.

It was an armadillo! According to Mr. Chen they are very good for you. He assured me that armadillos prevent cancer. Apparently we're having that for lunch too. I don't imagine that this group will be too thrilled when they find out.

"You must let me know their comments," he said. I promised that I would.

It's hard to believe that this trip is almost over. But I can't wait to see you. Mr. Chen has given me a wonderful recipe for shrimp with scallions; I'm going to make it for you the first night I'm home.

"How did the Americans like the animal with hard feathers?" Mr. Chen asked at our farewell banquet.

"I liked it," I hedged. "It was very tender, and the flavor was mild. It tasted sort of like chicken."

"But the others?" he insisted.

"To be honest," I said reluctantly, "they refused to taste it."

"Why?" he wanted to know.

"Most Americans aren't very adventurous about tasting new things," I admitted. "The people I am with won't eat frog, or jelly-fish, or bird's nest."

He shook his head sadly. "But they eat Chinese food in America, don't they?" he asked.

My impulse was to give him a half-truth. But I was exasperated by the cloudy mystery of China, and I felt that I owed him an American answer. "Mr. Chan was right," I said slowly. "The food in America is not real Chinese food. I don't think that Americans are ready to appreciate your cooking. I'm not sure we would under-stand that shrimp peeled in ice water taste better."

"Thank you," he said. He drew himself up very tall and said, with great dignity, "You have helped me. Please tell my old friend Chan that I will be staying. Tell him that life here is better."

"Is it?" I asked. But I remembered that cool, dark kitchen with its view of the lake. And then I thought of Mr. Chan's face behind the mountain of laundry in the hot streets of New York.

▪ ▪ ▪

My own mountain was waiting for me. A big, white paper moun-tain sitting on my father's desk. A mountain of letters, all un-opened. *"No!"* I cried, wanting to tear my clothes and put ashes on my face. I began ripping up the letters, which offered some sort of physical relief. "How could you keep this from me?" I sobbed.

"Your father made us promise," said Doug. "He didn't want to cut your trip short. He loved thinking of you in China. We couldn't refuse." He held me as I cried. "Be happy for him," he whispered into my ear. "It was what he wanted. Think of the alternative."

"Dad would have hated being stuck at home," I admitted, but it did not make me feel less forlorn.

■ ■ ■

When the tears were finished, I walked down to Chinatown. My face was still red and swollen, and I thought of my father as I bought shrimp and scallions, scrutinizing all the shops before making my selection. At home I rinsed them under the coldest water I could stand, until my fingers burned.

"Dad would have loved this," my mother said. She was being generous. I smiled, grateful. She had so much to do now—the estate to settle, lawyers to see—that she had forgiven me for leaving. "Maybe I'll go to China myself," she said, rather wistfully. "I'll have the time now."

■ ■ ■

There was no reason to stay in New York, but before leaving I tried to deliver Mr. Chen's message. Mr. Chan had disappeared. He was not in the Fluff and Fold Laundry, and the people there disclaimed all knowledge of a man called Chan. Mr. Bergamini was gone too, and the Chinese grocer who had taken over his store could not tell me where to find him.

Standing in the street, in the gray New York November, I tried to imagine Mr. Chen in Taishan, but I could not conjure him up. I began to wonder if he was real. From here Mr. Lee and his endless suspicions seemed equally fantastic. Had old ladies really searched my suitcase? I had traveled to China to please my father; I had spent my time collecting stories for him. But my letters were unread and my stories untold. How could I possibly make sense of the trip?

▪ ▪ ▪

When I went home to Berkeley the mystery deepened. I was having lunch with Marion Cunningham and Cecilia Chiang at Cecilia's restaurant, The Mandarin, telling them about the food I had eaten in Taishan. Cecilia nodded when I talked about frogs and broccoli and bird's nests made of pig skin. But when I got to the armadillo she became very still.

"How was it cooked?" she asked.

"In a rich sauce with cinnamon," I said.

"Did you like it?" she asked. She was looking at me with an expression I could not fathom. "Not much," I said. "But Mr. Chen assured me that it prevents cancer, and if you think of it as medicine it's not bad."

"Ruth," said Cecilia, "I think there is something you should know."

"Yes?" I said.

Cecilia took a deep breath and said, "I am sorry to have to doubt you. But there are no armadillos in China." She stared at me and said sharply, "Are you all right?"

It was a small thing. It was everything. Armadillos did not roam China; I could not believe anything I had been told. My father was dead.

Suddenly I heard his voice. "Everybody changes," he had said. Had he been aware that he was dying? I would never know. What I did know was that I had traveled farther than I had anticipated, and that everything had changed. And that without my father the world was going to be a very different place than the one that I had known.

DRY-FRIED SHRIMP

I can never cook this dish without imagining my father by my side. I wish he could have tasted it; he would have loved its classic simplicity.

Because Mr. Chen's recipes are so unadorned, they will reward you for using the very best ingredients. If you can find shrimp that have not been frozen, you'll be startled by the taste and texture of this dish.

3 scallions
2 tablespoons vegetable oil
½ teaspoon salt

1½ pounds large shrimp in shell
1 tablespoon soy sauce
2 tablespoons chicken broth

Accompaniment: cooked rice

Thinly slice enough of the green part of the scallions to make ¼ cup. Cut the white part of the scallions into ½-inch-long pieces.

Wash the shrimp in cold water and pat them dry. Heat a large wok (about 14 inches in diameter) over high heat until hot but not smoking and add the oil, swirling the wok to coat its sides with oil. Lower the heat to moderately high and add the salt and shrimp. Stir-fry the shrimp until almost cooked through, about 3 minutes. Add the white parts of the scallions and the soy sauce and the chicken stock and stir-fry until the shrimp is cooked through, about 1 minute. Remove the wok from the heat and add the green parts of the scallions, tossing to combine. Serve with rice.

Serves 4 to 6.

SOY SAUCE CHICKEN

One of the easiest ways to track changes in the world is to watch the availability of ingredients. Twenty years ago, when Mr. Chen gave me this recipe, most of these ingredients seemed impossibly exotic. It took serious research to find out about galangal, a member of the ginger family that is an important ingredient in Thai cooking. Today many of these roots and spices can be found in supermarkets, and the rest can be easily ordered over the Internet. Still, for me part of the fun of cooking this dish is going to Chinatown to search out the ingredients; the other part is the wonderful aroma that your kitchen acquires as it cooks.

10 cups water
20 whole star anise (about ½ cup)
¼ cup (about 1 ounce) anise seed
1 ounce dried galangal
2 ounces dried licorice root
10 cups soy sauce

8 cups sugar
1 large piece dried mandarin orange peel
1 (3-inch) cinnamon stick
1 (1-inch) piece peeled fresh ginger
1 free-range chicken (about 3½ pounds)

Accompaniment: cooked rice

In an 8-quart pot, boil the water with the star anise, anise seed, galangal, and licorice root, uncovered, for ½ hour. Pour the liquid through a fine-mesh strainer set over a large bowl and, reserving the spices in the strainer, pour the liquid back into the pot. Transfer the spices to the middle of a 12-inch square of cheesecloth. Gather the cheesecloth up and around the spices and tie it closed tightly with a piece of string to form a purse. Add the soy sauce, sugar, orange peel, cinnamon, and ginger to the pot and bring the liquid to a boil. Put the cheesecloth bag into the pot, along with the chicken, and simmer, covered, turning occasionally, until the chicken is cooked through, about ½ hour. Use tongs to transfer the chicken to a platter, and discard the cheesecloth bag. Pour the sauce through a strainer set over a bowl, discarding the solids, and keep warm.

To serve the chicken, remove the wings and legs with a sharp knife. Split the chicken lengthwise down its back with a cleaver or kitchen shears, then cut crosswise into 1-inch-wide pieces. Serve the chicken over rice with some of the sauce.

Serves 2 to 4.

COOK'S NOTE

This recipe makes a lot more sauce than you will need. But it's delicious over rice, roasted meats, or poultry, and it makes a great dip for Asian dumplings or pot stickers. It will keep in the refrigerator for 4 days, or in the freezer for up to 2 weeks. Boil it for a minute before using it again.

7

THE SAGE
OF SONOMA

■ Ordinary people become depressed by the loss of a beloved spouse. My mother was not ordinary. "I keep expecting the black cloud to descend," she said in a kind of wonder, "but it hasn't. I wake up every morning grateful to be alive. I know I'm going to get depressed again. But in the meantime, I have to try to enjoy every minute."

She went on a music tour of Vienna with the philharmonic. She visited Moscow and made reservations for Japan. "My doctor says I'd better travel while I'm feeling good," she said. "One never knows how long it will last."

"Very wise," I said, surprised as always by my mother's moods.

"Young people are such good company," she said as she invited an NYU student to move into my old room. She had a decorator redo the apartment. She dashed off to every play that opened in New York, stayed up all night writing letters, attended lunches and dinners and teas. Mom seemed to have achieved a permanent high. She was like a runner when the endorphins kick in or a drinker after the first martini. She was happy.

I knew I should be grateful. The year I was seven Mom became so depressed she took to her bed and spent months eating candy bars and thumbing through the same book, reading the pages over and over as the mail piled up in front of the door. Now I tried to be happy for her and struggled not to interpret this mood as a betrayal of my father.

But Mom did not make things easy. "Oh, PussyCat," she announced one day, "I forgot to tell you. I've joined a video dating service."

"A what?" I asked, more loudly than I had intended.

"Don't shout at me," she said. "A video dating service. They come to your house and film you talking about who you are and what you're looking for in a date."

Groping for an appropriate response, I came up with, "How much does this service cost?"

"It's quite expensive," she said, "but I think it will be worth it. I can't tell you how much I miss having a man around. Some days I feel as if I would like to just go out on the street, find the nearest man, drag him home, and make him get into bed with me."

I found this revelation so embarrassing that I could feel myself blushing. I repressed my first reply and merely asked again how much she was spending on this service.

"Well," my mother said in a tone I can only describe as defensive, "a few thousand dollars. I told you it was expensive."

"It's your money, Mom," I said lamely, and then thought to ask, "Have you had any results?"

There was a sort of silence and then she said, "The problem is that most people are looking for someone younger. Even the older men seem to want young women." Making a valiant attempt to change the subject, she asked, "Don't you get lonely?"

"I'm married, Mom, remember?" I said, taking the bait.

"It's none of my business," she replied, "but it seems to me your husband isn't home very much. Dad loved Doug so. He was thrilled by his success. But if he were here I know he'd be worried."

"I'm not," I said. It was a lie. Doug was very supportive during my father's illness, and for a time we'd crawled back into the familiar comfort of our relationship. But now Doug was concentrating on his career again, traveling more than ever. These days even when he was in Berkeley, he hardly seemed to be home.

My response was to throw myself into my work. *Metropolitan Home* had liked the China piece and asked me to become a contributing editor, and the food magazines were beginning to call. But my greatest triumph was the interview assignment from *Ms.*

"Do you know who M. F. K. Fisher is?" the editor asked.

"Doesn't everyone?" I replied. Mary Frances Kennedy Fisher was my hero, and I had read every word she'd ever published. I was a Fisher encyclopedia, and I went off to the interview with a catalog of questions. What did her first husband, Al Fisher, do after she left him for the great love of her life? Had she grown arugula in her garden in Switzerland? Did the extraordinary waitress in "Define This Word," my favorite Fisher story, actually exist? "That was fifty years ago!" she replied indignantly. And then graciously answered every one.

Unfortunately, it turned out that the editor's interest in America's most famous food writer was very different from mine. The magazine considered Ms. Fisher the model of a single working mother, and they wanted stories of her struggle. "Oh, pooh!" she said when I showed up a second time with a list of feminist questions to which *Ms.* required answers.

She was very vague about the way she had managed her money, and even vaguer about her second divorce and raising her two daughters on her own. "Of course women are different than men," she said crossly when I hauled that one out. Although she clearly considered these questions annoying, she offered a few answers, and I dutifully worked them into the article. But the editors were not fooled: They sensed that I lacked the requisite gravity to be one of their writers, and they did not offer me a second assignment.

I found I didn't mind as much as I had expected to. After Dad's death I retreated into the cocoon of Berkeley, grateful for the support of commune life. My father was dead, my mother was manic, and my husband was away, but in Berkeley I had another family.

It was, at the moment, slightly larger than usual because it included Ellen Frank, one of the many people who turned up periodically on Channing Way. Ellen never outstayed her welcome as others often did; one friend was with us for a year before we told him it was time he found a place of his own. But Ellen came when the weather back East got cold, spent a few weeks, and then moved on to Santa Monica and other friends. And she was a very good guest.

"I bought some shrimp," she said, walking in with a bag one day. "Let's make a big curry for dinner."

"I love curry," said Jules, coming into the kitchen and washing his hands. "I'll peel the shrimp."

I was tempted, but I had work to do. "Count me out," I said reluctantly. "I have to go research an article I'm writing about restaurants at the top of big buildings. The food will be terrible; it's almost impossible to get a good meal with a view."

"Cancel your reservations and go tomorrow," said Ellen. "The shrimp won't keep." She saw me hesitating and added, "If you put it off a day, I'll come with you."

"Me too," said Jules.

"You'll both have to bring guests," I warned them, reaching for the phone.

"Gee, how are we ever going to find people willing to go out and eat a fancy free dinner?" said Jules as Ellen began melting butter in a skillet. She added chopped onions and an apple, then stirred in turmeric, cumin, ground cardamom, and some chilies. As the aroma began to fill the kitchen Ellen turned and said, "Remember that cute guy I met last time I was in town? Can we invite him for dinner?"

"Who?" I asked.

"The investigative reporter," she said. "The one who works at your magazine. He did that piece on nuclear terrorism, the one that started on the cover and everybody made such a fuss about."

"Oh," I said. "Him. Michael Singer. I'm all for improving your love life, but I hardly know the guy."

Jules put down his shrimp and said, "I know him. I'll call."

In those years there was always enough for one more, but just to be on the safe side I made extra rice. Nick went out to get another gallon of wine, and Susan bought an extra loaf of bread. By the time Michael Singer walked in with a bottle of wine under his arm, ten people were tapping their toes in the kitchen, dancing and chopping while Muddy Waters blasted at full roar. As I wiggled my hips and stirred the curry I thought how lucky I was to live in such a lively house.

I could see why Ellen had remembered Michael; he was good-looking in a macho way that was rare in Berkeley. He had a barrel chest and slim hips and he walked with a kind of swagger, as if he were a gift to the women of the world. When he held out the bottle and asked, "Got a corkscrew?" I felt myself swell with irrational irritation.

"Real wine," I heard myself say. "Can the people stand it?"

He was not fazed. "The people?" he threw back at me. "You're a restaurant critic, aren't you? That's not exactly the people's profession."

"I may write about the life of leisure," I replied, "but I don't live it. And I'll have you know that the hospitality industry is America's largest employer."

"I see," he said, laughing. "You write about restaurants to keep all those nice people employed. How silly of me not to have known that you had a serious political mission."

He opened the wine, pulling the cork as if it were the pop-top on a can of beer. He flexed his fingers, reveling in his strength, and I saw that he had the sexual confidence of a big cat. He seemed to be sucking up all the air in the room, and Ellen was preening and purring as if she were in heat. I was embarrassed for her, and then embarrassed for women everywhere. Who did he think he was?

"I don't suppose," I said, "that you might deign to set the table?"

"Just point me to the silverware," he replied, laughing at me. "Jules and I were in the same men's consciousness-lowering group. I think I can handle that."

"I'll bet," I retorted, rather lamely, and returned to stirring the pot. By the time we got to dessert and I was asking if there was anyone who didn't want ice cream on the apple pie, all he had to say was, "None for me" to make me reply, "Watching our weight, are we?" And for him to shoot back, "Yeah, you got a problem with that? All of us aren't quite as disciplined as you are."

■ ■ ■

"What was that about?" Ellen asked when he left.

"What?" I asked, even though I knew perfectly well what she meant. I had barely recognized myself.

"I thought you said you didn't know him. You acted as if you've been hating each other for years."

"A man like that you can hate on first sight," I replied.

"Well, please don't hate him too much," she said. "Because I asked him to come to dinner with us tomorrow night."

"Oh no!" I said, although the thought of seeing him again thrilled me.

"Well, you said I should bring a friend. He's it."

"Some friend," I said.

"He's so cute," she protested.

"Not my type," I replied. "You'll notice he did not offer to do the dishes."

▪ ▪ ▪

Michael Singer was standing by the glass elevator at the St. Francis Hotel, wearing a suit and tie. "Figures," I muttered to Ellen, "a radical in a suit. What a phony."

"God he's good-looking" was all she said.

I ran my eyes over him, searching for a flaw. "His feet are too small" was what I came up with.

"Look at his hands," she said. They were so big they swallowed up the reporter's pad he was holding as he inclined toward a middle-aged couple, writing as they spoke. "For those prices," I heard when we reached him, "they *should* put paper umbrellas on the drinks. You're absolutely right. And the view?"

"Oh," the woman said, patting the navy silk dress that pulled too tightly across her stomach, "that was worth every penny. They sure don't have anything like that in Iowa." She gave Michael a big smile, touched his arm tentatively, as if she knew him, and said, "You be good, hear?" as she and her husband walked away.

"What do you think you're doing?" I asked him.

"Trying to be helpful," he said, showing me his pad. "I was early."

"I bet you always are," I heard myself say.

"Yes," he said curtly, "I am. It's rude to be late."

"So now I'm rude," I said.

"You are," he said. "But if you can manage to let me say something, I interviewed these people to get you some color."

"Look," I said coldly. "If I need local color, I can manage on my own. Let me worry about my work; you're just here as a hired mouth."

Taking Ellen's arm he swept into the elevator and pushed a button. The door shut in my face, and as the car ascended I could hear him laughing. From the glass cage he gave a jaunty salute. Ellen looked very happy.

I gritted my teeth and got into the next elevator. "What a jerk!" I said, punching the button. By the time I reached the top, Ellen and Michael were already seated at a big table by the window with Jules and his date. Michael was obviously enjoying himself; his arm was draped loosely over the back of Ellen's chair and he was laughing a big, boisterous laugh. As I approached the table he jumped up and poured wine into the glasses all around him, like a gracious host.

"I see you didn't wait to order wine," I said. I had meant the words to be light and easy, but they sounded sour.

"Anyone who's late," said Michael easily, handing me a glass, "has to accept the consequences."

"Even if she's paying?" I asked.

"Especially if she's paying," he said. "It's only money, and it's not even yours."

I sat down in the only available seat, directly across from Michael. He held up his glass, mockingly clinked it against mine, and said, "Welcome." I had invited everyone to dinner, but he had appropriated the party. I tried to ignore him, but he pointed out the window where the sun was starting to set, spreading a pink glow across the city sprawled at our feet. "It's so beautiful," he said, his tone suddenly reverent.

"And all it costs is money," I said. Even to me it sounded mean.

Michael shot me a dark look. "Am I the only person here who's hungry?" he asked.

"No, but you're the only person impolite enough to talk about it. I bet you're used to eating at six," I shot back.

"Where I grew up," he said, "we ate at five."

▪ ▪ ▪

What did we eat? I can't remember. Just drinking wine and more wine as the conversation flowed around me. He talks a lot, I thought and had a sudden vision of Doug, so silent, sitting across from me as I struggled to keep the conversation going. I looked up, startled to find Michael staring at me. He was talking as he watched me, shouldering the conversation that eddied around us like water, like silk. After a while he wasn't talking anymore either, and we were just staring at each other.

"Let's go." He was the one who said it; I didn't even like the guy. But I stood up and walked out with him, just like that. And when the elevator doors closed and he pulled me to him, my heart lurched with the elevator, and I melted into him. We stood in that glass cage, locked together, going down. I had left my friends at the table holding the bill, but I was suspended in the air, flying, in the grip of something I did not understand and did not question. In the morning I had one strong thought: This is going to hurt.

But by then it was too late.

■ ■ ■

He lived in North Beach, in a third-story walk-up apartment over Malvina's coffee shop. When we went downstairs for coffee he borrowed ten dollars from Franco, the owner, and stopped at each table to talk. He promised one woman to go running with her the following morning. She asked if he would crack her back before he left, and when he did a sharp arrow of jealousy shot through me. He seemed to touch everyone he passed: a dark man who asked if he'd meet him for a drink that night, and a couple who invited him for dinner the following week. And when a little girl sitting with her parents tugged on his shirt as he walked by, Michael knelt down beside her, took her hand, and said, "Hello, sweetheart, still waiting for me?" She nodded, her big green eyes looking worshipfully into his.

But at our table he kept his hands to himself, and his eyes were masked, guarded. When I tried to touch his hand, he withdrew it, and when he finally looked at me, I shivered. "Is something wrong?" I asked.

"I don't think I can survive another affair with a married woman," he said.

"So don't," I replied, and walked out, past all those people he had touched. I could feel my face burning, a slow fire just above my cheekbones. There's probably one of me every morning, I thought as I tried to remember where I had parked my car.

■ ■ ■

Nobody on Channing Way said much, but Ellen walked around looking miffed for a few days, and it was easy to imagine what she was thinking. Jules was the same as ever, but when I tried to draw him out about Michael he just turned away. Nick made it very clear that he couldn't understand what I was up to. It was that pre-AIDS time when people did not judge each other, and I knew that none of them would say anything to Doug. Still, knowing that my friends disapproved did not make me feel good.

But all I had to do was think of those big hands and my heart went swooping down an interior roller coaster. I replayed moments of that night, over and over, and they never lost their thrill. When I went to write "Rooms at the Top," I found myself searching through my purse for the interviews Michael had done. I inserted them into the article, just to spite him, but found they gave the piece new life. Remembering that couple from Iowa, how excited they were to have seen the view, changed the article for me. I started seeing the restaurant with their eyes. In fact, I liked having their opinions so much that I began to do interviews myself when I went to other restaurants.

But I didn't have Michael's ease with people, and I was awkward in my approach. After a while I discovered a trick: All I had to do was pretend to be my mother, a person who could ride a bus and know everyone's life story before she got off. "People like to talk about themselves," she always said. To her, and to Michael, they did.

▪ ▪ ▪

I knew he would call. I sprang for the phone each time it rang. He had to call. Surely, I thought to myself, this kind of connection doesn't happen that often, even to him. I lost my appetite. I dreamed of him. I waited for him to call.

He didn't. I began thinking up excuses to call him. Could I have left something at his house? No, too transparent. I couldn't just invite him for dinner. What could I ask his advice about?

In the end, I just called. "Hi, it's Ruth."

His voice was distant. "Yes."

"Do you remember me?"

"Yes." It had gotten icy.

"I'd like to see you again."

"I'm sorry. I can't do this, Ruth. There's nothing in it for me."

It was like being splashed with ice water. He hung up, and I wished I could recapture the past few minutes, rewind them so they hadn't happened. How could I have made such a fool of myself? I was trying to rationalize all this, organize my thoughts, make some excuse, when the phone rang.

"That's not exactly true," he said, no less coldly. "I do want to see you. I just don't think it's a good idea."

"Could we talk about it?" I asked, grasping.

"Okay," he said reluctantly. "Why don't you meet me at the Savoy Tivoli."

"When?" I asked.

"How soon can you get there?"

I calculated. Half an hour on the bridge, a few minutes to park . . . "An hour?" I said.

"An hour," he said.

"I'll be on time," I said, trying for lightness. "I know how much you hate it when people are late."

He did not laugh. "It always has consequences," he said.

■ ■ ■

He was sitting at the bar when I walked in, wearing a navy blue shirt and rimless glasses that gave him an intellectual air. He was fingering a glass of scotch, joking with the bartender. He was laughing, but when he turned and saw me the laugh died and he looked grim. I thought of some apocalyptic figure; this was not a guy who took things lightly.

He touched my hand. He slid off the bar stool and grabbed me, kissing my mouth and then pressing his whole body against mine so the electricity went everywhere. Without releasing me he threw some crumpled bills on the bar, said, "Forget about drinks," and walked me out the door and down the street.

When we got to his building he opened the door, pushed me inside and up against a wall. It was still light, and we were standing on the staircase, but he put his hand up my shirt and rubbed my breasts so hard that it hurt. I threw my whole weight on him and we began tearing off our clothes.

"No, wait," he said, pulling me up the stairs. We stopped on each landing, so that by the time we reached his door we were completely naked, and when the door closed behind us we fell on the floor and made love with a sort of gentle violence I had never experienced before. When we were done he pulled me into the bedroom and we sank onto the bed and did it again. And again. Finally, exhausted, we fell asleep.

I woke up feeling that I had entered a foreign country I had read about but never before visited. I had been living with my best friend, my brother; sex with Doug had never been an important part of our relationship. Sleeping with Colman had not been the main point either. With Michael, I felt I was in new territory, in the grip of some force larger than myself. It was as if all the ions inside of us yearned toward each other, and for the first time in my life my body felt completely awake, as if it was in the place that it was meant to be.

Michael ran his hands gently, lovingly, across my face. "I can't do this," he said, not angry anymore. "I can't give my heart to a woman who's not available."

"Very sensible," I said, turning to kiss him.

"I won't see you again," he said.

"Fine," I replied, and we made love so sweetly that I found myself crying at the end.

We went to dinner afterward and he told me how the civil rights movement had changed his life, and then the war in Vietnam had goaded him into action. "I joined a collective of antiwar filmmakers and lived out of cartons, sleeping on people's floors," he said happily. When he talked about the movement it sounded wonderful, exciting, and I asked myself what I had been doing while he was following his conscience.

After dinner we went back to his house and, because it was the last time, I stayed the night. We talked until it was light. In the morning we went to the coffee shop, and although he had a word for everyone, I somehow wasn't jealous. Even when he made a date to go running with a woman with long blond hair and good legs it didn't bother me. He went off to get us cappuccinos, and when he came back he kissed the top of my head as he placed the cup in front of me.

"I don't think I've ever felt this happy," he said. "Once," he added thoughtfully, "when I was eight years old, I asked my mother why I was so unhappy."

"You knew you were unhappy at eight?" I asked.

"Oh yes," he said. "I would go to my friends' houses and see what nice lives they all had. In my house all we ever did was fight.

But all my mother said was 'Where is it written that you should be happy?' "

"Are you telling me this for a reason?" I wondered.

He smiled and said, "I think you better go now."

I was convinced I would never see him again. I felt the drama of unhappiness, as if I was watching this all happen to someone else. I touched his face but he didn't touch me back. "Go," he said. "Please go."

■ ■ ■

Doug was back but I couldn't stop thinking about Michael. I found myself wanting to talk to him, ask his opinions about books, about music, about things in the news. I felt that I could spend the rest of my life talking to him and never run out of things to say.

"You seem very far away," Doug said one afternoon when we were walking to the post office to buy stamps. "Is everything all right?"

"I don't know," I said. It was an honest answer. The deep sexual connection I had felt with Michael both thrilled and frightened me. It occurred to me that the kind of calm, loving friendship Doug and I had might make great sex impossible. There had never been any tension between us, and there had never been any heat. Maybe, probably, he had discovered that he too could have great sex with someone who was not me. But I did not know how to talk about this with him; we had never discussed sex, never admitted to our lack of sexual interest in each other. And so, I merely said, "I don't get the sense that we're together anymore. We're not even sure we want the same things."

Doug didn't say anything, and I wondered if he was also struggling with the need to be honest about our relationship. But instead of pressing him I simply asked, "Is everything all right with you?"

"I think so," he replied. Which was, I realized later, not an answer at all.

I thought about that the next day when I walked into his studio and he slammed down the phone. Too quickly. "Who were you talking to?" I asked.

"That woman in Seattle," he said.

"You mean the one you stayed with?"

"Yes," he said. "Her. She has another project she wants to discuss with me. I may have to fly back up there."

"Again?" I asked.

"She's interested in my career," he said.

"So you are going for sure?"

"I guess so," he said. "But I'll only be gone a week."

▪ ▪ ▪

"Doug's in Seattle again?" my mother asked. "Doesn't this worry you?"

"Should it?" I asked.

"If my husband kept disappearing," she said crisply, "I'd worry about it."

"Oh, Mom," I said, "he's just pursuing his career."

"Take it from me," she insisted, "life without a man is lonely. If I were you, I'd be pursuing him. Try to save your marriage before it's too late."

"I'm not the one in Seattle," I replied.

"Maybe you should be," she said. "Have you thought about that?"

I had. But what would I say when I got there? "Remember me? I'm your wife"? Meanwhile I tried to think up an excuse to call Michael. It arrived in the form of a postcard from M. F. K. Fisher. "It would be so nice to see you again," she had written in her fine, thin hand. "Come to lunch. Bring a friend, if you like."

■ ■ ■

Michael agreed to come, but I could tell that he was uncomfortable about succumbing to the lure of lunch with a famous writer. He sat in hostile silence as we drove. I chattered on, too much, trying to fill the air between us. "Just shut up," I kept telling myself.

Then I began to worry about having a panic attack on the bridge. By the time I was pulling onto the Golden Gate Bridge my palms were wet and I could barely breathe. I can't do this, I thought. But then I saw that they had closed the lane closest to the rail for painting, and I realized that if things got bad I could pull over. It was like an escape clause, and it was all I needed.

It was beautiful on the Marin side, the hills like soft, dark humps above the Bay, and it got even lovelier as we drove north. By the time we turned off the highway, heading toward the delta, the air was smooth and we rolled down our windows. When I glanced over at Michael, the harsh lines in his face had gone away and he looked young, even vulnerable. "How did you get to know her?" he asked.

"I wished," I said, "wished so hard I actually made it happen. I've been reading M. F. K. Fisher since I was a little girl. For years, when nobody else had any intelligent interest in food, she was always there. It made me feel okay about myself, you know?"

He nodded, but said nothing.

"She can make you taste things just by writing about them, but that's not the point. She actually makes you pay attention to your next meal, feel more alive because you're doing that. When you read her you understand that you need to respect yourself enough to focus on the little things of life. She celebrates the everyday by making it seem momentous."

I realized that I was doing my best to make my subject seem worthy to this radical who had given up so much for his principles. But all he said was "You're very beautiful when you're animated like this."

"I knew that she lived in Sonoma, but I never would have just called and asked to meet her. I mean, it seems like such an intrusion. But I was wondering how I could manage it when *Ms.* magazine asked if I would write a profile."

"*Ms.,*" he said, sounding impressed. I felt a surge of pride. "How did it go with them?"

I hesitated. Should I tell the truth? And then I recklessly plunged forward. "Not as smoothly as it might have. When I first went to see Mary Frances she said I could interview her on the condition that I let her read the piece before I turned it in."

"You agreed?" he said, sounding appalled. "You let her read it before publication?"

I was sheepish. "I didn't know you weren't supposed to do that. My editor was horrified. But I'd given my word."

"What happened?" he asked, very cool again. He had backed away, and I was sorry I'd said anything.

"She was very nice. She said the piece was fine. She didn't ask for a single change. And later, after the piece appeared and she saw the changes the magazine had made, she wrote to say that she liked my original better than the one they'd printed. I did too."

"Why?"

"Because they made me put in all this feminist crap."

He looked amused. "You're not a feminist?"

"It seemed so silly to get her to talk about all this stuff that doesn't interest her. She's a woman who really likes men. And likes being a woman. In ways that people of our generation don't. If I was going to talk about her politics, I'd rather have talked about her year in Mississippi."

"Her year in Mississippi?" he said, genuinely interested now. "What year was that?"

"Nineteen sixty-four."

"Sixty-four?" He swiveled around so that he was facing me fully. "Are you sure? Sixty-four was the year Schwerner, Chaney, and Goodman were killed. That's really interesting. Why'd she go?"

"She told me that she worked at the Piney Woods School that year. Have you heard of it?"

"Of course I have," he said, as if he was insulted by the question, "it's a famous institution." I did not tell him that I had never heard of the place before Mary Frances mentioned it, that I had been forced to look it up. Started in 1909, it was dedicated to giving black children a serious education.

"I tried to get her to talk about it," I told him, "but every time I brought up Piney Woods she changed the subject."

"I'm going to try," he said. "I really want to hear about that."

Mary Frances was different with Michael there, softer somehow. We sat on her sofa, eating what she called "benne biscuits" and drinking small, icy glasses of wine. She had looked him up and down, openly, when I'd introduced them, and from that moment she addressed all her remarks to him. She really was a woman who liked men.

And Michael was a man who could draw people out. When he asked about Mississippi she did not say, as she had to me, "Maybe after I die some of what I've written about that difficult year will be published." She reached down and picked up Charlie the cat, stroked him softly, settled back into her chair, and said, "The kids were all gone, and my father was dead. So I went down there to teach." The tone of her voice was flat, as if *a* plus *b* equaled *c,* as if it were a trip to the grocery store, something that everyone did.

"How did you even know about it?" he asked. His voice caressed the words, as if just knowing about it were something to be proud of. She walked right into the trap.

"I'd known about it all my life! In the twenties a group came to La Jolla and gave a gospel concert to raise funds; after that I started sending them books and clothing. I did it for years. When the civil rights movement happened, I thought I'd find out if the South was as bad as everyone up here thought it was."

Michael looked at her admiringly. "And was it?"

"It was worse." She disappeared into herself for a moment, walking the streets of Mississippi, then said, as if from a distance, "I didn't go to town at all while I was there."

"So you fought your battles at the school?" he asked.

She gave him a long, cool look and said, "God no. I didn't go there to fight anything. I just went."

"But the murders happened in 1964!" he said, as if it was impossible for him to believe that while freedom riders were pouring into Mississippi she had gone merely to teach. "Yes," she said mildly. "Actually, I got to Piney Woods on June nineteenth. Later we found out that it was the same day the murders took place."

"Was the school in an uproar about the murders?"

"Oh no," she replied. "We lived a very isolated life. We had TV and radio, but we all worked so hard that there was no time for anything else. I remember writing to a friend that it was like being pregnant with a tornado outside the delivery room. You know it's there, but you can't stop for it." She paused for a moment, looking backward, and her face changed. "God, I hated that place," she said vehemently.

"Why?" said Michael, so softly that I could hardly hear him. It was as if he wanted her to think she was asking the question of herself. And she answered that way, as if she were very far away.

"There were signs everywhere saying things like 'Work is the mother of contentment.' The kudzu grew so fast you could watch it move up to destroy everything. I got up at five, finished my last class at nine-thirty at night, and I was exhausted all the time." She shook herself a little, coming out of it. And her face grew warmer. "But the students were wonderful. It took six months before they would eyeball me. But after that I was without color, and so were they."

"Did you ever figure out why you really went there?"

"No," she said. "All I know is that I was not invited back. Because I was a troublemaker." Then she stopped talking. The subject was closed.

Afterward she gave us lunch, and we sat, languidly discussing her Hollywood years. She was charming, but after an hour she rose and took a small basket from the refrigerator. She handed it to Michael and said, "Now I'm going to send you on a walk."

She took us to the door and pointed up a path winding away from the house. "Just follow it until you get to a special place. You'll know it when you get there. Save the contents of the basket until then. I won't expect you back for a few hours." Gently pushing, she set our feet on the path and went inside. We turned to see if she was waving us on, but of course she wasn't. That would not be her way.

"What a wonderful woman!" Michael said, taking my hand as we walked up the country lane. Birds were singing and we could smell the honeyed hay scent that you get in country that is more gold than green. "The first time I came to see her, Mary Frances gazed out the window and suddenly said, 'I love my tawny hills,' " I told him. He turned and looked back. "Yeah," he said, "like great lions lazing in the sun."

I was happy walking up the path, and I was aware that I was happy. I had seen what it would be like to be with someone whose interests were the same as mine, with someone who cared more for books than for art. I saw the possibility of a future that was one long conversation. But for this moment we did not talk much. Just held hands, walking and wondering what the place she had sent us to would be like.

"Do you think we'll really know when we get there?" I asked. "How far do you think it is? What do you think it will be?"

Michael laughed, a great low, lazy laugh, and I loved him just for the sound of it. "Yes," he said. "And I don't know. And I don't know." Then he began singing, his voice deep and beautiful. He put his arm around me, and I could feel the start of each song, a low thrum in his chest.

The path turned away from the golden hills and into woods, and suddenly it was almost dark and very cool. The trees above us grew close together, forming a leafy tunnel, and the scent changed to a darker one, of earth, leaves, and mushrooms. Twigs crackled beneath our feet. Bits of sunlight filtered through the leaves, making the path sparkle.

"It's like being in a cathedral," Michael said, his voice improbably reverent. "Like walking beneath stained glass." He was almost whispering as he went on: "I love churches. Sometimes when I'm really sad I go in and light candles. I love the dark, and the waxy smell, and the feeling of hope in the air. If God were anywhere, he'd be in a place like this, don't you think?"

But all I said was, "Look!" Because we'd found the place. The trees ended just ahead, and we started running, laughing, delighted. It was a deep pool at the end of the forest and straight ahead was a waterfall. Just as we arrived a bird started to sing, loudly, on a branch above our heads.

And finally I replied, "Yes, if God were anywhere, he'd be here."

▪ ▪ ▪

There was a bottle of wine in the basket, a long green one, and we stuck it in the pool to chill before pulling off our clothes and jumping in ourselves. The water was soft, in the way that only spring-fed ponds can be, like a caress against the skin, and we swam in circles, talking. When we reached the waterfall we found there was a hidden ledge behind it, a shelf of smooth rock we could lie on, hidden from even the squirrels and birds that were our only neighbors. We snuggled together there, then emerged into the sunlight to drink the wine and eat the cool cucumber sandwiches Mary Frances had packed in linen napkins. And as we lay in the sunshine, a line of Mary Frances's went shooting through my head.

"Chexbres was there of course. And we celebrated with the first of ten thousand completely enjoyable drinks. . . . Everything was all right after that."

■■■

It was dark when we got back to Mary Frances's house, and she looked at us and smiled. "It's magic, isn't it?" she said.

We did not go home that night. Or the next.

CHANNING WAY
SHRIMP CURRY

Afterward I knew I should move out of Channing Way and spend time by myself. I felt as if I was in love with both Doug and Michael, and I didn't think that was possible. I didn't even know if either of them wanted me.

It was time that Doug and I told each other the truth, no matter how hard that might be. But Doug was always away, and it was easier to keep quiet; once everything was said there would be no turning back. In the meantime, I clung to the comfort of my commune. I felt safe on Channing Way, and I cooked a lot of shrimp curry. It was my way of saying thank you.

This is a classic American curry, and very much a product of its time. It is also perfect commune food: It's delicious, good for a crowd, and doubles or triples easily.

1 onion, chopped

2 garlic cloves, smashed

½ stick (¼ cup) unsalted
  butter

4 tablespoons curry powder

½ teaspoon ground ginger

½ teaspoon ground
  cardamom

¼ teaspoon cinnamon

¼ teaspoon turmeric

½ teaspoon pure red chili
  powder, or to taste

1 tablespoon all-purpose
  flour

½ cup heavy cream

1 cup well-stirred canned
  coconut milk

2 cups chicken broth

2 teaspoons freshly grated
  lime zest

2 pounds large shrimp,
  peeled and deveined

2 tablespoons fresh lime
  juice, or to taste

salt and pepper

Accompaniment: cooked rice and mango chutney

Garnish: raisins, salted roasted peanuts, chopped candied
  ginger

Cook the onion and garlic in the butter in a heavy 5-quart pot over moderate heat, stirring, until the onion is softened, about 4 minutes. Add the spices and flour and cook, stirring constantly, for 1 minute. Whisk in the cream, coconut milk, broth, and lime zest and bring just to a boil. Simmer the mixture, stirring constantly, until it begins to thicken, about 2 minutes. Add the shrimp and simmer, stirring, until the shrimp turns pink and is cooked through, about 4 minutes. Stir in the lime juice, and add salt and pepper to taste.

Ladle the curried shrimp over rice and top with garnishes. Serve the mango chutney on the side.

Serves 6.

8

FIVE RECIPES

Winter: Sweet Potato Pie

■ And then, as if things weren't confusing enough, I got mugged. Afterward I started baking sweet potato pies, standing in the kitchen at Channing Way for hours, cutting flour into butter, watching the fat disappear into the soft white powder. I found solace in the precision of the gestures: filling a glass with ice cubes until the water was so cold it made my fingers ache, dribbling the icy liquid into the flour until it came together in loopy clusters. I liked the softness when I gathered them up, liked pressing them into the suggestion of a ball.

Sweet potatoes would not have been my filling of choice, but it was winter and they were cheap.

Rolling out the dough I replayed the mugging, over and over. I was going to dinner with a colleague, a wine writer. We had gone into his garage and climbed into his car. I heard a voice say, "Stop." And then I saw the black gloves come up against the car window, and the tall body doubled over to peer into the Porsche. I saw the gun, with its long barrel, and its sight on the end like an ugly snout. I did not see a face, ever.

I heard, vaguely, as if from a great distance, a voice telling us to open the door. I saw Jeffrey reaching over to open it, his voice cracked with fear. And then the long black leather body folded itself into the car next to me, and the gun, cold, metallic, came to rest against my head.

But what I remember most was Jeffrey trembling and crying, and reaching into his jacket for his wallet. I remember thinking that he shouldn't do that—they would think he was going for a gun—but wondering even more why he was so scared. I was not afraid.

I was nothing. I could feel the gun against my head, but my emotions had disappeared. I was like ice. I did not even wonder why they wanted Jeffrey to close the garage door, did not consider what their intentions might be.

From a great distance I heard Jeffrey say, all his hip bravado gone, that the garage could not be closed from inside. And then I felt myself being pulled out of the car, out of the garage, being told to hurry.

I heard, "Don't make any noise and no one will get hurt."

Heard, "Move it, motherfucker."

Heard, "Get going, bitch."

Heard, "Now we are going into the house."

And then I heard the clang and clatter of Jeffrey's keys as he heaved them into the bushes.

I felt, rather than heard, his fall to the ground, and felt the crack of the gun against his head, like a shot, over and over. I felt the air shift as the arm holding the gun came down, felt Jeffrey's sigh each time it hit his head.

And then the man who had me pressed his gun deep into my temple and said, "Give me your purse." As I obeyed him he let go of my arm, and without knowing that I was going to do it I took off as if I had been pushed, screaming and running as fast as I could.

Will he shoot me? I wondered, ducking behind the nearest car for cover as I shouted, "Help, help, please help me!" No one was following me, and I went running down the middle of the street, feeling ridiculous.

Afterward there were cops and ambulances and doctors—the whole sorry aftermath of crime. But it was months before I understood what kept me anchored to my kitchen, baking endless pies.

I had run off and left Jeffrey lying in the street without a second thought. It probably saved our lives, and he was only an acquaintance. But I knew he would never forgive me.

I roasted sweet potatoes and mashed them with a fork. I added sugar and eggs and rum. I heard the policeman's voice as he finished taking depositions. "You're lucky to be alive," he'd said. "God must have wanted you to have a second chance."

For what? I wondered, as I put the pie into the oven.

SWEET POTATO PIE

2 medium sweet potatoes
   (about 1¼ pounds)
½ stick (¼ cup) unsalted
   butter
¾ cup sugar
¾ cup whole milk
3 large eggs
1 teaspoon vanilla

½ teaspoon cinnamon
¼ teaspoon freshly grated
   nutmeg
¼ teaspoon salt
1 tablespoon dark rum
1 tablespoon all-purpose
   flour
1 unbaked 9-inch pie shell

Preheat the oven to 350°F.

Prick the sweet potatoes with a fork and roast them on a shallow baking pan in the middle of the oven until very tender, about 1¼ hours. Cool to room temperature.

Raise the oven temperature to 400°F, and place a shallow baking pan on the bottom rack.

Scoop the flesh from potatoes into a bowl and discard the skins. Mash the sweet potatoes with a fork until smooth. Melt the butter in a small saucepan and stir in the sugar. Add the melted butter mixture to the sweet potatoes with the milk and the eggs and beat with a whisk until smooth. Whisk in the remaining ingredients (the filling will be quite liquid). Pour the filling into the pie shell.

Carefully transfer the pie to the heated shallow baking pan on the bottom rack of the oven and bake until the filling is just set, about 40 minutes. Transfer the pie to a rack to cool.

Serves 8.

Spring: Apricot Pie

Grabbing for second chances, I opted for honesty. That spring I finally got the courage to say to Doug, "Let's talk."

I told him about Colman. I told him about Michael. He sat looking at me as if he had never seen me before and uttered these three words: "It's not possible." I knew that he was just beginning to understand what I had known for quite some time: We were no longer the people we had been when we'd married. For a moment he saw me as some new exciting creature and seemed thrilled by the possibilities. Then his face fell and he began asking all the obvious questions—when, where, why? I told him as much as I could, as much as I knew myself.

I said that they were both just friends now, that I was trying to give our marriage a chance. I told him that I knew two things for certain: I would always love him, and I wanted to have a child.

And then it was his turn. Doug told me about his women; I was not surprised that they existed, but I was shocked at how many there had been, and for how long. I had suspected there was a woman in Omaha, and I had been almost certain he was sleeping with someone in Seattle. But I had not anticipated the lovers in Chicago and New York. Or Berkeley. He had even slept with someone from The Swallow. It was a blow, and I suddenly remembered the way I had felt that first morning in L.A., when I woke up in Colman's bed and wondered where Doug was, and with whom. But the most painful part of all was hearing him say that he did not want children. At least not now.

Later, when we had said all that there was to say, I looked over and saw that his face was wet with tears. "I'm so scared," he said. "We've taken it apart and we'll never put it back together."

"I'm scared too," I replied.

Doug had work to do and he flew off, to Minneapolis, to Seattle, to New York. "If he really cared," I told myself, "he'd stay home and try to make this work." But we were angry with each other now, angry because we had grown up to be different people than we had anticipated. Neither of us had counted on that.

When Doug came back I went to the airport to pick him up, ready to steel myself against him. But he walked into the terminal looking so much like my husband that I held out my arms and said, "Welcome home!"

"You are my home," he replied. My heart melted, and we drove out to Point Reyes, to watch the sunset on the beach.

There was a spectacular neon sky, and as the fiery ball sank into the sea Doug put his arm around me and said, "We belong together. You're my family." And I put my head on his shoulder and my arms around his waist and agreed.

But then he was off again. He was going to Buffalo, to build a piece and meet a woman. The night he left I baked apricot pie. It was his favorite, and he stood for a long time watching me roll out the dough. It sailed smoothly across the counter, the little bits of butter in ragged layers, glistening through the flour.

"I don't want to lose you," he said.

"Me either," I replied.

"Will you bake me another when I come back?" he asked.

I shook my head. "By the time you come back," I said, "apricots will be out of season."

APRICOT PIE

1 recipe pie dough	¾ cup sugar
2 pounds apricots	¾ cup flour
1 stick (½ cup) unsalted butter	½ teaspoon nutmeg

Roll out the pie dough and fit it into a 9-inch pie pan. Crimp the edges and put the pan in the freezer for 15 minutes.

Preheat the oven to 400°F.

Wash and dry the apricots. Do not peel them. Break them in half with your fingers, and remove the pits.

Melt the butter over medium heat. Stir in the sugar. Add the flour and nutmeg.

Put the apricots into the unbaked pie shell. Cover them evenly with the sugar mixture. Put the pan in the oven, on the bottom rack.

After 10 minutes turn the oven down to 350°F. Bake for 35 minutes more, or until the top is crusty and brown.

Transfer the pie to a rack and cool before serving.

Serves 8.

Summer: Chocolate Cake

When Michael asked if I would bake a cake for his fortieth birthday party, I could not say no. It was what I would have done for any friend. But as I watched myself cream ten pounds of sugar into seven pounds of butter I began to understand what I was really up to. My unconscious had taken over; I had made a decision. The cake took rivers of chocolate and dozens of eggs, and by the time it was finished I needed four men to help me lift it into the car.

Michael blanched when he saw my creation coming toward him. This was more than a cake; it was a declaration of love in front of three hundred people, and we both knew it.

People at the party drank too much. They became maudlin and sad. They confessed things they were sorry about later, and threw up in the bathroom. We had planned to be forever young, and now middle age had come riding into our midst. It was time to make choices. And I had made one.

"Let's go somewhere," said Michael in the morning. "Let's just get in the car and get out of town." We packed what was left of the cake and headed north on Route 1, curving up the rugged California coastline.

We drove for half a day to a remote windswept village where the earth and the sky and the sea converged until it was impossible to know where one ended and the other began. "Here," said Michael, stopping the car. He went inside and I stayed in the car, thinking how nice it was to be carried along, to be with a man who would make the decisions.

He climbed back into the car and threw me a key. "I've rented a house," he said, pulling up in front of a gray-shingled structure on the edge of a cliff. It walked so lightly on the earth it seemed to vanish into the landscape.

We lived on chocolate cake and wine—when we ate at all, which wasn't often. We could not get enough of each other, and I felt myself drowning in sensuality. Every pore of my body yearned for this man, opened up to him. I had not known that sex could be like that: sweet, tough, funny, tender. He looked at me and my bones melted. He touched my hand and I felt it to my toes. When he played the blues my whole being vibrated to the music.

But this was more than sex. We talked, endlessly, and I could feel my mind stretching to meet his. His brain was quick and restless, and he was curious about everything. I imagined our life together and now I could not imagine settling for less.

Driving back he said, "When we make love I feel that I've come home. I feel that we are in this dance that's been going on for thousands of years. It feels right. I want to have children with you. Leave Doug. Marry me. Why are you so frightened?"

But all my fears had come back, and now I was no longer certain that I had made the right choice. Looking into the future I could not imagine it without Doug. It had never occurred to me that you could love someone and leave them, and I was terrified.

"You had better make up your mind," said Michael. "Soon."

We drove across the Golden Gate Bridge and I fed him the last piece of cake, crumb by crumb. By the time we reached San Francisco, it was gone.

BIG CHOCOLATE CAKE

FOR CAKE LAYERS

1½ cups boiling water

1 cup plus 2 tablespoons
  unsweetened cocoa powder
  (not Dutch Process)

¾ cup whole milk

1½ teaspoons vanilla

3 cups all-purpose flour

2 teaspoons baking soda

¾ teaspoon salt

3 sticks (1½ cups) unsalted
  butter, softened

1½ cups firmly packed dark
  brown sugar

1½ cups granulated sugar

6 large eggs

FOR FROSTING

5 ounces unsweetened
  chocolate, chopped

1½ sticks (¾ cup) unsalted
  butter, softened

1 cup whipped cream cheese

1 teaspoon vanilla

2½ cups confectioners' sugar

⅛ teaspoon salt

MAKE CAKE LAYERS

Preheat oven to 350°F. Butter two 13×9×2-inch baking pans and line bottoms of each with wax paper. Butter paper and dust pans with flour, knocking out excess.

Whisk together the boiling water and the cocoa in a bowl until smooth, then whisk in the milk and vanilla. Sift together the flour, baking soda, and salt.

Beat together the butter and sugars in the large bowl of a standing electric mixer until pale and fluffy, then add eggs one at a time, beating well after each addition. On low speed, beat in flour and cocoa mixtures alternately in batches, beginning and ending with the flour mixture (the batter may look curdled).

Divide batter between pans, smoothing tops. Bake in the middle of the oven until a tester comes out clean and layers begin to pull away from the sides of pans, 25 to 35 minutes.

Invert cakes onto racks, remove wax paper, and cool completely.

MAKE FROSTING

Melt the chocolate in a double boiler or a metal bowl set over a saucepan of simmering water, stirring until melted. Cool to room temperature.

Beat together the butter and cream cheese until light and fluffy. Add remaining ingredients and beat until well combined.

ASSEMBLE CAKE

Put one cake layer, rounded side up, on a cake plate and spread with 1¼ cups frosting. Top with another cake layer, rounded side up, and spread top and sides with remaining frosting.

Serves 20 to 25.

COOK'S NOTE

This is a classic sort of birthday cake, the kind of chocolate cake that pleases children. I made it for Michael because it is a recipe that is very forgiving and easily expandable. The cake I made for Michael was ten times the size of this one.

If you're going to double or triple it and bake the cake in larger pans, you will have to adjust the baking time.

Fall: Mushroom Soup

That fall, in New York, I made mushroom soup almost every night for my mother. And for myself. It's the most soothing soup I know, with no sharp edges to jar the palate, no sneaky unexpected spices. It is the perfect prescription for those in need of solace.

And we were definitely in need of that. Mom was running out of money, and the only solution was to sell her country house. I went east to help her clean it out, but she soon found this so depressing that she washed her hands of the entire project and took to her bed. "It's too much for an old lady," she protested, refusing to leave the apartment. "You and Doug are breaking up and I'm losing my house. You'll have to do it all alone."

I took the train to South Norwalk every day, walking from the station to the house. I hauled boxes from the attic, cleared closets, dismantled beds and bookcases. The Goodwill truck arrived every afternoon to collect another roomful of furniture.

In my parents' bedroom I emptied the dresser drawers, caressing the soft cotton pajamas that had belonged to my father. I found a pair of shorts I remembered Mom wearing when I was in kindergarten, and the halter top she had paired with it. I unearthed the dress she wore to my wedding.

Bit by bit my parents' bedroom disappeared, and I moved into the bathroom, where I swept old lipsticks, bobby pins, and compacts into a box. Then I moved into my bedroom, reducing it to another blank space.

In the living room I took down the paintings, rolled up the rugs, pushed the teak coffee table from Copenhagen into the middle of the floor. I boxed up the silver in the dining room, packed up the books in the den. Day by day the house grew emptier. Even its smell began to change.

Every night I went back to New York and made mushroom soup. Then I went out to walk the windswept sidewalks, trying to tire myself enough so that I could sleep. But I could not keep from seeing the city through Doug's eyes, noticing the arc of a curb, the reflection of a traffic light, the way electrical lines went singing through the streets. I had made a terrible mistake. When I was so exhausted that I could not stumble down another block, I turned and headed home for bed.

"Doug called," my mother said one night when I walked in the door. "He's in New York. He's on his way over."

It was painful to see Doug in my mother's apartment, surrounded by all my father's books. It was such a reminder of what we had once had, what we had lost, that we clung to each other, entwining our hands as if we would never let go.

In the morning my mother was furious. "People don't behave this way!" she cried when he had left. "He's leading you on." And then she looked at me and added, "I've never seen you so miserable. He's in love with someone else, and now he's leaving you."

▪ ▪ ▪

It was easier to be angry at my mother than myself, and I spent the day in the attic viciously throwing out things I knew she would want: old curtains, ugly linens, an atrocious table she had always, inexplicably, loved. It gave me a certain satisfaction. When Goodwill rang the doorbell for their daily pickup I sang out, "Come in."

But it wasn't Goodwill. "I drove out to see you," said Doug. "There's a full moon, and I thought maybe we could go to The Pier for dinner. Just for old times' sake."

We had stuffed shrimp and lobster and key lime pie. We talked about my father and had too many drinks. And then we went back to the empty house and pulled a mattress off the Goodwill pile and put it in the middle of the living room floor. The moon was shining in the window, turning the wooden floor into a sea of silver. We snuggled together on the mattress, sailing on a vast shimmering ocean of light.

But sometime during the night, after the moon had set, I felt Doug jerk and come awake. It was pitch-dark.

"What's wrong?" I asked.

"I had the strangest dream," he said. "I was holding a power tool and it exploded in my hands."

I woke up knowing that it was really over. I made coffee and toast in the empty kitchen; Goodwill had already picked up all the pots. We sat on the floor in the dining room and wrapped our hands around the two cups I had saved out for the very end.

"There will never be a day when we won't miss each other," I said, savoring the melodrama of the moment. He drove me to the train station and we stood there on the platform, like in all the movies, waiting for the train to pull in.

"It's too good," he replied, "we have to save it."

"A week from now," I replied, "you won't feel that way." The train arrived. I climbed on. I was going back to town, going to make mushroom soup.

MUSHROOM SOUP

½ pound mushrooms	1 cup beef broth
½ stick (¼ cup) unsalted butter	2 cups half-and-half
	salt, pepper
1 small onion, diced	¼ teaspoon nutmeg
4 tablespoons flour	1 bay leaf

Thinly slice the mushrooms.

Melt the butter in a heavy sauté pan. When the foam subsides, add the onion and sauté until golden. Add the mushrooms and sauté until brown.

Stir in the flour, and then slowly add the broth, stirring constantly.

Heat the half-and-half in a saucepan or in the microwave. Add it to the mushrooms, along with salt, pepper, nutmeg, and bay leaf. Cook over low heat for 10 minutes; do not boil.

Remove the bay leaf and serve.

Serves 4.

Winter Again: Swiss Pumpkin

The night Doug moved out of Channing Way I made Swiss pumpkin. As I cooked I reminded myself of a famous Brillat-Savarin aphorism: "The invention of a new recipe does more for mankind than the discovery of a new star."

I invented Swiss pumpkin.

Watching Doug pack had been unbearable. "You should move out too," he said as he carefully layered his drawings into boxes. "You should get a place of your own, try living alone for a while, without the safety net of Channing Way." When I didn't reply, he said bitterly, "You're planning on moving right in with Michael, aren't you?"

"I don't know what I'm doing," I replied. It was true. Some days I went apartment hunting with Michael. Some days I went apartment hunting alone. Paralyzed by indecision, I stayed on at Channing Way. Doug had been away so much that if I willed myself not to notice that his belongings were gone, the house did not seem very different. It was the same big mess it had always been, filled with too many people and too few rooms. It was easy to fool myself into thinking that Doug had just gone off on another trip.

Then I went to visit his new place. It was just like him: calm, spare, quiet. The walls were old bricks, the ceiling was high, and Doug had painted the trim a blackened green. The space was un-cluttered, with a few beautiful objects strategically placed to cap-ture the eye.

I wandered around, touching the things that had once belonged to us both. The stone bird we got in Italy was perched on his kitchen shelf; the star quilt from our bed covered his bed. He'd built himself a small round table for the living room with Charlie Chaplin legs that gave it a human air. It looked like no place we had ever lived together.

There were letters on the table in the hall. When I saw that they were addressed to him it finally sank in. He lived here now; he was home. I had done this. I had pulled my life apart. I would never, ever be safe again.

Doug ground coffee beans and put his arms around me while we waited for the water to boil. "We've done the right thing," he said. "Our relationship has given us the strength to live without each other. We've made each other independent."

Words, I thought. So many words. My quiet man was becoming a talker, and I no longer even knew if he meant what he said. Now he kissed me and added, "I care more about our relationship than I do about our marriage. That's why I want to let it go."

"Mmm," I sighed, turning to leave. As I got to the door he said, "I think I'll roast a chicken. Can you tell me how to do it?"

"Don't worry," I replied, "you'll figure it out."

And then I went down the stairs and out the door. I was going home to bake a pumpkin.

SWISS PUMPKIN

1 pumpkin, about 4¼
   pounds
a 14-inch baguette, cut into
   ¼-inch-thick slices, then
   toasted lightly
¼ pound Gruyère cheese,
   grated

1¾ cups half-and-half
2 large eggs
1½ teaspoons kosher salt
1 teaspoon freshly ground
   black pepper
¼ teaspoon nutmeg

Preheat the oven to 350°F.

Carefully cut a 1-inch slice off the top of the pumpkin. Reserving the top, scoop out and discard the seeds and strings. Make 3 layers each of toast and cheese in the pumpkin cavity, alternating layers and ending with cheese. Whisk together the half-and-half, eggs, salt, pepper, and nutmeg and slowly pour the mixture into the pumpkin. Replace the top of the pumpkin and bake on a shallow baking pan in the middle of the oven until the pumpkin is tender, about 2 hours. Serve by scooping out the pumpkin flesh with the bread and cheese.

Serves 4.

9

RAINING SHRIMP

RESTAURANT CRITIC
CHOKES TO DEATH
IN RESTAURANT

■ The headline flashed through my head; if I could have laughed, I would have. But I couldn't. I couldn't swallow, couldn't breathe, couldn't talk, and I seemed unable to make anyone around me understand that I was in trouble. I was in a small restaurant surrounded by twenty of my closest friends, but in the general exuberance my silence went unnoticed.

I was wedged into the back corner, one wall behind me and one to my side, unable to extricate myself from my seat. Time slowed down, and I began to understand that if I didn't do something quickly I was really going to die. The irony of the situation was not lost on me: I had just fallen in love with Thai food and it was about to kill me.

I hadn't expected much from this little Berkeley joint. When the first course turned out to be a bright magenta soup, I sneered down into the bowl and said, "Food coloring" in my most disparaging restaurant-critic voice. Then I deigned to take a spoonful.

My head flew off. I felt my cheeks getting hot and my eyes getting moist. My palms prickled. Shivers swooped down my spine. Suddenly I was so attuned to sensation that I could feel my watch ticking against my wrist. No food had ever done this to me before.

The hot-pink soup was dotted with lacy green leaves of cilantro, like little bursts of breeze behind the heat. Small puffs of fried tofu, as insubstantial as clouds, floated in the liquid. I took another spoonful of soup and tasted citrus, as if lemons had once gone gliding through and left their ghosts behind.

Afterward there were tropical fish cakes flavored with coconut and bursts of ginger. And then curries—green ones and red ones— exploded into my mouth. I was getting high, my whole body flooded with a feeling of well-being.

And that was my undoing. Exhilarated and eager for the next sensation, I had become so silent that when the satay stuck in my throat, no one noticed.

As my breath gave out I began to panic and wave my arms around. Jules, who was sitting next to me, said mildly, "Do you want something?" and handed me his beer. I took a sip and watched him watch it dribble out of my mouth, slowly realizing that I could not swallow.

At that moment Michael leapt across the table, pushed everyone away, and grabbed me. He put his arms beneath my rib cage and squeezed upward with such force that the piece of meat that had been stuck in my throat flew halfway across the room. Air rushed back into my lungs, color back into my cheeks. I was going to live!

"Thanks," I said. "You saved my life."

"Don't mention it," he replied.

"I have to go to Thailand," I said next.

"I get it," he said. "As you were dying your whole life flashed before you. You had an epiphany. You realized you had to see Thailand before you died."

"Something like that," I answered.

▪ ▪ ▪

Every Thai man, the woman at the Tourism Authority of Thailand had told me, became a monk at the age of twenty. I thought about that as I flew. There were, she said, more than three hundred temples in Bangkok alone, and I imagined myself meandering down quiet streets, watching monks file past in saffron robes chanting softly, musically.

I had put the trip together with uncharacteristic speed, begging every editor I knew to give me an assignment. Within days, three of them had said yes, and I had enough work to make the trip a reality.

"You're not going to Thailand," said Michael, "you're just running away. It's easier than deciding what to do with your life. You're drifting, waiting for something to happen so you won't have to make up your mind." He had a very clear picture of my future: He wanted me to file divorce papers and move in with him. He wanted to get married and have children.

Doug also thought I was being irresponsible. And he too had a plan for me. "You need to live alone for a while," he said. "You should get your own apartment." Although we no longer lived together, neither of us had made a move toward a divorce, and when we were together, we spoke as if we had a future.

Going to Bangkok, I knew, was a coward's move, but I wanted to get away from both of them. Southeast Asia seemed exotic and unfamiliar, the perfect place for an encounter with destiny.

As the plane began the approach to Bangkok, I looked down and saw flooded green fields dotted with small thatched huts, and rivers snaking everywhere. It was hazy, and I remembered the other thing the woman at the Tourism Authority had said: "Our land is so lush that in monsoon season we say it is raining shrimp."

But no shrimp rained down as the taxi inched toward the hotel. And as we bumped and skidded through the gray industrial landscape, no temples peeked through the murk. The sky was dark, the streets flooded, the air so polluted it was hard to see the ugly buildings we were passing. Horns blared, engines whirred, and tailpipes spewed smoke. My head ached; my eyes stung. "Welcome to Bangkok!" shouted the driver.

"What?" I shouted back.

"Ninety-five percent of all the cars in Thailand are here in Bangkok," he yelled.

"I thought people rode boats along the canals," I shouted.

"You probably thought we shopped at the floating market as well," he called over his shoulder.

"You don't?" I had an assignment from *Cuisine* magazine to write about the floating market of Bangkok.

"Only for tourists," he shouted. "The central market is much more convenient."

"Were you ever a monk?" I asked, suddenly suspicious.

"Of course," he said solemnly. "I went to study scripture and purify myself. It is our tradition."

"I'm glad to hear that," I said.

"What?" he screamed. Bangkok might have most of Thailand's cars, but it did not seem to have a single muffler.

"I'm glad," I bellowed, making a megaphone of my hands.

"Don't worry," he yelled. "Your hotel is like a temple. Very quiet."

▪ ▪ ▪

A woman with smooth skin, hair to her waist, and orchids at her neck stood at the entrance to the hotel. She bowed as I walked in. Another sarong-wrapped beauty led me along hushed corridors. She flung open the doors to my room and I entered, walking across thick white carpets to a white marble bathroom. The bedroom was filled with flowers. A bottle of champagne sat cooling in an ice bucket; a basket overflowed with rambutans and mangosteens. The woman led me to the window and out to the terrace. Below us the sun sparkled off the river, as if the curtain of pollution hanging over the city had been pulled aside. In Bangkok, I thought, the sun shines only for the rich. The woman smiled again, put her hands together in a prayerful attitude, and went out the door, walking backward.

I tumbled into bed, jet-lagged and already overwhelmed by the strangeness of it all. My eyes closed. I was back in San Francisco, lost, trying to meet Doug for dinner. I was late, I was naked, I was running. Every street was a dead end, and Michael kept popping out of doorways, grinning wickedly, like the target in a penny arcade game. Bells were ringing, and I was running, trying to cover myself as the bells got louder and louder. Way down at the end of the street I could see Doug, but the more I ran toward him, the farther away he got. The noise was becoming unbearable . . .

And then I was awake, sweating and disoriented, and the bells were the telephone. I grabbed it.

"Ruth?" said a deep French voice. It was Jacques, my one friend in Thailand. He would pick me up in an hour.

■ ■ ■

Jacques was the most romantic figure who had ever turned up on Channing Way. He was a friend of Nick's, a burly man with vigorous brown hair and a well-used face that made him look like a former prizefighter. Jacques was actually the Bangkok correspondent for a French newspaper, and we knew him because in his spare time he composed electronic music. He was an amiable man, passionate about wine and reputed to be friendly with both John Cage and Prince Sihanouk. None of us had ever met anyone quite like Jacques, and when we had nothing better to do we sat around and speculated that he was a spy. Seeing him standing in the lobby of my hotel was like discovering a little bit of Berkeley in the middle of Bangkok.

"Tonight," he said, giving me a lopsided grin, "we will eat like

Thais." He led me into the steamy, raucous Bangkok night. "People here eat in little bites, moving from one restaurant to another. I hope you like hot food?"

"I've never tasted anything that was too hot for me," I bragged.

Jacques's eyes twinkled. "Bravo!" he said. "Then we will start at the restaurant near the boxing stadium."

"I love it here," he said as the valet came riding up on his motor scooter. "But you have to be a little bit crazy." We climbed onto the scooter and plunged into the whirlpool of traffic.

It was instantly clear that Jacques did not intend to take me to tourist places. Likit was a dump, an enormous, bare room with hundreds of chickens roasting on flat beds of charcoal in the front. Fans circulated above our heads in a vain attempt to clear away the smoke. The aroma was delicious. "They are famous for their charcoal chicken," said Jacques, kicking at some papers on the floor. The papers fluttered up, momentarily, and settled back onto the wooden slats. "At New Year's people line up for hours to get it to take out."

The chicken was crisp and moist, spicy and fragrant. It was dripping with a thin chili sauce that prickled pleasantly in the back of my throat. "This is great," I said, licking my fingers, as the waitress set a platter of fried pork with garlic and pepper on the table. I looked around for cutlery.

"Where are the chopsticks?" I asked.

"In Thailand chopsticks are used only for noodles," said Jacques, ladling some rice onto his plate. He took a spoon in his right hand and a fork in his left. "The Thai eat with spoons," he said, demonstrating. "The fork is a pusher." He pointed out dishes of small chilies on each table, and plates heaped with cabbage, lettuce, basil, long beans, and cilantro. Bottles of hot sauce and vinegar stood sentinel behind them. "Here when you eat you have to be a little bit of a cook too," he said, sprinkling hot sauce on his pork. He added some cilantro and a splash of vinegar. "The food is al-

ways served with condiments, and you make each dish to your own taste." I followed his lead and took a bite. The flavors jumped around in my mouth, layered, intense. There was one, very green and earthy, that I could not identify.

"What is that flavor that goes to the side of your mouth?" I asked.

Jacques looked very pleased. "Cilantro root," he said. "It is used a great deal in Thailand and hardly at all in the rest of the world."

"Delicious," I said, a little disappointed that none of the food was spicy.

The waitress set a big bowl filled with crabs on the table. They were fragrant with chilies and redolent of beer. "Steamed nippers," said Jacques, adding more chilies and basil to his plate.

I followed suit, but the dish was still not very hot, and I was starting to think that real Thai food was different from what I had been served in California.

Then the waitress set another platter on the table. "How dong," she announced.

"Game," explained Jacques. "I'm not quite sure what kind. How dong can be many things, but it is always something from the forest."

"Oh, I love game," I said, taking a large serving. I ostentatiously sprinkled some hot sauce across the top, added a few leaves of basil and a couple of chilies, and took a bite.

It was a mistake. The dish was incendiary. I reached for the water.

Jacques laughed and grabbed the glass from my hand. "Water will only make it worse," he said, handing me a small ball of sticky rice. "This should help." I took a bite, and the pain began to abate.

"What *is* that?" I asked.

"How dong," he said. "It is always cheap, and it is always hot. It is made of miscellaneous meat; it could be anything—snake, muskrat, baby lion. The recipe calls for lots of chilies, pepper, and

spice to mask the flavor of the meat. If you want heat, order how dong. Ready for the next adventure?"

▪ ▪ ▪

We raced through the electric streets, screeching around corners, sideswiping cars, grazing the sidewalks, until we came to the night market. We meandered past stalls piled high with dishes, stopping for skewers of grilled squid and neat little bundles wrapped in banana leaves. Unfolding the green envelope, I uncovered a rectangle of sticky rice so rich with coconut milk that when the sweet tropical smell wafted up, it obliterated the surrounding aroma of curry, ginger, and limes.

We went on to bars, where we drank Thai whiskey and beautiful women threw themselves at Jacques as if I were not there. Around midnight it started to rain and Jacques took me to a place down one of the small dirt alleys that shoot off the main avenues. Barely more than a shack with a corrugated tin roof, it had a primitive barbecue in the back, where a man stood grilling cockles; we snatched them from the fire, drenched them with lime and chilies, and poured them down our throats. The rain thundered down, like drums, like music, and Jacques threw back his head and laughed. We drank more whiskey mixed with bottled water and Jacques showed me the pots of food simmering on a stove. "You just point at what you want," he said, ordering something submerged in a sauce the color of Tabasco.

The thunder on the roof ended, abruptly, and the silence was startling, as loud as the music. Jacques grabbed my hand and pulled me outside. "Time for the next course," he said.

The streets were still filled with people. Women in improbably tight dresses beckoned from doorways; behind them we could see men at tables, throwing dice, drinking beer. Music drifted toward us in the dark.

We rode through the thick, humid air. Occasionally a breeze

caressed our faces. A temple loomed in front of us, and Jacques slowed down. Through the darkness I could just make out the form of the pointed roof and an old woman sitting in the doorway, cross-legged on the ground. Jacques got off the cycle and squatted beside her. He whispered something in Thai and beckoned to me.

The old lady patted the ground, and I sat down facing her. She held out her right hand; I put mine in hers. She ran her left hand across the top, barely touching it, as if she could read my thoughts through my skin. Then she turned my hand over, picked up a candle, and sat peering at my palm for a long time.

"Do I ask a question?" I said.

"That is not necessary," Jacques replied. "She will speak when she is ready." The old lady was very still, watching my hand, and then she began to talk.

"You are strong and successful," Jacques translated. "She says that you do unusual work and that this supports your family." The old lady was silent for another moment.

"She says that you have no child, but that you want one."

I nodded.

"She says," he continued, "that you are separated from your husband. She says that the question you want to ask is whether you should return to him."

The old lady was silent for a few minutes. The wind rustled through the leaves above us. Then she began to speak, slowly, carefully.

"Yes," said Jacques. "The answer is yes. There is only one man in your hand. She says your destiny is with him."

The woman abruptly dropped my hand. The reading was over. I held out a handful of baht; she took each coin individually, looked at my face, then blew out the candle and faded into the dark.

"I need a drink," I said.

We got back onto the motor scooter and rode very quickly. Suddenly Jacques made an abrupt turn into an alley and came to a stop in front of another tin-roofed shack. "The best place in Bangkok after a long night of drinking," he said, leading me inside. The room was small and dimly lit. "They are specialists in congee. The rice is good—it absorbs the alcohol. And then you eat these, with a little more whiskey, to get you back to zero."

He was pointing at plates covered with small, beautifully translucent crabs, their shells faintly blue against the bright red roe. "Pu dong," he said. "They are marinated, raw." I picked one up and put it in my mouth, wondering for just a second if it was smart to eat raw crabs in Thailand. But it was in my mouth, the thought was gone, and I was savoring the sensation of the slippery meat. It was chewy and very hot, but behind the heat was a startling, pleasant sweetness.

Jacques showed me how to the scrape the roe from the crab and chew on the shells, which were so soft they melted away, leaving only flavor. In my mouth was the cool of the sea, the sunshine in the chili, the taste of rice growing in the paddies. My head was swimming. I had another shot of whiskey. Another crab. And then my eyes were closing.

I clung to Jacques, barely awake as we dodged traffic. The night air was hot and sticky; you could smell the rain that was still to come. Neon lights flashed, horns blared.

And then, suddenly, the noise stopped. Trees swayed, cooling the night. Flowers opened to perfume the air. Doors swung silently open on well-oiled hinges. A woman, her long hair braided with orchids, was bowing me in. I tumbled into bed.

▪ ▪ ▪

That night I did not dream, and when I woke up I was calm, as if a great weight had lifted off my chest; after all this time it was good to know my destiny. I would go home, pack my things, and move in with Doug. If he would have me. The future felt clear. Wrapped in this cocoon of confidence, I meandered through Thailand, focused only on the food.

The flavors changed, dramatically, as I traveled. Up north, in Chiang Mai, the very air was perfumed with garlic, which was eaten on everything. In the morning, even breakfast arrived sprinkled with preserved garlic.

"Northern food is much better than what they eat in Bangkok," said a woman in Chiang Mai. She pointed at the sticky rice that appeared in a basket at each meal, then showed me how to roll it into a ball with three fingers and use it to sop up the sauce.

I found myself memorizing dishes I liked: the little pumpkins filled with coconut flan; the chopped raw meat, larb; the tiny ears of grilled corn sprinkled with chili powder.

In Chiang Rai I sat at a roadside stand watching long-horned water buffalo lumbering through flooded rice paddies while children fished with hooped nets and little yellow ducklings paddled around them. The local specialty, kang kee lek, was a spicy, creamy mush made of pork, coconut milk, and acacia seeds that I found absolutely irresistible.

In Phuket, where the signs along Patong Beach read U.S. NAVY, PATONG OFFERS YOU WINE, WOMEN AND SONG, the people were pickle crazy; on my first visit to the market I tasted pickled pineapple, pickled guava, and sweet-water olives. The sweet olives were so strange I made a face, and the woman standing next to me burst out laughing. "You do not like this?" she asked.

I shook my head. "Also I do not like," she said. "Where are you from?"

I told her, and she looked impressed. "American men, we get many," she said. "American women, none." I said that I had seen the signs, and that I found the beaches disappointing.

"Have you been to Karon Beach?" she asked. When I told her I had not, she insisted on meeting the next day so that she could show it to me. We took a bus to the end of the line, where men pulled boats filled with fish onto an expanse of pure white sand. You chose what you wanted and they cooked it right there, over a little fire at the edge of the sea.

Eating that crisp-skinned fish with a friendly stranger, I thought of Doug, wishing he were there to share it with me. Over the next few weeks I found myself saving up little details I knew he would like. I barely thought of Michael; he was my old life, behind me. I was moving on.

▪ ▪ ▪

I went back to the sexy stew of Bangkok for my final nights in Thailand. "I've missed you and your expense account," said Jacques when I called. "I've found a restaurant you have to try." He laughed and added, "It's very expensive."

It turned out to be a supermarket with cases filled with every imaginable fish and vegetable lining its sides. In the middle, where the aisles should have been, were tables. Chic people strolled through the space, filling their carts with prawns and celery, porgy and water chestnuts, lobsters and crabs. "You have to invent your own dishes," said Jacques, piling shrimp as large as his fists and pale, delicate stalks of baby celery into the cart, "and after you have checked out you take the ingredients to the chefs and tell them how to cook what you've bought. There is a separate cooking charge."

We invented three dishes, and after we had watched the chefs cook them over the leaping flames I said, "Take me back to the fortune teller."

"I don't blame you," he said. "You want to know when you'll be coming back."

He hadn't asked a question, so I didn't have to tell him that it was another question I wanted answered. I wanted to be sure that I was making the right decision.

■ ■ ■

The old lady was still sitting in front of the temple, as if she had not moved in the month since I'd last seen her. I sat down before her. Once again she took my hand.

"You are strong and successful," Jacques translated. "She says that you do unusual work and that this supports your family." The old lady was silent for another moment.

"She says that you have no child, but that you want one."

I had heard all this before. He continued, "The question you want to ask is whether you should return to your husband." And then, without a pause he went on: "She says there are two men in your hand, and your destiny lies with the second."

I looked up and began laughing at myself. I was on a tawdry street in a strange town looking for magic answers. "At least the food was good," I said, handing the old lady some coins.

MIANG KAM

Maybe the old woman knew exactly what she was doing. Because she made me realize the sheer stupidity of my behavior, made me see that I had come too far to turn back. The whole way home I thought of Michael, missed his company and realized how lucky I was to be with a man who was constantly interesting to me.

And then I got off the plane and saw him standing by the gate, talking to a tall, tawny woman. His hair was very black against his tan skin, his teeth very white. The woman leaned into him for a moment and they were so handsome, so appealing, that every eye turned. I threw myself into his arms, felt the heat rising off his body. "She's glad to see me!" he said, laughing.

We went back to his house and I made him this dish, from a recipe given to me by a wonderful Thai chef named Boonchoo Pholatawarna. It's street food, the sort of thing that is sold in every Thai market. It makes great cocktail-party food, but it's also a wonderful little snack to feed your lover.

FOR THE SYRUP

½ *cup water*

½ *cup packed light brown sugar*

2 *tablespoons Asian fish sauce*

2 *teaspoons finely chopped peeled fresh ginger*

2 *tablespoons roasted salted peanuts, finely chopped*

¼ *cup unsweetened (desiccated) shredded coconut, toasted*

FOR THE PACKETS

¼ *cup small dried shrimp*

½ *cup unsweetened (desiccated) shredded coconut, toasted*

¼ *cup finely chopped shallot or red onion*

¼ *cup finely chopped peeled fresh ginger*

¼ *cup roasted salted peanuts, chopped*

¼ *cup finely chopped fresh small Asian chilies or serrano chilies, seeded if desired*

1 *lime, cut into thin wedges*

1 *head butter lettuce, leaves separated*

TO MAKE THE SYRUP

Whisk together the water and sugar in a heavy small saucepan and boil, stirring occasionally, until reduced to ½ cup, about 5 minutes. Remove the pan from heat and stir in the fish sauce, ginger, peanuts, and coconut. Transfer to a serving bowl.

TO ASSEMBLE THE PACKETS

Arrange all the remaining ingredients in separate mounds on one platter.

To eat, each diner fills a lettuce leaf with some of each condiment, then squeezes lime juice over it and drizzles it with sauce before folding the leaf over the filling to form a neat little bundle.

Serves 4 (makes about 16 bundles).

10

MIDNIGHT DUCK

■ When the gate swung open I caught my breath. All I could see were four stone steps, curving up toward a lawn. Michael took my hand, and we started climbing. With the first step deep green walls came into view, covered with ivy and so old I knew they would be soft when I touched them. The second step revealed a jasmine-covered trellis leading to a cottage. By the third step we could see the cottage itself, small and red, its crooked chimney set at a jaunty angle. But it was only on the final step that the entire scene became visible.

We were in a sheltered garden, hidden from the world by mossy walls. A carpet of lawn spread beneath our feet, and off in a corner a little frog leapt into a tiny fountain with a quiet splash. Daisies gathered sunlight in front of the cottage, and it seemed to me that every ray in San Francisco must be concentrated here. The quiet was so profound that despite the traffic on the street outside, we could hear the warbling of the robin welcoming us from the top of the wall.

"It's hard to believe we're in San Francisco," I whispered. "It feels like we're in a hill town in Tuscany."

"You don't have to whisper," said Michael. "It's ours."

"How did you find it?" I was still whispering, afraid to break the spell.

Michael smiled and took my hand. For a moment he was quiet. At last he said, "I knew I had to, so I did."

"I guess I should call you Rumpelstiltskin," I said, for he had accomplished the impossible. After Bangkok, I had told Michael I would live with him when we found a perfect place. It sounded like a decision, but I was still hedging my bets; rental property in the Bay Area was nearly nonexistent, especially for people with very little money.

But Michael was not like me or Doug; he went after what he wanted, and he knew how to turn no into yes. Now he led me into the house, saying, "Please don't make me slay another dragon."

Inside, the cottage was even better. The living room was spacious, with a big fireplace at one end and a wall of windows overlooking the garden at the other. The kitchen was compact, but it had a wood-burning grill with an electric rotisserie. One bedroom had a little porch, and from the other you could see a small slice of the Bay, peeking between two buildings. I felt as if Michael had waved a wand and conjured a magic cottage from thin air.

But after ten years on Channing Way, the sheer perfection of the place was hard to take. And compared to the easy camaraderie of the communal life, I found living with just one person extremely stressful. "Now you'll see how easy it isn't," said Doug when he came to visit. There was a note of satisfaction in his voice that made me suspect that he was as frightened as I was. "I still dream about you every night," he admitted.

"I dream about you too," I said, confessing that moving into the cottage had depressed me. I tried to hide these feelings from Michael, but with no crowd to surround me I felt exposed, naked. Living with a lot of people was so much safer.

And then, to make matters worse, my mother announced that she was planning a Thanksgiving visit. The idea of the three of us in the cottage was almost unbearable. Michael was even less enthusiastic than I was.

"Can't your mother come ruin Christmas or something?" he cried. "Thanksgiving is my favorite holiday, and I was looking forward to celebrating our first one together, just the two of us in our own house. Besides, you know she's going to hate me. She's going to spend the entire visit telling you how much better off you were with Doug."

"If that's all that happens we'll be lucky," I muttered.

"What?" he asked.

"Oh, nothing," I replied hastily. "I'll see if I can't get her to come for Christmas instead."

My mother was not pleased. "Let me see if I understand what you are saying," she said icily when I suggested the switch. "You don't want me to come for Thanksgiving."

"I just thought it might be better if you came for Christmas," I said carefully. "You know, you're not a food person and you don't care all that much for turkey. But Christmas on your own can get really depressing."

"If *that's* all you're worried about . . ." said Mom, her voice melting, "you don't have to worry. It's very sweet of you, but I'm spending Christmas in India. I've already bought the tickets. And I've bought the tickets to San Francisco too."

"You might have asked first," I demurred.

"Ask my own daughter for permission to visit her?" she demanded. The chill was back. "When she's living with a man I haven't even met? When she's ruined her life by leaving the most wonderful husband a girl could ever have?"

"Maybe you'd like to stay with Doug?" I suggested. I couldn't help myself.

"My psychiatrist," she said suddenly, "says that I'm jealous of you. You have a glamorous life, a man who loves you, interesting work. You're young. I suppose he's right, but I never thought mothers could feel that way about their kids."

"I didn't either," I said, accepting defeat. "Give me your flight number. I'll pick you up at the airport."

▪ ▪ ▪

My mother was hard to miss. She came swinging into the terminal dressed in every color of the rainbow. A huge straw hat was perched on her head, its bright red poppies vibrating with each step. "PussyCat!" she cried, bending to kiss me. She stood up and began waving, crying, "Good-bye, good-bye, I'll phone," as she blew kisses to her new friends. Perfect strangers were watching me with knowing eyes. What had she told them?

"Such *nice* people on the plane!" she gushed as we drove home, launching into the intimate details of the lives of people she would never see again.

"I'll have to work while you're here," I warned when she'd wound down. "I'm doing a story about this guy who thinks you can tell everything about a person just by asking one simple question."

"What?" she asked.

"What does your family eat for Thanksgiving dinner?"

"Ridiculous!" she said.

"He's pretty impressive," I replied.

"So what did he say about you?" she asked.

"Oh, I was easy. It took him about a minute to say that at least one of my parents was not born in America. I asked how he could tell, and he said that the biggest clue was that you sometimes forgot to make gravy."

"I never forgot to make gravy!"

"Yes, Mom, you did. A few times. Once you forgot to make dinner altogether!"

"But I was sick!" she said. "I was depressed. That doesn't count."

"Actually, it wasn't the gravy that got his attention. It was the 'sometimes' part. For real Americans this is a tradition, and nothing is supposed to be 'sometimes.' He said that our family had not learned the interior semiology of the symbols."

"What was the other clue?" she asked.

"No mincemeat pie. For some reason, and he doesn't know why, Jews never serve it."

"It's interesting," she conceded. "More interesting than most of the stuff you write."

"Oh," I replied, "it gets even better. He told one friend of mine that he could tell her mother regretted having married beneath her because of some cranberry ice she always made."

"How could he possibly know that?" Mom asked.

"Elise told him that nobody ever ate it, and he said that it didn't fit with the rest of the meal. It's all in the details. She said he was absolutely right; they all resented that ice, which belonged to their mother's fancy background. They didn't eat it, but she insisted on serving it anyway and it just sat there, melting."

"Clues in the cranberries," she said as we pulled up in front of the cottage. "It's still just food, but it's interesting."

I opened the gate and led her into the garden. It was green and still. Squirrels chased each other across the lawn, and the flowering vine twining over the door gave off a honeyed scent. "What a change from Berkeley!" said Mom, and I began to have some hope.

I stuck my key into the lock and prayed, uncertain about what I would find when it opened. Michael was so irritated by this invasion that I would not have been surprised to discover clothes strewn across the house I had so carefully cleaned. But when the door swung open, I saw a vase of flowers that had not been there when I'd left. The hall smelled like furniture polish; the floor gleamed, and not a thing was out of place. Michael had even put a little note on Mom's pillow telling her he couldn't wait to get home from work and meet her.

He came bustling into the house an hour later, filled with good cheer and charm. He kissed her cheek and said brazenly, "You're so much prettier than your pictures!" My whole being flooded with relief; in this mood he was irresistible to any woman. I went into the kitchen to get cheese and crackers, and when I emerged he was bending toward my mother, teasing her about having waited so long to come and meet him. I went back for the wine, and as I stood in the kitchen pulling the cork I heard him say how happy he was.

"Who ever thought I'd be living like this?" he said. Even from the kitchen I knew that he was nodding toward the garden. "I had nothing when I met Ruth," he confessed. "My best friend told me that if I really wanted to be with her, I'd have to grow up, give up freelance writing, and get a real job."

"And how did you do that?" Mom asked.

I hadn't heard this before. I stopped to listen. "I sat down one day and listed my options," he said. "Television seemed like the obvious choice."

"But you'd never worked in television before!"

"I was a journalist. I had made films. I didn't think it could be that different. I decided where I wanted to work and applied at all the others. By the time I went to KRON I had figured out how to pass the test, and they hired me as a substitute news writer. Within a couple of months they had given me a full-time job."

Michael had told me none of this. He had simply called one day and said, "I've got a job. Now will you throw in with me?"

"Once I was inside," he continued, "it was easy to become a producer."

"And you like it?" Mom asked.

"It's the most exciting work I've ever done," he replied.

"Oh yes," I said, coming back into the living room and handing her a glass of wine. "Very exciting. A few days ago I picked up the phone and a deep voice said, 'Tell your nosy boyfriend we know where he lives. Tell him he'd better stop looking into matters that are not his business.' "

"Your work is dangerous!" said Mom happily.

"Not really," said Michael. "I'm doing a story about police corruption in a little town near here. They make threats, but they don't kill reporters."

"Police corruption," Mom repeated in a thrilled voice. I could almost hear the story she was formulating for her friends. It would begin, "Ruthie's new beau does really useful work . . ."

▪ ▪ ▪

We took Mom to Chez Panisse for dinner. Alice had set little nosegays of wildflowers all around the table, and she sent us a bottle of champagne. As people turned to see who was getting this special treatment, Mom puffed with pleasure.

"No steak tonight, Mom." I smiled at her. She smiled back and then, simultaneously, our smiles faded. A cloud descended over the table as we both remembered the last time we had eaten together at Chez Panisse, and with whom.

Michael stepped valiantly into the silence. "Cheerio," he said, clinking both of our glasses, "have a nice visit." The champagne smelled like spring and tasted like icy bubbles. The oysters were cold, with that deep, mysteriously ancient flavor they have when they first come out of the ocean.

Alice had made mushroom soup so intense and untamed that it was exciting rather than soothing, like taking a walk in the wilderness. I was somewhere else, lost in the flavors, when Alice wafted over to the table to inquire how we had liked the grilled wild duck and poached pears.

"Fabulous," breathed Mom. Alice beamed and turned to me. "I

had lunch today in a restaurant I want to take you to. They grow all their own food!"

"Everything?" I asked. "How big is their garden?"

"Huge," she said, envy in her voice. "They're growing mulberries, fava beans, cardoons, and wild artichokes. They've planted nine different kinds of peppers. You should see the herbs! They raise rabbits and chickens, and they milk their own goats to make cheese."

"Where is it?" I asked.

"Far," she admitted. "Boonville."

"That's almost to Mendocino!" I said.

"True," she said dreamily. "But today I had the most amazing BLT."

"You drove three hours for a BLT?" I asked.

"It was a perfect sandwich!" she exclaimed, with such passion that we all put down our forks and listened, really listened, to her.

"Imagine this," she said in the same tone that you might use with children when you were about to read a fairy tale. "They bake the bread, right there, that morning, so it's just a couple of hours old. They make their own mayonnaise too, from the eggs of their own chickens. Have you ever tasted an egg that was just laid?"

We hadn't.

"A fresh egg doesn't taste like anything else on earth," she said. "It's a real treat; once you've had one you can never go back. You should see the color of the yolks! Bright orange, which makes the mayonnaise absolutely golden. They pick the tomatoes and the little lettuces at the last possible moment, so when you eat the sandwich they're still warm from the sun."

"And the bacon?" I asked. "I suppose they smoke that too. Right before they serve the sandwich?"

"No," she admitted, and I could tell that it cost her something. "They wanted to make their own bacon, but they got the wrong kinds of pigs. So they have to get their ham and bacon from a farmer down the road. But when it's layered with those ripe, warm tomatoes . . . you can't imagine how good it tastes."

I could. "I've known Vernon for a long time," she went on, her voice deepening. "Vernon's got wonderful taste. One year he made me dinner for my birthday . . ."

An old boyfriend! I thought, as she began describing a meal that was both earthy and elegant. "There was a raw beef salad and an old white Margaux, which is still one of my favorite combinations," she said. "And now he's planning to do this special Thanksgiving dinner that sounds so interesting. He's found a medieval recipe where you kill the turkey, pluck it really fast, and get it into the oven before rigor mortis sets in. He showed me the drawings from an old manuscript. I'd love to try it."

"I think we should go there tomorrow!" my mother announced.

"Good idea," I said. It would give us something to do. "It sounds like a place I should write about."

■ ■ ■

"I don't envy you the trip," said Michael as he went off to work the next morning. "Three hours each way, locked up in a car with her. I'd much rather spend time with corrupt policemen."

"Well, at least she doesn't want to kill me," I said.

"Don't kid yourself, honey," he said, going out the door.

■ ■ ■

"Do you think Doug might want to come with us?" Mom asked as we were leaving.

"Oh, I don't think—" I began.

"We don't have to tell Michael," Mom added mischievously, and before I could stop her she had dialed Doug's number.

"I told him we'd pick him up," she reported when the call was finished. "I'm dying to see his place."

"Oh, good," I said. "Then you can tell me how much nicer it is than mine."

"No, dear," she said with seeming sincerity, "it couldn't be."

■ ■ ■

Doug had left the downstairs door unlocked. His loft was above an old hardware store, and as we walked up the stairs we inhaled the clean scent of paint and wood chips. "It reminds me of that place on the Bowery where you lived right after you were married," Mom said. I took a deep breath and realized it did smell exactly the same. It gave me an eerie feeling, as if Doug had just erased the time we had spent together and begun again.

But when Doug opened the door I had the rush of instant gladness I always felt when I saw him. He was wearing clean blue jeans and the shirt with the peacock blue stripes I had given him for his thirty-third birthday. His cheeks were very pink. He kissed Mom, easily, and then me, less easily.

I watched Doug showing my mother the plans for Sound Garden, the piece he was building up in Seattle. He had become more articulate, and she was clearly impressed.

"And will you be spending Thanksgiving in Seattle?" she asked as we got into the car.

"Oh no," he said. "My girlfriend and I are going to cook in my studio." I felt a physical pang as he said that, and Mom gave me a sidelong glance, trying to see how I had taken it. "Actually," he went on, and I could feel his eyes slide toward me, "I'm going to be doing the cooking. It will be my first turkey."

I struggled to betray nothing. "What are you making?" I asked.

"The usual," he said, "just the traditional Thanksgiving dinner. You know: turkey, stuffing, gravy, potatoes."

"Are you making mincemeat pie?" I asked.

"I might," he said.

■ ■ ■

From the outside, The New Boonville Hotel wasn't much: a two-story white clapboard building with deep porches on both floors that gave it the air of a nineteenth-century boardinghouse. "I don't see a garden," said Mom, sounding disappointed.

"Give them a chance, Miriam," said Doug. "It must be in back."

Inside, the first impression was sunlight and new wood, but as you stood in the entranceway the details began to come into focus. Despite the jars of jams and wildflowers perched along the windowsills, the restaurant had a pared-down elegance. A fire burned in a stone hearth, and the walls were filled with art. Looking up, I discovered little surprises among the paintings: an artist's clock, and a framed bit of calligraphy signed Gregory Corso.

"Nice," said Doug.

"Thanks," said a rumpled man, ambling into the room, his long black hair strewn with strands of hay.

"You must be Vernon," I said, thinking that he did not seem handsome enough to have ever been Alice's boyfriend.

"I'm hungry," said my mother petulantly. "It was a long drive."

"Why don't you sit down and let me get you a drink," said Vernon, leading us to a table. He smiled ingratiatingly at her, and I began to see what Alice had. "I'll bring you a little something while you look at the menu. Then you can go out to see the garden." He pulled out Mom's chair and she smiled, almost flirting.

Vernon brought a long, slim bottle and filled our glasses with cool, pale wine. "Smell it before you take a sip," he said. I stuck my nose into the glass and the light scent of spring flowers came drifting up. "Gewürztraminer!" I said. "The perfect afternoon wine."

"It's from Navarro," he said. "They're our neighbors. I love being able to serve the wine right where it's grown. You'll see; it goes perfectly with our food."

Vernon disappeared for a minute, and when he returned he was carrying three plates. "It's all made here," he said. One contained slices of warm bread spread with fresh, creamy goat cheese sprinkled with fresh herbs. He set down the second saying, "I picked these tomatoes just now and splashed some of our own vinegar on top." The smell of the vinegar rose up, lively, prickly, just a little bit sweet. "And these," he said, setting down the third plate, "are grilled duck livers. They're our own ducks too."

The food was simple, true and good. Doug took a bite of the velvety liver and said suddenly, "I don't know why, but this reminds me of that first meal we had on Crete." He touched my hand.

"It does," I said dreamily, filling my mouth with the fragrant cheese. "It tastes of the land."

"Why don't you children go look at the garden?" Mom suggested. "I'm very happy just sitting here."

We went out, following the sound of the ducks. They were cooing at the bottom of the garden, strutting around the silvery leaves of the wild artichokes. The beds stretched off into the distance, all the vegetables edged with flowers. "What are those?" Doug asked, pointing at great purply plants raising their leaves toward the sun. When he lowered his arm he took my hand. A thrill went through me, and then I settled in, anchored to him.

"Amaranth," I said. The herbs gave their fragrance to the air. Bees droned sleepily. The sun was very hot. A lazy curl of applewood smoke wafted across the garden. I half-shut my eyes and rainbows danced in front of me. I leaned against Doug and said, "Let's never leave."

"Mmm," he said, holding me tight. We aren't making this easy, I thought as we stood there, dreaming of the past. And then I had an image of Michael, standing on the hill looking down at us, and a chord of guilt resonated through my chest.

We went back through the kitchen, a large, airy, open room that smelled like wild yeast and raspberries. Glasses filled with herbs and flowers danced among the shelves, which were lined with jars of preserved fruits. Big wooden barrels of homemade vinegar sat under a counter that was heaped high with vegetables. A pie cooled in the window. Just inside the door a cat lay curled, purring happily.

"I could live here," I said.

"Welcome," said a woman with short black hair. We both jumped; we hadn't seen her standing by the stove. "I spend eighteen hours a day in here, so I try to make it nice."

"Eighteen hours a day?" I asked.

"I'm Charlene," she said, wiping her hands on her apron and sticking one out. I surveyed her as I took it: Her hair looked as if she had chopped it off with a carving knife, and her hands were chapped. She was wearing a green T-shirt that gave her face an unattractive pallor, and her feet were thrust into chipped wooden clogs. She seemed like a woman who had not glanced in a mirror in months. She looked exhausted.

"When do you take time off?" I asked.

"I don't," she said matter-of-factly. "I haven't been off the property in a year and a half."

"Maybe we should reconsider that plan," Doug whispered in my ear.

▪ ▪ ▪

Back at the table, my mother was all smiles. "I've been having the *best* time," she announced. "Vernon's been telling me all about the restaurant. It's an absolutely fascinating story." She twinkled flirtatiously up at Vernon. "May I tell them?" He inclined his head.

"Once upon a time," she began, "Vernon and Charlene met at a party at Chez Panisse. They discovered that they both had the very same dream. They've been together ever since. Isn't that romantic?"

"Uh, let me go see about your lunch," said Vernon, excusing himself.

"They are totally self-sufficient!" said Mom. "I think this is the most wonderful restaurant."

"But all you've had is a little goat cheese!" I said.

"I know the food's going to be wonderful," she said. "I just know it."

And, of course, it was. We began with a deep green vegetable purée sprinkled with herbs. It was followed by pasta that looked like a Jackson Pollock painting on a plate: The noodles were as bright as marigolds, and they were tossed with goat butter and tangled with deep purple hyssop flowers. Then there was a sun-warmed salad, followed by duck grilled to the color of polished mahogany and surrounded by Pinot Noir grapes. A plate of new potatoes sautéed with butter, tart apples, and mint sat on the side.

Afterward we had raspberry ice cream that was the color of a Renaissance sunset. I held it in my mouth, loath to let the flavor vanish. Just churned, it did not taste as if it had been made by human hands. The cream seemed straight from nature, from happy cows who had spent their lives lapping up berries and sugar.

"This is the best meal I've ever had," said Mom.

"Thank you," said Vernon, who did not know that Mom thought every good meal was the best she'd ever eaten. He held out a plate of tiny apple turnovers. "Charlene just baked these." They were still warm, and they crumbled in your mouth when you took a bite.

"Wasn't it *wonderful*?" Mom kept saying as we drove home.

"Yes," I said, still back in the garden with Doug's hand in mine. "And you didn't even get to meet the gardeners. They go out at night with flashlights looking for slugs; they don't believe in pesticides, they don't believe in hybrids, and they do amazing things with plants. Like the tomatoes: After they begin to leaf out, the gardeners bury them in dirt again so that they get a double root system. They say the tomatoes taste better like that."

"And they do," said Mom, a true convert. "That was the best tomato I ever ate." But the garden was fading, it was beginning to rain, and by the time we could see the San Francisco skyline, all the sunshine had evaporated.

I dropped Doug in front of his house and we kissed, lightly, lips brushing. Over Mom's head we made longing, anguished faces at each other, and I suddenly remembered Doug saying his girlfriend could always tell when we had been together. "I'll see you in my dreams tonight," he said. "In my dreams we're not apart."

"Mine too," I murmured, thinking again how difficult we made things for ourselves. It must be so much simpler when you hated each other after you broke up.

Doug turned up his collar and faced into the rain. "I think I'll go get some bourbon to chase away the chill," he said as he headed down the block.

▪ ▪ ▪

"Listen," said Michael.

"What?" I asked, rolling over sleepily. I peered at the clock. "It's three A.M. Go back to sleep."

"What's that strange sound?"

I lay still for a minute, listening to an eerily rhythmic whooshing float through the house. It was very familiar. I strained, trying to remember where I had heard it before. And then I remembered that Mom was with us. "She's taking a bath," I said.

"At this hour?"

"She doesn't sleep like normal people. When I was a kid she was always getting up to take baths in the middle of the night. She likes to leave the plug out and let the water run so it stays really hot. That's the sound you hear."

Michael groaned.

"Shh," I whispered. "Don't talk. If she hears us she'll demand breakfast or conversation or something. Just go back to sleep."

Michael groaned again. I went back to sleep. And then he was shaking me. "Get up, get up, something terrible has happened."

I surfaced slowly, swimming up through the layers of a dream. I blinked at the light. "What time is it?" I asked, sitting straight up.

"Five-thirty. I woke up feeling that something wasn't right and I went to look around. The front door is wide open, banging in the wind, and your mother is gone."

"Don't worry," I said. "She probably just went for a walk and forgot to close the door."

"At this hour? In the dark? She's an old lady. It's dangerous."

"Pity the person who tries to stop her," I said, rolling over and diving back into sleep. But then—when?—Michael was shaking me again. "What now?" I asked.

"Your mother's on the phone. She wants to talk to you." He handed me the receiver.

"Good morning, PussyCat," my mother trilled in her most obnoxiously cheerful voice. "It's time you got up. I've had the nicest walk, but now I'd like to please be picked up."

"Where are you?" I asked. Mom turned, and I heard the buzz of another voice. Somebody was standing next to her at the phone booth. "She says it's Jones and Turk."

"It can't be," I said. "That's the middle of the Tenderloin. And you would have had to walk uphill most of the way."

"It wasn't easy," she admitted. "The sidewalk seemed to go straight up. I've never *seen* such hills. There was one point, when I was getting right to the top of that street you live on . . . what's it called?"

"Leavenworth."

"Leavenworth, when I just couldn't go any farther. But the nicest man came along and got behind me and literally pushed me up to the top."

I laughed; I could just picture her, huffing to the top, propelled by a stranger in the dark.

"It's not funny!" she said. "But after that, of course, it was all downhill. It was a little hard on my knees, but I kept going."

"And now you're there having a pleasant conversation with a prostitute?"

"Is *that* what she is?" said Mom. "I wondered. Come get me, please. I'm very tired."

■ ■ ■

Michael was gone when we got back. Mom went to take a nap, and I sat down to work on my Thanksgiving story. I did not emerge from my studio until I heard a deep groan coming from the living room. I went rushing in to find my mother energetically pushing the sofa across the floor.

"What are you doing?" I asked.

"I was thinking that the sofa would look much better if you put it on the other side of the room," she replied.

"I don't know much about decorating," I demurred. "And neither do you."

This had never, in the past, been known to deter my mother. It did not do so now. Before I knew it, we were on an excursion to Macy's. We bought new curtains, new towels, a new rug. By mid-afternoon the house had an entirely new look. Mom was extremely pleased with herself. "Won't Michael be happy!" she said.

But when Michael came home happiness did not seem to be his dominant emotion. "Say you like it," I whispered.

"But I don't!" he shot back.

I pulled him into the bedroom. "We can put it all back after she goes," I pleaded. "She had such a good time doing it. Don't make a fuss."

"But it's *our* house. I liked it exactly the way it was. She had no right to do this."

"You're right," I said. "But she's my mother."

"She's impossible."

"You knew that before she came. What does it matter? It's just a few days. Can't you just let it go?"

He couldn't. I stayed in the bedroom, listening to him pushing the furniture back where it had been. "Don't, don't," I heard her say as the sofa slid across the room. "It looks so much better where I put it."

"Not to me it doesn't," he said grimly. An armchair scraped the floor. A table thudded.

"I was planning on having a little tea party for the people I met on the plane," she said. "I just couldn't invite them with the house looking the way it did."

"I suppose you'd also like to paint the bathtub gold," he was saying as I went out to try to make peace.

"It would be an improvement," she said.

Michael stalked into our bedroom, and I was left in the living room. My mother stood in the middle of the floor, wringing her hands. "It looked so nice," she kept saying.

"Well, it *is* his house," I soothed.

"No," she said, "it's your house too. And if you ask me, you let him push you around. He seems upset by my staying so long."

The thing to do now was reassure her, tell her it wasn't true, that he'd had a bad day at the office. Instead I heard myself say, "It's a small house. It *is* difficult for him."

My mother looked as if she had been slapped. She was silent for a second. "Well, isn't that too damn bad!" she finally managed to come up with. "I feel sorry for him." Gathering herself for an announcement, she said, "Don't bother making dinner for me. I've lost my appetite." Her bedroom door slammed, hard, behind her. She stayed behind it all evening.

"Why on earth did you choose this moment to have a bout of honesty?" cried Michael angrily. "Why couldn't you have said something conciliatory? You spend most of your time making nice and then you suddenly decide to tell the truth? Why? Now she's going to campaign against me."

▪ ▪ ▪

She would have anyway, I thought, lying in bed, hating them both. I wished Doug were there. With him I always had an ally. Now I felt like a bewildered shuttlecock batted between two energetic forces I could not control. How had I made such a mess of my life?

I listened to the hours pass. The clock ticked. The refrigerator clinked. The windows rattled. My mother got up, went to the bathroom, went back to bed. The pump went on. A horn sounded. Michael snored lightly. It was unbearable.

I got up and tiptoed into the living room to try to sort out my feelings. "Oh, PussyCat," I heard my mother whisper. I turned; she wasn't there.

"That's some name," said a voice, and I jumped. Where did it come from? I looked around, but I was alone.

"Some name," the voice said, growling now inside my head.

"Who is this cute little PussyCat?" I folded my arms against my chest, hugging myself. "Me?" I asked.

"Oh," said the voice inside my head, "grow up."

It was not a pleasant voice, but for some reason it calmed me down. I went back to bed and fell into a deep sleep.

When I woke up, Mom was sitting at the table wearing her poppy hat and surrounded by her suitcases. "I can't stay here anymore," she said regally. "I can't sleep feeling so unwelcome."

"Please don't leave," PussyCat tried to say. But I pushed her out of the way, crossed my arms, and said, "I'm sorry you feel that way. I'll drive you to the airport."

Mom looked so taken aback that I realized she had been expecting PussyCat. She was always expecting PussyCat.

"You'll be sorry," she sniffed as we drove. "I'm glad your father's not here to see what you've done with your life. You were much better off with Doug. You should beg him to take you back. You should have children with him. You've made a terrible choice."

"Maybe," I replied. "But it's my choice. What are you going to do for Thanksgiving?"

"I guess I'll just have to eat a little bowl of cereal," she said in a pathetic voice. "Think of me when you and that Michael are dining on turkey in your cozy cottage. I'll be all by myself, eating a cold meal in my lonely apartment."

"Mom," I said, putting my hand over hers, "don't leave. We've invited you for Thanksgiving. We'd like you to stay."

"I couldn't stay now," she sniffed. "I'd rather be alone."

"You won't be," I said, suddenly seeing the truth. "You'll have a thousand invitations." As I said it I realized that I was the one who was going to be alone. Alone with Michael. And suddenly I knew what I had to do.

■ ■ ■

"You're not cooking Thanksgiving dinner?" Michael asked. "My favorite meal? My favorite holiday? We can't have it at home?"

"Not this year," I said. "We'll eat at home next year, I promise. I'll invite a hundred people if you want. But this year we're going out."

Michael did not look happy. But since he had driven my mother out of the house, he was not standing on high moral ground.

"You'll love Boonville," I said. "It's a wonderful place for Thanksgiving. Wait until you see the garden. There's a huge fireplace in the dining room. We can spend the night in Mendocino. It'll be perfect."

■ ■ ■

San Francisco was foggy when we left, shrouded in a soft mist that muffled sound and obliterated sight. We were wrapped in a cocoon, heading north, feeling like the only people on the road in the early morning. All over America, I thought, women were getting sleepily out of bed, turning on the oven for the pies, melting the butter for the stuffing.

The fog was worse when we got to the Golden Gate Bridge, and it didn't lift as we passed the turnoff for Point Reyes. It was still with us when we got to Petaluma, and I was beginning to despair. And then, suddenly, the sun began to peek through. By the time we turned off toward Route 1 the fog had burned off, leaving one of those clear, bright days that make you happy to live in the Bay Area.

"It's probably snowing in New York," I said, taking Michael's hand.

"Feeling sorry for your mother?" he asked.

"No. Right this minute she's telling her friend Dorothy how terrible I am, what an unfeeling child. She's saying that I've ruined my life. And, by extension, hers. But I know it's not true. She'll have dinner with friends. She won't have any dishes to do. She could have stayed. She chose to leave." It was going to be all right. I could feel it.

The New Boonville Hotel looked particularly beautiful, filled with people and festooned with fall leaves. Logs burned in the fireplaces, snapping and shining. The room smelled like applewood; promises of pigs and turkeys, apples and onions hovered in the air. Above it all, like the blare of a trumpet, rose the high, wild note of cinnamon. The tables were laden with dishes of walnuts, bowls of applesauce and crimson cranberry relish that glistened like jewelry. Vernon poured wine into crystal glasses. We settled in.

"You were right," said Michael, "it's perfect for Thanksgiving. And I've never been hungrier." He kissed me and said, "I can't wait to find out what medieval turkey tastes like."

Half an hour later all the walnuts were gone and Michael was beginning to attack the applesauce. The people around us were restlessly playing with their knives, tapping their spoons, rustling their napkins. No food had appeared.

"The people in the other dining room ate more bread than we expected, so Charlene's baking a new batch," the waiter said apologetically. "It will be out any minute. She's even churning new butter."

"I need more than bread and butter. We spent three hours on the road. I'm starving," said Michael.

By the time another half hour had passed, his tune had changed. "Bread, a cracker, anything," he pleaded as the waiter rushed past. He was checking his watch, tapping his feet. "It's been an hour. Are we going to get anything?"

"Soon," promised the waiter. "Very soon."

When the bread arrived in the dining room a cheer went up, and we fell on it like starving people. Soup appeared soon after. The squash purée was bright orange with an earthy sweetness. Cream was drizzled through it, making patterns. Chives were strewn across the top. "Okay," said Michael. "I'll admit it. It's the best soup I've ever tasted. I could eat ten bowls." He looked at the waiter. "Is there more?"

The waiter shook his head dolefully. He removed the plates. Outside it was growing dark. We waited, uneasily, listening to joyous sounds in the next room. "I think I heard someone say something about suckling pig!" said Michael. "I'm going to go see."

He came back looking glum. "They've got suckling pig in there. They've got roasted sweet potatoes and bowls of Brussels sprouts and something that looks suspiciously like dressing." He stared at his empty plate and cried, "What are we, the Vietcong?"

A waiter scurried past, his head down, carrying a bowl. He was attempting not to make eye contact, but Michael stopped him. "Can we please have some of the suckling pig they're eating in there?" he asked in his most polite voice. The waiter held out the bowl with a guilty air. "This is all that's left," he said. "We mixed it with the stuffing to stretch it, make it go around, but there's still not very much." He ladled a minuscule mound onto each of our plates.

"It's delicious," I said hopefully.

"It's one bite," said Michael. "Did they eat all the Brussels sprouts and sweet potatoes too?"

The waiter nodded unhappily. "But don't worry," he said. "We're going to serve the turkey in here first. And Charlene's making mashed potatoes for you. And the most wonderful Savoy cabbage. And, of course, there's salad. Not to mention all those pies."

"Can we expect to see any of this before tomorrow?" asked Michael.

"I hope so," said the waiter fervently, making his escape. "I'll just go see how it's doing."

"Next time you decide to come to the perfect restaurant for a meal, remind me to pack some candy bars," said Michael morosely.

"I know this is a drag," I said. "But I'm sure the turkey's going to be amazing. It will be worth it."

"It couldn't be," he said.

The waiter came back bearing two big bowls as if they were crown jewels. He presented them proudly. One held a fluffy white mound of mashed potatoes crowned with streams of melting butter; little puffs of steam hovered over the top. Ruffled curls of Savoy cabbage lightly scented with chives and vinegar filled the other. "How much would you like?" he asked ingratiatingly.

"All of it," growled Michael. In the end he settled for about a third. "The turkey will be out any second," said the waiter, piling vegetables onto our plates. "We just took the birds out of the oven, and they look gorgeous. So golden. And the smell! I'll be right back."

But when he returned to the dining room, his hands were empty.

"Don't tell me," said Michael. "They ate all the turkey in the other dining room?"

"No," said the waiter.

"They're just sharpening the carving knife?" I suggested brightly. The waiter shook his head.

"The dogs made off with it?" I asked.

The waiter looked as if he was about to cry. "You know that ancient recipe Vernon wanted to try?"

I nodded.

"Well, it turns out there's a reason they stopped using that recipe eight hundred years ago. We've got turkeys all right. They're beautiful. They're brown. They smell great. Just one small problem: They're so tough you not only can't carve them, the knife actually bounces off the bird."

Michael looked stricken. And then he started to laugh. I began to laugh too. And then everybody in the dining room was laughing and clinking classes. "One more thing to be thankful for," said Michael.

"What's that?" I asked.

"We will never, ever have to come back here again."

We had apple pie and walnut pie and pumpkin pie topped with home-churned ice cream and followed by port and fresh walnuts. We had preserved peaches and homemade goat cheese. Sometime around midnight, after almost everyone else had gone home, Charlene appeared carrying a platter of duck.

"And what does your family eat for Thanksgiving dinner?" I asked Michael.

"Midnight duck," he said. "It's going to be an old family tradition."

■ ■ ■

The New Boonville Hotel was an ambitious dream that didn't last. Although there were spectacular disasters like the medieval turkey, there were also spectacular successes. These recipes, which are adapted from the ones that ran with the article I wrote about the restaurant in *Metropolitan Home,* are definitely among the successes.

CHARLENE'S SEMOLINA EGG NOODLES WITH SMOKED HAM, ASPARAGUS, ONIONS, AND GARLIC

Charlene Rollins made noodles in her own particular fashion; I've never seen another recipe quite like this one. But they are delicious, the dough is very easy to work, and the abundance of egg yolks makes the noodles a bright, astonishing gold. It goes without saying that the better the ham you toss into the topping, the more delicious the dish will be.

FOR THE PASTA

2 cups all-purpose flour

½ cup semolina flour, plus additional for dusting

½ teaspoon salt

18 large egg yolks

3 tablespoons olive oil

FOR THE SAUCE

1 large red onion, chopped

salt and pepper

1 stick (½ cup) unsalted butter

2 tablespoons finely chopped garlic

¼ cup finely chopped flat-leaf parsley leaves

½ cup water

¾ pound sliced smoked ham, cut into 1- by ¼-inch strips

1 pound medium asparagus spears, trimmed and cut diagonally into ½-inch-long pieces

TO MAKE THE PASTA

Pulse the flours and salt together in a food processor. Add the egg yolks and oil and process just until mixture forms a ball of dough. Divide the dough into 6 pieces and form each into a disk. Wrap each disk of dough in plastic wrap and let stand at room temperature for 1 hour.

Dust 3 baking sheets with some semolina flour.

Unwrap 1 piece of dough and roll it out on a lightly floured surface with a floured rolling pin until paper thin, making a rectangle about 11 by 13 inches. Cut the dough crosswise with a pizza wheel or sharp knife into 11- by ½-inch-wide strips. Carefully transfer the pasta, overlapping strips slightly, to a sheet pan to dry at room temperature, gently turning occasionally, for about 2 hours. Repeat the rolling and cutting with the remaining dough.

TO MAKE THE SAUCE

Cook the onion, with salt and pepper, in 4 tablespoons of butter in a heavy skillet over moderate heat, stirring, until softened. Add the garlic and parsley and cook, stirring, for 2 minutes. Cover and keep warm.

Combine the water, ham, asparagus, and remaining 4 tablespoons of butter in a large heavy saucepan and simmer, covered, until the asparagus is crisp-tender, about 2 minutes. Stir in the onion mixture and season with more salt and pepper. Keep sauce warm, covered.

TO ASSEMBLE THE DISH

Cook the pasta in an 8-quart pot half full of boiling salted water until just tender, about 1 minute, and drain in a colander. Return the pasta to the pot, add the sauce, and toss to combine. Season with salt and pepper.

Serves 4 to 6.

WARM SALAD

You don't need a garden to produce this salad. You don't need sun-warmed greens and homemade goat cheese either. But they help.

⅓ cup olive oil
½ pound sliced bacon
1 cup coarsely chopped
  walnuts
1 clove garlic, minced
8 cups assorted bite-size
  greens, such as curly
  endive, escarole, or baby
  kale

2 tablespoons fresh lemon
  juice, or to taste
4 ounces fresh mild goat
  cheese, crumbled
salt and pepper

Heat the oil in a large heavy skillet over moderate heat until hot but not smoking and cook the bacon, turning it occasionally, until crisp. Use tongs to transfer the bacon to paper towels to drain, reserving the fat in the skillet. Crumble the bacon. Add the walnuts and garlic to the skillet and cook, stirring, over moderate heat until the nuts and garlic are golden. With a slotted spoon, transfer the walnuts to a large salad bowl and season them with salt.

Add the greens, bacon, lemon juice, and goat cheese and toss. Drizzle some of the hot drippings from the skillet over the salad and toss again, adding salt and pepper and more hot drippings and lemon juice to taste.

Serves 4.

RASPBERRY ICE CREAM

Charlene didn't use quite as much lemon as I've put into this recipe, but I think that the lemon juice brings out the sweetness of the berries. Like all ice cream, this tastes best just after it is made.

4 cups fresh raspberries
2½ cups sugar
¼ cup eau-de-vie de framboise

3 tablespoons fresh lemon juice
4 cups chilled heavy cream

Purée the raspberries in a blender until smooth. To remove the seeds, force the purée through a fine sieve into a 2-quart heavy saucepan. Stir in the sugar and bring the mixture to a boil. Cook, stirring occasionally, until the sugar is dissolved. Continue to boil the mixture until a candy thermometer registers 220°F (about 15 minutes).

Transfer the mixture to a large bowl and cool, stirring occasionally, to room temperature (the mixture will thicken as it cools). Whisk in the eau-de-vie and the lemon juice, then slowly whisk in the cream, gently but thoroughly.

Freeze the mixture in an ice-cream maker. Transfer the finished ice cream to an airtight container and put it in the freezer to harden.

Makes about 2 quarts.

11

DALÍ FISH

■ Barbara Lazaroff told me a dozen different stories about her past. I never knew which ones to believe. On Tuesday she claimed to be a chemist. On Wednesday she said she had gone to college on a music scholarship at the age of fifteen. She once told me she had been an inhalation therapist. On another occasion she'd talked about her life in the theater. And I could not begin to count the times she'd mentioned that she was going to be a doctor. This beautiful woman turned heads wherever she went, but she yearned to be respected for her mind. She went on endlessly about her accomplishments; unfortunately, she seemed to forget, from one day to the next, what they were. Was any of it true?

"Who cares?" said my editors when I pointed this out. "We want you to write about Wolfgang Puck as he opens his new restaurant. We want all the dirt. Spend as much time as you need. You should spend *weeks* making yourself a nuisance."

"But Barbara is his fiancée and business partner," I protested. "Chinois is her restaurant too."

"He's the famous one," they replied. "He's the one we care about. You're going to have to be into everybody's business, but concentrate on him."

I tried. I followed America's favorite chef as he went in and out of markets. I tagged along as he went to duck farms, to fruit stands, and to the wholesale vegetable district. I was with him while he tested new equipment. When the American Express representative came to beg for his business, I was there. I learned that Wolfgang gained weight when he worried about money, and as the delays stretched endlessly on I watched Chinois very nearly make him fat.

At first Michael liked the idea that I was going to Los Angeles to write about the opening of the city's most eagerly anticipated restaurant, but each time it was delayed he became a little more impatient. "You're flying to Los Angeles *again*?" he would cry. I couldn't blame him; Chinois was supposed to open in March, but by August the restaurant was still under construction. "You're not seeing Colman again, are you?" Michael asked as I headed to L.A. one more time.

"Of course not," I replied.

He gave me a searching look. "Maybe you're hiding another rendezvous with a criminal?" he inquired.

I blushed; this was a sore point. When L.A.'s chef du jour, Joachim Splichal, started cooking at the private Regency Club, I did my best to finagle an invitation. The magazine's publisher invited me to join him and his friend for lunch and I was ecstatic. I accepted before he told me the friend's name. "We're having lunch," he said, "with H. R. Haldeman."

What am I doing here? I thought, sitting in a staid room filled with suits. The conversation was dull; the food turned to sawdust in my mouth. Sitting across from that beefy blond man, I remembered watching the Watergate hearings on Channing Way's grainy television and felt sick to my stomach.

"Good," said Michael when I told him. It was all he said for an entire week, and it was another week before he looked at me with less than loathing.

But I was not concealing lunch with the enemy, and I had no clandestine dates. Still, Michael was right; I did have a secret.

During one of my trips to L.A., an editor at the *Los Angeles Times* had tracked me down and asked me to come in for an interview.

"I won't beat around the bush," Robert Epstein said when I arrived at his office. He was thin, with wiry gray hair, attractively pocked skin, and an ironic air; he looked so much like Richard Boone that every time I glanced at him the theme from *Have Gun Will Travel* played in my head. "We're looking for a new restaurant critic."

"I hate L.A.," I said. "I'd never move down here. Why don't you call Colman Andrews? He lives here and he'd be perfect."

"Yes," Robert Epstein agreed, "we've thought of that. But he fills in for our critic from time to time and we're looking for a new voice."

"Not mine," I said.

Robert Epstein acted as if I had not spoken. "Take your time," he said blandly, "we're in no hurry. We're offering you the best job in America. The *Times* is the most powerful paper on the West Coast. You won't turn this down."

Although his assurance was irritating, I was intrigued. *New West*'s new owners had changed the magazine's name to *California* and given me a contract, but at thirty-five I was still a freelance writer. I had no health insurance and no pension and my expense account was twice the size of my meager earnings. This was the first time I had ever been offered a full-time job that paid real money and provided benefits. And there was one more consideration: I was surprised and flattered that the editors of the *Los Angeles Times* considered me to be in the same category as Colman.

They obviously did not realize that he knew more about food than I ever would. How could they possibly think I had enough experience for this job?

"You know more than you think you do," said Colman when I called to ask for advice. Over the years our relationship had mellowed into a slightly competitive friendship, and I still loved spending time with him. "Of course you should take the job," he continued. "Why wouldn't you?"

I could think of lots of reasons. I didn't want to leave my friends. I didn't want to leave our little red cottage. I hated L.A. I was scared. And even though Michael and I had been living together for two years, I was not divorced. Just thinking about living in a different city than Doug took my breath away.

Those same reasons, I knew, would cause Michael to be thrilled by this unexpected opportunity. We would be able to start out fresh, with no baggage. Unlike me, he thrived on change and with his drive and energy he would easily find a new job. When Michael wanted something, he made it happen. Telling him about the offer from the *L.A. Times* would be tantamount to accepting it. And so I said nothing and mulled it over, on my own.

Meanwhile I went down to L.A. every few weeks and watched as Wolfgang created a new crossover cuisine. I stood at his elbow as he reinvented tempura, added glace de viande to classic Chinese recipes, and made dim sum out of goat cheese. I diligently took notes, dutifully recording everything that he did.

But looking back I see that most of my notes concerned Barbara. I obsessively wrote down every word she uttered, as if I were trying to uncover the truth about her. I knew that it mattered, but it took me a while to understand why.

■ ■ ■

The office above Spago did not seem like a place where a famous chef did business. The room was quite small and very old, with inconvenient widows. It looked like your grandmother's attic, and it was filled with funky desks and too many people screaming into too many phones.

"Hello?" I called before I had even gotten to the top of the stairs. From where I stood I could see Wolfgang Puck leaning all the way back in a torn office chair; his feet were up and he was wiggling his toe through a hole in his sock. He was pudgier than he had been at Ma Maison, and he had traded his toque for a baseball cap with *Spago* scrawled across the front. He grinned at me and swiped a finger across his cute pug nose; he looked about fifteen.

"I'm sorry," he was saying into the phone, his Austrian accent very thick. "But what am I going to do? Tell fifty people with reservations they can't come?" He hung up and said to the room in general, "That was David Bowie. He wanted to bring fifty people to dinner. I told him no." The phone rang again and he picked it up, cradling the receiver beneath his chin as he casually munched on nuts. "Billy Wilder," he explained, after hanging up. A few minutes later Itzhak Perlman called; could he have pizza with scallops? "Of course," said Wolfgang. Celebrities did not scare him. He had been peeling potatoes at thirteen, but that was a distant memory. He had fed the famous, catered to them, studied them for so many years that when fame came knocking on his door it was no stranger.

Barbara sat across the room, tugging at her long black hair with scarlet fingernails. She was addressing invitations for Spago's annual Academy Awards party, and she was agonizing over the task. Wearing fake eyelashes, mascara, eyeliner, lipstick, and powder she looked as if she had dressed up to honor the job, as if the stars would see her right through the invitations. "Should it be Mr. and Mrs. Paul Newman?" she mused. "Who wants to be *Mrs.* Robert Redford?"

Hanging in the air, unspoken, was another question. "Who wants to be *Mrs.* Wolfgang Puck?"

■ ■ ■

Their house surprised me: I had not imagined Wolf and Barbara living in a dear little gingerbread cottage with a pointed roof and a jumble of furniture. In a neighborhood bristling with signs declaring ARMED RESPONSE, theirs didn't even have an alarm. "Wolf never locks the door," said Barbara. "We don't even have water in the swimming pool. He wants to turn it into a duck pond. Come in, come in, I want to show you the kitchen."

She led me through the living room into a large kitchen stuffed with impressive equipment. "It was my first design job. When I met Wolf I said, 'Magazines are going to want to take pictures of you cooking in your kitchen, and you can't do it in a slum. How will it look?' Then I wrote to all the companies and said that the kitchen was going to be in magazines, so they gave me stuff for free and half price and stuff. And then," she announced jubilantly, pointing out the wok stove, professional range, and giant refrigerator, "it *was* in magazines."

Another career, I thought, looking around the room. My eye fell on a framed picture sitting above the stove. "That was when I was a model," she said nonchalantly. I wrote it in my notebook, followed by a big question mark. "I only weighed eighty-five pounds," she said, as if to assuage my doubts. "But now I have to change. Why don't you come upstairs with me?"

Barbara shepherded me into a cluttered bedroom, flung open her closet, and stood trying to decide what to wear. She pointed at the dresser and said, "Could you reach into that top drawer and find me some socks?" I pulled the drawer open and her cats, Greystone and Alchemy, jumped in and nosed around as I held up first one pair of socks and then another. There were dozens.

"The women who sell hosiery are always the most awful people, so I buy five hundred dollars' worth at one time to get it over with," said Barbara. "Stop, stop, those are good." I was holding black-

and-white striped socks that seemed like a strange choice to go with yellow polka-dotted shorts. I threw them across the room, barely missing the bird Wookie in mid-flight. Barbara pulled on the socks and screamed, "Ohmygod, we have to go. I have an appointment to look at art." Blowing kisses at cats, dogs, and assorted birds, she made her exit. I followed in her wake.

She drove down La Brea in her new BMW, talking nonstop and peering at the numbers on the buildings. "Rauschenberg wants to give me a piece, but I like showing young artists," she said. "I have a very good sense of direction," she went on, passing the gallery three times in succession. She finally spotted the building, and a potential parking spot right in front. "We just need to get that guy in the Jaguar to pull up a couple of inches," she said.

"I'll ask," I said, reaching for the door handle.

"No," she replied, "better let me." She saw my face, understood what I was thinking, and added kindly, "I have a bigger mouth."

Men rarely refused her anything; she came back, smiling. The BMW purred smoothly into the space.

I followed as Barbara swept through galleries, squealing each time she found something she liked. "I love it, I want it," she said as she looked at an enormous red ceramic sculpture. "I like screaming art; otherwise you put it on the wall and no one notices it." She turned to the dealer. "I have to have it. I've bought this piece."

"But you haven't even asked the price!" I protested.

"Don't worry," Barbara whispered in my ear. "Whatever it is, we can get it down."

She drove back to Spago, fast. I bit my nails and asked a question, hoping the answer would slow her down. "How did you meet Wolf?"

"I was at a disco with a girlfriend," she said, cutting off a car to our left. "I'm an excellent dancer, by the way." I half-expected her to tell me about her professional career in dance, but this bit of information was not forthcoming. A horn blared angrily. Barbara accelerated and continued. "Wolf looked so cute dancing in his whites that I went over and asked him to dance. And then he asked me to come visit his cooking class at Ma Maison the next day." The man in the next car was gesticulating angrily. Barbara ignored him.

"I was living with someone, but I went anyway. I was late, and when Wolf looked up and saw me he dropped the stick of butter he was holding."

She finally slowed down and looked at me. "And you?" she asked. "Are you married?"

"Sort of," I said.

"You're either married or you're not," she said.

"Well, I'm married to one man but I live with another."

"So you don't plan to have children?" Barbara's directness startled me. I was supposed to be interviewing her.

"I do want children," I said.

"Me too," she said. "I would be the most wonderful mother. How old are you?"

"Thirty-five," I replied.

"You'd better make up your mind," she said. "You don't have much time." She gave me a sidelong glance as she started up the hill. "I know, I know, I'm pushy." She pulled into the parking lot and added, "But I'm usually right."

■ ■ ■

The office at Spago was in complete chaos.

"Charlton Heston on line one. He can come to the Academy Awards party!"

"David Bowie on line two. Do we want tickets for the concert?"

"Janet De Cordova, line three."

"The White House on line four! They want to know what you're going to cook for the economic summit in May."

Wolfgang leaned back in his chair. He had no notes, no papers, and as he stared into space he seemed to be snatching the ideas from the air. "Tell them," he said with casual authority, "American caviar and then . . . I don't know. Maybe warm goat cheese toasts and my American lamb salad. Maida Heatter's making cheesecake brownies for dessert. The Europeans will love it."

He looked up as if noticing me for the first time. "I know," he said, "this is different from the food I used to cook at Ma Maison." I blinked; he was answering a question I hadn't asked, and it always took me a moment to get accustomed to his almost telepathic prescience. "But there didn't used to be anything to eat here, and now everything has changed. With good ingredients you can cook it more simply." He leapt out of his chair, as if I had reminded him of something, and started down the stairs. "Come with me to the kitchen; I am going to try out some things for the new restaurant. It's so much fun because nobody really knows about it, so you can throw anything in and say, 'Oh yes, it comes from a Far Eastern province. My uncle lived there.'"

Wolfgang guided me through the kitchen, dipping one finger into this bowl, another into that one, shouting directions as he munched his way across the room. "You're cutting back on the coffee in that ice cream," he told one cook. "Don't do that."

"You can never fool him," she sighed, throwing in extra espresso. "You think he won't notice if you make a change, but he always does. How does he do it?"

"Make more sour that sauce," he told another cook, swiping a taste as people scurried behind him doing his bidding.

The procession reached the far corner of the kitchen and came to a halt in front of a tall, thin man with a big black mustache. Heaps of fish, vegetables, and shellfish were laid out on the counter in front of him. "This is Richard Krause," said Wolf. "He's going to be the chef at Chinois. What do we have today?"

"Two kinds of shrimp," said Richard, demonstrating. His right hand held a small, pale specimen that hung limply in the air. With his left he grabbed one that was twice as large, its dark red meat glowing through the shell. He wiggled the one in his right hand. "Chinatown," he said. He wiggled his left. "And these are spot prawns from Santa Barbara."

"Look at the difference!" said Wolfgang, cutting off a little piece of raw prawn and popping it into his mouth. "The local products are so good now. And look at those beautiful squabs!"

He stared down at the birds as if they were saying something that he wanted to hear. After listening for a moment he said, "Let's try them with Szechuan peppercorns."

"We don't have any," said Richard.

"Okay," said Wolf, cheerfully scooping up a handful of black peppercorns and crushing them with the back of a pot. "We'll use these." He pressed the pepper into a squab and groped for a bottle. "You forgot the peanut oil!" he scolded. Then he shrugged and said, "Oh well, olive oil will have to do."

When he had finished he slid the bird into the oven and turned to the catfish. "How come such a good fish has such a bad name?" he mused, tweaking its long mustache. For a moment he just stood, patting the fish, as if the answer he was seeking would come to him through touch. "We should call you Dalí fish," he said. "That way you would sell more. Should we roast you?" The fish apparently didn't answer, so he stood another moment, waiting for inspiration. At last it came. "We should steam it really nice with stripes of scallions and cilantro. We could serve the broth on the side, to drink, and put the fish in one of those sizzling pans."

"We don't have one," Richard pointed out. Wolf shrugged and said, "Well, in a wok, maybe."

"We don't have any of those either," said Richard.

"How can you cook Chinese food without a wok?" I asked.

"It doesn't matter," said Wolf cheerfully. "We just cook very little in a big pan. Chinese food tastes good to us because they sear everything instead of letting all the juice go out. Even in French cooking most people put too much in the pan." His confidence was captivating; I hadn't tasted a morsel of this food he was busily inventing, and yet I was certain that it was going to be a hit. I watched him arrange the fish in a steamer and begin to concoct a sauce of fresh plums, plum wine, ginger, and scallions. It made me hungry.

"We have to go out to the site," said Barbara, bouncing into the kitchen and grabbing his hand. "We promised to meet the contractor." Before he could answer she simply swept us both out the door.

"Well," I heard Richard sigh, "that's that. It's almost impossible to get uninterrupted time with Wolf."

▪ ▪ ▪

The restaurant that would one day be Chinois was just a big, empty, rubble-filled building. Wolfgang looked distressed. He looked more distressed when the contractor ambled over to say he was going to need more money. "The thing is," said the man, holding out the plans, "this isn't a restaurant, it's a museum. There isn't a straight line in the place."

Wolfgang turned to his girlfriend. "If you worked harder, Barbara," he said, drawing her name into three long syllables with the accent on the first, "we'd be done by now." It was almost a joke.

"He thinks I don't work hard because I need more than two hours of sleep," Barbara explained.

"I work better when I don't sleep too much," he said.

"We aren't all like that," Barbara replied. There was a bitter edge to her voice, and Wolfgang hastily looked down at the plans. He pointed to a curve. "What is this, here?" he asked.

Barbara gave it a cursory glance. "We went over the plans a hundred times," she shouted. "I designed this restaurant. I know exactly the look I want. Just keep out of it."

"No, no, all right," he said. "Are we going to eat lunch or not?"

As we drove to lunch Barbara challenged, "Ask us anything."

"Look out!" said Wolfgang nervously.

"Let *me* drive the car," she replied. And then, because I hadn't spoken quickly enough, she posed a question of her own. "Ruth wants to have a baby," she announced. "What do you think?"

"Babies are good," he said, which seemed a perfect answer.

"You just want a child to take to the tennis courts and to teach how to cook," she said. "But I would be the most fabulous mother in the world. It's true! I'll do that in my next life." She looked at me in the mirror and asked, "What are you planning to do in your next life?" She said it casually, as if it were the kind of question people asked each other every day.

I answered in that spirit. "I've been thinking about that," I said. "The *Los Angeles Times* offered me a job. I think I'm going to turn it down."

Barbara looked at me, and her astonishment showed. "Turn it down?" she asked. "Why?"

"I don't like Los Angeles," I said. "And I don't think I'm ready to be the restaurant critic of a big-city newspaper."

Barbara didn't say anything. She didn't have to. I knew what she must have been thinking. She had been a musician, a chemist, a medical student, a designer. And I was merely a wimp.

After a moment she broke the silence. "You can like anyplace," she said, "if you put your mind to it."

■ ■ ■

The *Los Angeles Times* was in no hurry; they were just planning ahead. *California* magazine, on the other hand, was in a panic; six months had passed, and they wanted their article.

"Isn't Puck ever going to open Chinois?" my editor whined. I couldn't blame him; they had spent thousands of dollars flying me back and forth to Los Angeles, and the restaurant was still unfinished.

"Wolf put on twenty-five pounds before Spago opened," I told him, "and this might be worse. There's been one delay after another. But now I think it's really about to happen. They booked a private party for David Begelman next week, and Barbara is determined not to let him down."

"Determined" was the wrong word. Barbara was going to get that restaurant open if it meant hammering every nail herself. The tension began to show. When the uniform company lost Barbara's complicated pattern, the owner tried to mollify her with a black satin jacket. He had embroidered *I'm not Wolfgang Puck's girlfriend—he's MY boyfriend* over the pocket. She was not amused. "Nice," she snapped, "but I'd rather have my uniforms." The skylight arrived broken. The building inspector refused to approve the fixtures. The state sent out a special inspector, who snooped around, examining the licenses. "They're out to get me," Barbara wailed.

"These things happen," Wolfgang said.

She turned on him. "You can laugh and play," she cried, "but I'm the one who takes the shit." He patted her hand and she said ardently, "We will open on time. I don't care. Whatever it takes. We will open."

Then Edison arrived to turn on the electricity and bad became worse. Chinois, the foreman announced, would have to be delayed. He took Barbara outside and pointed to the rotting electrical pole behind the restaurant. "We can't climb this, and we'll need the hundred-and-fifty-foot crane to replace it," he said. "I can't get the crane here for at least two weeks."

I watched Barbara to see how she would handle this situation. I was expecting an explosion, but Barbara surprised me. For a moment she just stood there in her purple-and-yellow polka-dotted shorts with her legs going on forever and her long black hair blowing in the wind. And then she began to cry.

A few hours later the foreman returned, riding to the rescue on the giant crane. But Barbara's triumph was short-lived. "Lady," he said, walking into the restaurant, "we can't get to the pole."

"Show me," said Barbara.

He led her outside and pointed to the fence behind the restaurant. "See," he said, "the only access is through your neighbor's yard. And the guy's not home. I'm sorry, lady, but it ain't going to happen today."

"Oh yes it is," said Barbara, turning on her heel. She went into the restaurant and returned with a couple of dishwashers. She pointed to the fence. "Take it down," she ordered.

The Edison man whistled admiringly. I must have looked less impressed, because Barbara took my arm and said, "Don't worry, I'll put it back up. I'll paint it. I'll do whatever they want. They'll be *grateful*."

We were watching the last of the fence fall when another neighbor showed up. He was so furious he could barely talk, but he composed himself sufficiently to make a speech about high-handed people ruining the neighborhood. Barbara listened quietly to his tirade. When he had finished she batted her long fake eyelashes and said with great earnestness, "That pole was about to fall on the house. We couldn't wait. It had to be done immediately."

A skeptical look flickered across the man's face, but Barbara stared him down. Watching her I suddenly understood the secret of her success. She clearly believed every word that she was saying.

■ ■ ■

"Where's Barbara?" asked Wolf. "We open in seventeen hours." It was two A.M. and he stood in the doorway with a box of pizza and a bag of beer, surveying the chaos. Workers on triple overtime stumbled about the room, giddy with fatigue. The windows were holes torn into the walls, the room was unpainted, the counters untiled. The restaurant lacked tables, chairs, and lamps. There was no electricity.

The contractor pointed to a sleeping figure wrapped in a paint-spattered drop cloth beneath the bar. "She couldn't stay awake anymore," he said. "She's been up for two days."

Barbara stirred at dawn, stretched, gave a little shriek of horror. Cans of soda, half-eaten cookies, and crumpled bags of potato chips surrounded her. "What time is it?" she asked. "We've got to get this place cleaned up!" She began clutching at the debris. "The inspector will be here at eight."

In the morning light the bones of the restaurant were starting to show. You could see that once it was tiled and painted, the many layers of the intricate Asian design would be stunning. Even the inspector was impressed. He was a burly man in an Easy Rider cap, but as he looked around he said admiringly, "Your copper hood looks nice." And then, quickly, he added, "Goddamn restaurants are driving me crazy. They all got to be open yesterday." He turned taps, checked joints, poked into the bathrooms. He went outside to inspect the new electrical pole. As he signed the papers he said to Barbara, "You're now officially open for business." Looking around he added, "Good luck."

It would take luck—or a miracle—to turn this mess into anything resembling a restaurant by nightfall. All morning Barbara raced around, wringing her hands, urging everyone to hurry. The contractor applied grout to the front of the counter and the carpenters hung windows. Busboys and waiters drifted about, begging for instructions. Painters were everywhere.

At noon the tables arrived, adding another level of chaos. A painter swiped each one with fast-drying latex as it came through the door and passed it to his partner, who laid on a second coat. Heaps of flowers were delivered and Barbara began arranging them, interrupting herself every few minutes to fly around the room, waving orchids like batons, crying, "Faster, faster."

Midway through the afternoon Wolfgang bustled boisterously through the door. He surveyed the mess with seeming unconcern.

"Do you ever wonder if all this is worth it?" I asked. "Do you ever wish that you had done things more simply?"

"No," he said cheerfully. He was about to make a joke, but he changed his mind. "Most chefs think if they serve good food they are going to be really successful, but that's not true. The package is important in L.A." He pointed at Barbara and added, "Don't worry, we'll open." But I noticed that when she came swirling toward him like a small storm cloud he suddenly remembered an urgent errand elsewhere.

At four the electricity came on and the cooks began to work in earnest, pushing workmen out of their way. "You should cover that food. I'll get dust on it," said an electrician as he climbed onto the counter to install lights directly above the men boning quail. They just shrugged and kept working.

Wolfgang returned at five wearing his whites. He hung two haunches of lamb in the rotisserie, and as they slowly started to sizzle the smell of food began to compete with paint and sawdust. "Wolfgang's not happy unless he's cooking lamb," said Richard under his breath.

The painters were painting more sluggishly now, as if their arms were so heavy they could barely lift them. The carpenters hammered in slow motion. The electrician climbed down from the counter, squinted back at the lights he had hung, and packed up his kit.

Barbara looked up and went pale. "They're too low!" she shouted.

"They are not!" the electrician shouted back. "They're exactly where you told me to put them."

Barbara planted her hands on her hips and stared at the man. She pointed imperiously to the lights. It was late; the man was tired; the first guests would walk through the door in less than two hours. He stared at Barbara. And then, wearily, he unpacked his bag and heaved himself back onto the counter. At that moment the air-conditioning system unloosed a slow, steady drizzle. The cooks and electricians worked on, numb beneath the downpour. "What else can go wrong?" asked Wolfgang.

"The uniforms," said Barbara anxiously, "they're not here yet." For the first time, he looked nervous. Seeing that, Barbara touched his arm and said, "Don't worry. We're going to open if we have to serve in our underwear."

▪ ▪ ▪

At 7:30 a man pushed through the crowd gathered on the sidewalk panting, "Let me through, let me through, I have the uniforms." When Barbara saw him her cheeks regained their color. She grabbed the package and began distributing uniforms, pushing the waiters outside as she did. "You'll have to change in the alley," she said.

It was 7:45 when Barbara walked up to the painters and removed the brushes from their hands. "You're finished," she said firmly. And then, frantically, she began to shove cans of paint, ladders, hammers, and saws out the side door. When the floor was empty she pushed open the still-wet rest-room door and went to change. She emerged, looking like an Indian princess in leather and spangles, turned down the lights, and held out her arms. She called, "Wolf!"

For a moment we all stood where we were, watching them waltz down the center of their brand-new restaurant. Then we burst into applause.

What did it matter, I thought, what Barbara had done in her former lives? She could have been a doctor or a musician; she could have been a model. But when it was time to put that behind her she had done so without a backward glance. Barbara had invented herself, and she was her own best creation.

If she could do it, so could I.

GRILLED CALIFORNIA
GOAT CHEESE ON TOAST

This is an adaptation of the appetizer Wolfgang Puck served at the White House during the economic summit of 1983. Goat cheese was an obvious choice: During the early part of the eighties it was impossible to imagine California cuisine without goat cheese. That is, however, no reason to disdain it.

a ½-pound log of soft mild goat cheese, cut crosswise into 16 equal pieces
2 tablespoons chopped fresh thyme leaves

1 teaspoon freshly ground black pepper
3 tablespoons extra-virgin olive oil
1 baguette, cut into 16 slices, each about ½ inch thick

Arrange the cheese slices in a shallow dish just large enough to hold them in one layer and sprinkle them with thyme and pepper, then drizzle with 2 tablespoons of oil. Marinate the cheese for 1 hour at room temperature, covered.

Preheat the broiler.

Broil the bread slices on a broiler pan 4 to 5 inches from the heat, turning them once, until golden. Top each toasted bread slice with a piece of marinated cheese, pressing slightly if necessary to fit the cheese to the toast, and drizzle the toasts with the remaining 1 tablespoon of oil. Broil again, 4 to 5 inches from the heat, until the cheese is slightly melted and hot, 1 to 2 minutes. Serve warm.

Serves 4 to 6.

CHINOIS CURRIED OYSTERS
WITH CUCUMBER SAUCE
AND SALMON ROE

This was an appetizer on Chinois's first menu. I've always loved it. I've adapted the recipe from the one Wolfgang distributed at the American Institute of Wine and Food's Cutting Edge of L.A. Cuisine dinner in 1985. The cucumber sauce is very easy and endlessly versatile; I sometimes use it as a vegetable dip.

FOR THE CUCUMBER SAUCE

¼ of a seedless cucumber, chopped

¼ cup rice wine vinegar, unseasoned

½ teaspoon salt

⅛ teaspoon freshly ground black pepper

2 tablespoons Asian sesame oil

2 tablespoons peanut oil

FOR THE CURRIED OYSTERS

1 tablespoon curry powder

1 tablespoon all-purpose flour

pinch of salt

16 oysters, shucked, shells reserved

3 tablespoons vegetable oil

6 tablespoons salmon roe

Accompaniment: lemon wedges

TO MAKE THE CUCUMBER SAUCE

In a blender, purée the cucumber with the vinegar and salt and pepper until very smooth. With the motor running, add the two oils in a slow stream and blend until emulsified.

TO MAKE THE CURRIED OYSTERS

Whisk together the curry powder, flour, and salt in a shallow bowl. Dredge the oysters in the curry mixture one at a time, shaking off the excess flour, and transfer them to a plate.

Heat the oil in a 10-inch heavy skillet until hot but not smoking and pan-fry the oysters in batches, turning them once, until slightly crisp on the outside, 1 to 2 minutes. Transfer the fried oysters to paper towels to drain. Spoon a scant tablespoon of the cucumber sauce into each of the 16 oyster shells and top with a fried oyster. Top each oyster with 1 teaspoon of salmon roe.

Serves 4 to 6.

12

FOODIEſ

■ A mockingbird lived in the tree behind the house Michael and I had rented in Laurel Canyon. He slept all day, but at night he perched in the branches belting out horrid, unnatural songs that twisted through my dreams. I'd wake up wondering why birds were singing after dark, thinking that even the stars were crooked in Los Angeles. I knew the midnight warbler was laughing at me, mocking me for leaving home.

Then the crashes began. The steep curve at the bottom of Laurel Canyon lurked outside our house, waiting to snare unwary drivers. First we'd hear the whoosh of a car taking the curve too fast, then the screech of brakes, then the sickening thud of metal hitting bark. Next came the horns, the sirens, the flashing lights. No wonder the rent had been so reasonable.

The house was dark, even in the daytime. The rooms, with their murky wooden panels and painted brown floors, seemed to repel sunlight, and the kitchen was dank, with scratched linoleum. There were far too many doors, and when Michael had to work late

I checked and rechecked them, making sure they were locked. The landlord, a nosy, unpleasant person, lived next door and popped in unexpectedly, as if it were his right. I'd come home from work and find him in the kitchen, pretending to fix a leaky faucet.

We'd rented the place for its large patio and spacious, shaded yard. We learned, later, about the coyotes who also considered it their home. You could watch them sneak through the hole in the fence and out to the street, sneering when they ran, howling when they stopped.

Coyotes prowled my *Los Angeles Times* office too. They were not as visible, but I could feel them padding around my desk, sense their hot breath on the back of my neck, hear them howling off in the distance.

"What are you worried about?" asked Michael, who loved his new job at KCBS. "You're just writing restaurant reviews. It's no different than the magazine."

But sitting at my shiny new computer, I knew that he was wrong. Even my friends seemed to think I had turned into someone else now that I had become the restaurant critic of California's largest newspaper, and people who had known me forever were suddenly afraid to invite me for dinner. Michael McCarty didn't punch me in the stomach anymore. Wolf and Barbara seated me on the celebrity schedule. And once, in a fancy restaurant, the man at the next table turned on his date as she complained about her meal to say, "Who do you think you are, Ruth Reichl?"

The words hit me like a hammer. Who did I think I was? I really wasn't sure anymore. More than a million people were reading my words, and half of them seemed to hate me. My predecessor had retired after almost twenty years, and for months her loyal readers filled the mailbox. "Another member of the Lois Dwan fan club," said Bob Epstein, striding up to my desk one morning. He waved a letter over my head and added, "He says we should send you back to San Francisco. This guy," he said, throwing a second letter onto my desk, "says you are personally responsible for lowering the quality of restaurants in Los Angeles. He wants us to bring back Lois Dwan.

"And this one," he said, gleefully adding another to the growing pile, "wants to know if we are aware of a loose cannon named Ruth Reichl running around Times Mirror Square." He laughed, delighted. "We've never gotten this much reaction to a critic."

"A critic *should* be controversial," I retorted jauntily. "If you don't make people mad, you're not doing your job."

Bob was not taken in. "Don't worry, kid," he said kindly, "I don't pass these letters on to the bosses." He leaned over and added, "I just let them see the positive ones. And believe me, we get those too."

"Yeah," I said. "I've gotten a few nice calls."

"Any celebrities?" he asked hopefully. This was, after all, Los Angeles. "It would help if I could drop a few names."

"Yes," I said. "Danny Kaye."

▪ ▪ ▪

I'd recognized the voice at once: masculine, slightly high, with the polish of the theater and just a whiff of New York. It was straight out of my childhood. The very sound of it had made me laugh.

"Danny Kaye phoned you?" said my mother during her daily call. "Why?"

"He's very interested in food," I replied. "He said he liked my writing, and he invited me to his house for dinner next Monday night."

"Danny Kaye invited you to his *house* for dinner?" she repeated, actually sounding impressed. "He's supposed to be a wonderful cook!"

"He certainly seems to think he is," I replied. "He told me that Paul Bocuse and Roger Verger say that the best restaurant in California is Danny Kaye's house."

"He must have been joking," she said.

"No, Mom, he wasn't."

"Too bad Daddy's not alive. Danny Kaye was his favorite actor. He'd be so pleased."

I thought of my father, singing "Hans Christian Andersen" to me as I fell asleep. I saw him laughing at *Me and the Colonel.* "Do you think he might finally approve of the work I'm doing?" I asked, hating the needy tone of my voice.

My mother ignored it. "He just loved Danny Kaye," she replied, making no concessions.

■ ■ ■

At first the thought of going to Danny Kaye's house was thrilling. But at the last minute Michael couldn't come; three gunmen had held up a bank in Santa Monica, and he was needed at the station. As I drove through Beverly Hills, alone, looking for San Ysidro Drive, I began to have doubts. What on earth were we going to talk about? By the time I found the house and walked up the path I was so nervous that I panicked as I was about to ring the bell. I stood there for a second, then ran back to the car.

"You're late," Danny said when I'd finally composed myself enough for a second attempt. He glanced at his watch. "Six minutes late. You could have ruined dinner."

"It's nice to meet you too," I heard myself say. He let out a short bark of laughter, shook my hand, and led me into the house.

He looked just as he had in all the movies of my childhood. He was not so much older as more wrinkled, like laundry that had not been ironed. His blondish hair was a little too long and fluffed around his face, and his lean body no longer moved with the boneless grace of an acrobat, but otherwise he seemed unchanged.

The best restaurant in California was huge—and echoing. We seemed to be alone as we walked through one silent decorator-designed room after another, and I began to hate those gunmen who had sent Michael back to work. It was a relief when we reached a cheerful sitting room and found it filled with other guests.

"Don't get comfortable," said Danny as he introduced me to his friends, "because I want to show you my kitchen." He rushed through the introductions as if they were an irritating chore and led me out the door. I felt like a very special guest of honor. For the first time since I had been in Los Angeles I was glad I had taken the job.

"Wow." I actually said it, then put my hand to my mouth and blushed. The kitchen was a theater, and the round table in the middle was set so that the people seated there would be facing the stove. The cook would be the star of this show, and as Danny strolled possessively around the stage, showing off exotic pots and expensive gadgets, I saw that the entire room had been built with this in mind. It was a one-man kitchen, designed exactly for his body: Each counter was precisely calibrated to his height, so that he could stand at the stove and reach anything he might need.

Danny picked up a cleaver lying on the butcher block and held it out. "Try it," he urged. "I have them hand-made just for me."

I took the cleaver, feeling the comforting heft of the thing. Danny handed me a carrot. "Cut it," he said, and I understood that he was conferring a rare privilege. "I don't normally like people to touch my tools, but I want you to." The cleaver felt good in my hand. I swung and felt it bite cleanly through the carrot.

"Great cleaver," I said, handing it back.

"Knives are very important," he noted, solemnly caressing the edge.

He went to the big refrigerator and took out something wrapped in white paper. "I hope you eat liver," he said, opening the paper and holding up a thick maroon slab.

"Of course I eat it," I replied. "I'm a restaurant critic. I eat everything."

"You have not eaten liver like my liver," he said confidently. "Just wait. There's only one butcher in the entire city worth buying it from. And then you have to slice the meat just so, on the diagonal." He demonstrated.

He showed me the vegetables, the fruits, the cheese, reciting the pedigree of each. As he offered to introduce me to his purveyors I realized that my opinion really mattered to him. I hoped, with all my heart, that he cooked as well as he believed he did; I did not think I would be able to lie to him.

Danny led me back to the sitting room, and then he disappeared for a while. The rest of us chatted, distant and polite, but the room seemed empty without him. Suddenly he was back, standing in the doorway imperiously calling, "Dinner, now!" Everyone in the room jumped up, scattering crumbs and spilling drinks, scrambled into the hall, and made a mad dash for the kitchen.

I stood in the doorway, staring at the scene. The table had been set with bowls of clear, golden broth that sat steaming at each place. The fragrance drifted intoxicatingly through the room. "Lemongrass!" I said.

"Sit down!" Danny shouted irritably from his post at the stove. We stopped milling and each of us rushed for the nearest seat, as if this were a game of musical chairs. We threw ourselves down as he commanded, "Eat!" We obediently picked up our spoons.

With the first bite I knew that no lies would be necessary. Danny's soup was extraordinary, with that resonance that goes on and on, like a bell still humming, long after the last note has been struck.

Danny did not sit down. As we ate he stood at the stove like a mad scientist, enveloped in the steam that billowed about him from a huge cauldron. I heard the sizzle of butter hitting a hot surface and sensed the high, clean note of lemon juice being added to the pan. Now there was a richer scent—cream, I guessed—and then the aromas began to mingle, so that lemon and cream and butter were dancing through the air.

Water drained; wet pasta hit a skillet with a hiss, and a cover went crashing down. Then Danny was rushing to the table with a plate in his hand and setting it in front of me. "Eat it now," he insisted, "don't wait for the others. This is a dish that can only be served to people eating in the kitchen. In a few minutes it won't be any good. I made the noodles myself."

I twirled the pasta around my fork and took a bite. And then, in spite of myself, I gasped. The pasta was so thin that it seemed to have vanished, leaving only a memory behind. What was left was simply the subtlety of the sauce, pure and light, as if the liquid had somehow taken solid form. It wasn't food; it was magic on a plate, and for a moment I disappeared into the flavor. When I returned Danny was standing over me, watching me so intently and with such pleasure that I knew I didn't have to say a single word.

I didn't listen to the conversation after that, or think about much of anything at all. I just ate, conscious of my luck at being there, trusting that each dish would be extraordinary. The liver was like little pillows of velvet between satin slivers of onion, and so sweet it was as if it had been dusted with sugar. "It's the onions," he said, answering my unspoken question. "They're grown in special soil. And, of course, the way they're cut."

The conversation flowed around us, background music, but I didn't try to join it. I understood that in his kitchen Danny was desperate for an audience; cooking for people who didn't pay attention ruined it for him. He was a creator, not a consumer, and the only thing he required was appreciation.

And so I said nothing as he snatched the lemon soufflé from the oven and rushed it to the table. High, light, rich, and eggy, it fell, slightly, as it was cut, collapsing onto itself with a fragrant sigh. I ate it slowly, savoring the way it disappeared in my mouth, and drank the espresso he served me at the end without sugar, liking the bitterness against the sweetness of the soufflé.

"I think it's the best meal I've ever eaten," I said as I left. Danny nodded. "You have to come back," he said. I understood that this had been a test, and I had passed.

▪ ▪ ▪

After that Danny called now and then, regularly. There was a French chef arriving in town whom he thought I should meet— could I come to dinner? He was going to the baseball game—did I like Dodger dogs? When he heard I'd had a car accident he went right to the hospital. He was furious to discover I had already checked out.

"What do you mean by leaving the hospital early?" he yelled into the phone. "I brought you something to eat."

"You're at the hospital now?" I asked.

"Yes," he said. I pictured him there, ranting around the bedside of the person now occupying my room. "I've probably set this poor woman's recovery back a week," he said accusingly, as if it were my fault. "I think I scared her silly."

"Well, leave the food for her, why don't you?" I suggested.

There was a silence on the other end of the line. And then he said, "It wouldn't be the same."

I understood that this was his idea of a compliment, and I wanted to reciprocate. "I wish all my readers were like you," I said.

"What do you mean?" he asked.

"There is a strange new tribe of people in the world," I told him, "who live only to eat out. They're groupies, obsessed consumers of the restaurant experience." I thought for a minute and then added, "They're sort of the opposite of you."

"Thank you," he said, understanding at once.

"You'll like this," I said. "One producer told me he's been so busy eating he hasn't made a movie in two years. But he has a hernia, which makes eating all that food painful. So he has to drink a bottle of Maalox every night. I asked him why he did it, and he said, 'Oh, I don't mind suffering for my art.' "

Danny let out a snort of laughter. "You ought to write an article about them," he said.

▪ ▪ ▪

It seemed like a good idea. Bob thought so too. And so I began interviewing the pale, rich fanatics whose lives revolved around restaurants. There were dozens of them, people who collected meals like baseball cards and chefs like trophies, and they were only too happy to discuss their addiction.

One couple drove down to the paper to show off their enormous menu collection. I sat for hours as they pulled one precious document after another out of a suitcase. "We find that most diners don't play their role," said the wife. "You don't go to important restaurants without doing some preparation for it. It's not just the food and the ambience and the people who are representing the experience. It's what you bring to it."

I looked to see if she was serious. She was. Her husband extracted a photo album from the suitcase and said, "Let's show her the pictures from Wolfgang's wedding in France." He shoved the album under my nose. There they were, flanked by Wolf and Barbara. "The wedding was fabulous," he said and turned the page. "Afterward we went on to Italy." He pointed down at pictures of his wife and himself with one smiling Italian chef after another. "Then, of course," he continued, turning the page yet again, "we went on to Switzerland and Frédy's."

The happy couple, their arms around an unsmiling Frédy Girardet, gazed up from the snapshot. "The problem with eating at Frédy's," said the wife wistfully, "is that once you've eaten there it is hard to eat anywhere else."

As she spoke I remembered what Darrell Corti had said when I'd met him: "What's the point of knowing a lot about food if all you get is disappointment?" But I kept my mouth shut and tried to look wise. I nodded. I changed the subject.

"I was praying that they wouldn't ask me what I thought of Girardet," I said to Michael later that night as we were dressing for dinner. "Because of course I've never been there."

"You had nothing to worry about," he replied. "People like that cannot imagine a world in which the L.A. *Times* would hire a critic who had never been to Girardet."

"You're probably right. One man told me his day was ruined if he couldn't tell his friends about at least one restaurant they didn't know about. Another told me he was using up his daughter's inheritance with his passion for restaurants. But my favorite moment of all was when I asked a woman if she ate out because she couldn't cook and she said, 'Oh no. Actually I'm an extraordinarily good cook. But I believe in doing what I do best. And I *eat* wonderfully.'"

"Well, I wish you were taking one of those people who eat wonderfully to dinner," he replied. "Are you absolutely sure I have to wear a jacket?"

"Yes," I said. "When I made the reservation they said they wouldn't let you in without one."

"Let's stay home," he said. "I hate these stuffy places."

"You promised," I moaned, "and you can't let me down now. I'll never find someone to come to dinner on the spur of the moment."

Michael sighed and put on a jacket.

▪ ▪ ▪

The restaurant was dark and intimate. The tails on the maître d'hôtel's tuxedo bobbed as he led us to our table. He pulled out my chair with mellifluous murmurings about cocktails and wine. He shook out my napkin and spread it on my lap. When he had finally taken himself off, Michael looked up at the chandelier and said wistfully, "I wish I were home watching the football game."

In that moment the Reluctant Gourmet was born. "Given the choice between a dressy dinner and a Dodger dog," I wrote when I got home, "the Reluctant Gourmet will choose the dog every time."

The Reluctant Gourmet began insinuating himself into my reviews, puncturing pretension, questioning authority, taking a skeptical view of the high price of eating out. He preferred beer to wine. He liked the fights and steadfastly refused any invitation that interfered with *Monday Night Football*. He was smart, irreverent, and funny, and he could say all the things a restaurant critic could not. Los Angeles was instantly enchanted with him; before long the R.G. was getting more mail than me.

"I like the Reluctant Gourmet," said Danny. "Is that your boyfriend? Why don't you marry him?"

"He keeps asking me the same question," I replied.

"Well, what are you waiting for?" And then he added, "Go ahead and do it. I'll come to your wedding." He seemed to think that this would clinch the deal.

▪ ▪ ▪

The success of the R.G. emboldened me to start taking more chances with my column. When somebody revived the moribund Perino's, an old Hollywood warhorse, I invited the glamorous ghost of Gloria Swanson to join me for dinner. She swooped through the ornately decorated rooms, fingering tablecloths, sneering at modern service, lamenting the way things had changed. "In my day," she drawled, holding up her cigarette lighter, "people knew how to dress for dinner." She admired the cheese toast, laughed at the captain's effort to flambé steak Diane, and noted that the soufflés of yore were decidedly higher. I was extremely pleased with the resulting review, and when Bob called me into the office I waited for him to tell me how brilliant it was.

But he was frowning. He looked into my eyes, cleared his throat, and said, "Ruth, this is a newspaper."

"I know that," I replied, irritated. "So what?"

"You can't make things up!" he blurted out. "The Reluctant Gourmet is one thing. I've met Michael. I know you exaggerate him a bit, but at least he's real. Gloria Swanson, on the other hand, is dead. She wasn't with you at the restaurant."

"But I can't spend the rest of my life writing about too much salt and the busboy clearing from the wrong side!" I said.

"Why not?" he wanted to know. "You know more about food than anyone I've ever met. Just write about that."

I shook my head. "Haven't you noticed that food all by itself is really boring to read about?" I asked. "It's everything around the food that makes it interesting. The sociology. The politics. The history."

"Well," he said, handing Gloria Swanson back to me, "choose one of those. Because this won't do. In journalism you have to tell the truth. I'm sorry."

I went back to my computer and stared at the screen. I had twenty-four hours to dump Gloria Swanson and find something real to write about. "A table at Perino's," I wrote, "used to mean something." Nah, too boring. I tried again.

"In the thirties, when Gloria Swanson swept through Perino's . . ." No, that wouldn't do either.

"The lamb at Perino's . . ."

I was stuck. I packed up my things, picked up my keys, and headed to the parking lot. I planned to go back to the restaurant and pray for inspiration.

Driving through Hancock Park I looked at its once-proud mansions. These stately homes had formed the first Beverly Hills, and long ago, in Perino's heyday, the lawns had been manicured, the garages filled with fleets of Bentleys. I tried to imagine what the neighborhood had been like back then, listened for the echoes of Carole Lombard and Errol Flynn. Then I shook myself; the stars had packed up and moved west, the houses were decrepit, and it was the present that mattered, not the past.

I pulled into the restaurant's large, dark parking lot and handed my car keys to the valet. A maître d'hôtel stood at the restaurant's door. "Welcome back," he said softly, and for a moment he was Erich von Stroheim. Did I detect an accent? He led me past mirrors and crystal chandeliers and around massive bouquets of flowers to a curved pink banquette. He handed me an enormous menu and bowed. I would have sworn he clicked his heels. . . . No! This would not do!

I peered over the menu, studying my fellow diners in hope of finding something remarkable to write about. Seeing nothing of interest, I strained to overhear fascinating tidbits of conversation. To my despair, the people to my right were analyzing real estate and the men to my left were deep into Dodger discussions. Nothing useful there.

The captain, as he had before, recommended the shrimp cocktail, the scallops, the pommes soufflées. I had tasted them all and found them perfectly acceptable. Desperate, I tried a classic restaurant critic trick: In a pinch you can always make fun of the food. All you have to do is order the menu's most outrageous item. This works beautifully when a chef is creatively moved to invent truffled salmon in banana sauce, asparagus-raisin ice cream, or guacamole with raw clams. But Perino's radicchio ravioli in cream cheese sauce wasn't all that absurd, and unfortunately it wasn't bad.

And then, as I took a bite of broiled salmon (overcooked), the moment I had been waiting for arrived. I heard a commotion at the front of the room and turned to see a fleet of policemen trooping through the restaurant. "What's happened?" I asked the captain.

He leaned over confidentially and whispered in a voice rich with excitement, "A man was just held up in the parking lot!" He seemed thrilled to have a tale to tell. "At gunpoint," he continued.

I had my story!

Without wasting time on dessert I asked for my check. I raced home and went right to my desk. "Eating at Perino's," I began, "can be a lot more exciting than it used to be." This was far better than Gloria Swanson: The piece now read like a detective story. It had a plot; it was a thriller.

"I've never read a restaurant review quite like this," said Bob when I turned it in. "I knew you could do it. Good work!"

"Don't expect me to come up with a holdup every time I review a restaurant," I warned him.

"I'm not worried," he said. "I'm sure you'll think of something." He smiled.

No mockingbirds sang as I climbed into bed. "You were right about moving," I admitted to Michael. "I'm glad we came. When Bob read my review he said I was going to breathe new life into the Calendar section of the paper. And I can't wait to see this one in print."

Michael yawned. "I knew you'd eventually be happy that we moved down here. But that holdup was a piece of luck." Turning over he said sleepily, "You got a police report, didn't you?"

"Police report?" I asked. Alarm bells went off in my head. "How do you get a police report?" Michael didn't answer; he was fast asleep. But I was sitting bolt upright with waves of adrenaline shooting through my veins.

It had never even crossed my mind to check the waiter's story. I had simply written down what he'd said and now, too late, I realized it might not have been entirely true. I suddenly remembered the waiter's avid face; he had been so excited. Perhaps there had been no holdup in the parking lot. The policemen could have been there for other reasons. Maybe a customer had been unable to pay his bill. Maybe they had simply come to question someone about something that had nothing to do with Perino's. Or . . . the possibilities were endless.

Was it slander or libel when you printed something that was untrue? I didn't even know. What were the penalties? I was ignorant of that as well. I'd lose my job, of course, but could I get sued? Could I go to jail?

And then I had a moment of crazy hope. Maybe I hadn't actually said that a holdup had occurred. Perhaps I had simply quoted the captain talking about the robbery. That was bad, but it was better than a bald statement of fact.

I sprang out of bed and went into my workroom to read the review. The mockingbird hooted loudly. As I turned on the light a coyote slipped out of the yard and slunk up the road. I picked up the review.

"A diner, waiting for the valet to fetch his car, was relieved of his wallet at gunpoint," I read, with a sinking heart. It was worse than I remembered; I had definitely reported a holdup at Perino's. I heard Bob saying, "Good work," and wondered what he'd say when he found out what an idiot he'd hired. Danny Kaye would never talk to me again. What had ever made me think I was a reporter?

It was two A.M. I was awake, turning in circles, wringing my hands. I was so restless inside my own skin that I didn't know what to do. I felt nauseous, and my head was light. My feet itched. I couldn't sleep. If only it was a few hours earlier and we could stop the presses. Did they still stop presses? I didn't even know that.

Should I call the police now and ask for a police report? No; if it turned out that there was none it wouldn't look good when I had to go to court. My only excuse was my extreme naïveté and utter stupidity.

By three A.M. I was convinced that I had imagined the entire episode. There had never been any policemen in the restaurant at all. "You have employed a seriously deranged woman to write reviews for your newspaper," the owners would write as they demanded millions in damages.

By four A.M. I was beginning to doubt that I had even been to the restaurant. Did Perino's even exist? I lay there, my imagination spinning out of control, watching the hands move around the clock, swearing that I would never write another restaurant review.

"You look pale," said Michael in the morning.

"I didn't have a good night," I replied.

"Too excited to sleep?" he asked, snapping open the paper. And there, in black and white, was my article.

"Yeah," I said, smiling wanly.

Driving downtown I thought about the misery I was about to face, about the way my life was going to be altered. When had this job become so precious to me? I was surprised to discover that I liked L.A. and didn't want anything to change. Even my horrible house suddenly seemed less bad.

I parked in the lot and dragged myself into the office, flashing my soon-to-be-surrendered ID card at the guard. Who did I think I was, Ruth Reichl? All of a sudden I wanted to be her. After all these months, the thought of moving back to Berkeley was no longer appealing.

The telephone on my desk was ringing. I picked it up. A deep voice said, "Ms. Reichl? This is Evelle Younger. I am the former attorney general of the State of California." I dropped the phone as the blood went rushing from my head. My life was over. I bent down and retrieved the receiver. When I put it back to my ear he was saying, ". . . I was in the restaurant the night of the holdup, and I respect the honesty of your reporting . . ."

"Thank you so much for calling, Mr. Attorney General," I managed to squeak. "You'll never know how much it's meant to me." And then I went home and slept for the rest of the day.

■ ■ ■

"It would have been bad," Michael said, "but not as bad as you imagined. It would have been embarrassing; the paper would have had to print a correction. You probably would have been fired. But in a suit the restaurant would have had to prove malice, and there wasn't any. Still, promise you'll do me a favor. You're a wonderful writer, but next time you decide to play reporter, let me take a look before it goes into print. I deal with hard news every day, and I could have saved you from all this."

"I know," I said. "I was stupid."

And then, without knowing that I was going to do it, I leaned over, kissed him, and said, "I've been stupid about a lot of things. Will you marry me?"

DANNY'S LEMON PASTA

I never asked Danny Kaye for the recipe for his lemon pasta—or for any of the other dishes that he cooked for me. But I loved the pasta so much that one day I simply tried to make it myself.

It took me a long time to perfect the recipe. It isn't as good as Danny's—nothing could be—but it's the closest I've been able to come.

½ stick (¼ cup) unsalted butter
1 cup heavy cream
3 tablespoons fresh lemon juice
1 pound fresh egg fettuccine
2 teaspoons finely grated fresh lemon zest
salt
freshly ground black pepper
freshly grated Parmesan cheese

Melt the butter in a deep, heavy 12-inch skillet and stir in the cream and lemon juice. Remove the skillet from the heat and keep it warm and covered.

Cook the pasta in a large pot of salted boiling water until al dente, 2 to 3 minutes. Reserve ½ cup of the pasta cooking liquid and drain the pasta in a colander. Add the pasta to the skillet with the lemon zest and 2 tablespoons of the pasta cooking liquid and toss well. (Add more pasta cooking liquid 1 tablespoon at a time, if necessary, to thin the sauce.)

Season the pasta with salt and pepper and serve with Parmesan cheese.

Serves 4.

13

MASHED BANANAS

■ We got married in our new house, which was old and gracious, set high up in the hills, with large rooms and expansive views of the San Bernardino Mountains. It was a sunny day; Bruce Cost came down from San Francisco to cook, and the food was so good that Danny said that, at least for the day, our house was the best restaurant in L.A.

Nancy Silverton baked the cake, and Alice cut it, along with Marion Cunningham and Cecilia Chiang. Watching them pass the slices I had a moment of total happiness. Nick and Jules were there, dressed up in the same clothes they had bought when I'd first become a restaurant critic and we'd started going to fancy restaurants. Colman was there with his wife, standing in the corner talking to Wolfgang and Barbara. My mother was swanning around, looking proud and beautiful, and for a moment I missed my father so much that it was a sharp, physical pain. I found myself looking for Doug, but of course he wasn't there. I had almost asked him to come, and I suspect that he would have. Just as I would have gone to his wedding a few months later if he had invited me. It was comforting to know that we were still family to each other, and that we always would be.

After the wedding, life calmed down. I liked working at the newspaper, Michael loved his job, and we both enjoyed living in Los Angeles. We had only one problem: Three years went by and I did not become pregnant.

▪ ▪ ▪

"You're old," said the fertility doctor we finally consulted. "Why did you wait so long? We'll have to start with a few tests."

"Will they hurt?" I asked.

"Oh no," he said. And then he conceded, "It's possible that a couple of them might be a little uncomfortable." His tone of voice suggested that anyone with a real commitment to having children would gladly endure a bit of discomfort. Especially when she was thirty-nine years old.

I remembered that tone when the technician said, "You might experience a bit of cramping now," and began to stick mysterious probes into my body. An electric pain went through me like lightning. I gritted my teeth.

When nothing remarkable came of those tests we advanced to phase two. This involved expensive drugs and daily six A.M. appointments in a room full of hopeful women. We sat in the clinic, newspapers rustling, watching the clock tick inexorably forward. By nine A.M. the air in the waiting room had become a thick cloud of rage. We were all late for work. "Men would never put up with this," we muttered, looking up resentfully each time the nurse came to call another name.

"I told you, drink more water," the nurse said every morning as she stared at the mass of bruises on my arms. "You don't have good veins." She jabbed at my arm, stabbing in first one place and then

another, attempting to take blood. Afterward she brought me down
the hall to take pictures of my ovaries, ramming the probe viciously
into my vagina. "You can get dressed now," she said each day when
she had done. "See you tomorrow."

I was so accustomed to the seeming senselessness of the rou-
tine that I was startled to hear something new emerge from her
mouth one morning. "They're blooming," she said in a lugubrious
voice.

"It's bad," I said.

"No," she said mournfully, "it means there are eggs. We might be
able to do the operation. You'll have to come back tonight and give
more blood." She looked at my bruised arms and said, her tone
canceling her words, "I hope we'll be able to find a vein."

The operations were called "procedures." They were expensive,
painless . . . and unsuccessful.

"You might want to start thinking about adoption," said the doctor after the third procedure. "If you wait until you're forty you'll
be at a disadvantage." I understood this to mean that he considered me hopelessly infertile. I was, in any case, ready to say good-
bye, so I took the piece of paper that he offered. It contained the
name of a lawyer specializing in private adoptions. "He's the best,"
said the doctor. "He's never had one go wrong."

"Call me Joshua," said the lawyer, holding out his hand. He was
a sleek, handsome man to whom adoption had clearly been very
good. His huge Beverly Hills office was filled with modern art and
big leather chairs that swiveled to face expansive windows with
fabulous views of the city. He chatted about restaurants for a
while, then lowered his voice to a mellower range as he riffled papers on a large, well-polished ebony desk.

"The point is to sound rich and friendly," he declared, as he out-
lined his method. He handed us a list of small newspapers from
the South and showed us a sample ad. Our targets were pregnant
southern women who lacked either the means or the desire to raise

their babies. "You have to emphasize what a wonderful life the baby will have. Remember, you are selling a dream."

The ad began, "Prosperous, loving white couple seeks baby. All medical expenses paid." Joshua put it down and said, "You're writers; you know how to do these things. Now," he continued, "get out a pen. I want you to take notes."

Michael and I simultaneously pulled out our reporter's pads. "Not you," said Joshua, turning to Michael. "They only want to talk to her."

"But I'm adopting this baby too," he protested.

"They want to talk to the mother," said Joshua briskly. He looked at me. "Ready? Okay. First, get a separate phone just for these calls. Second, keep a pad and pencil next to it. Take notes, so you remember what they've said and what you've said. You think you won't forget, but you will."

I nodded and wrote.

"Rule Number One," he intoned. "Ask no questions. Not at the outset. Your initial job is to charm them. Remember that you're selling yourself. And this will be the most important sale you'll ever make."

He looked at us appraisingly and added, "There's no need to be too truthful. Michael will do, but with a name like Ruth no one will call. I'd suggest Tammy."

"Tammy?" I said. "You want me to call myself Tammy?"

He shrugged. "It's up to you. But in our experience few young women are willing to give a baby to someone named Ruth. We've been very successful with Tammy. Dusty works well too."

"Shall I change my name to Joe-Bob?" asked Michael.

Joshua did not crack a smile. "That won't be necessary," he said. He stood up and held out his hand. "Good luck," he said. "You're about to embark on a wonderful adventure!"

■ ■ ■

"So how do you feel about this wonderful adventure?" asked Michael as we left.

"You hated him, didn't you?" I replied.

"Admit it, you did too," he said. "Do you think we should find another lawyer?"

"We don't have to spend time with him," I said, reluctant to admit that this man, this dealer in pain, had made my skin crawl. "Anyway, he's supposed to be the best. I imagine they're all the same."

"You may be right," said Michael reluctantly. "I'll do whatever we have to do. But can we agree on one thing? I don't think you should be Tammy. Let's not start off with a lie."

▪ ▪ ▪

The first call came at midnight. "About the baby?" said a very young voice. It burst into tears.

"How old are you?" I asked, forgetting Rule Number One.

Thirteen. Roxanne was thirteen. She was four months pregnant, and I was the very first person she had told. "My daddy'll kill me if he finds out," she said. And then she added dreamily, "I want my baby to grow up around movie stars. Which ones do you know?" She had never heard of Danny Kaye and soon hung up.

Joshua should have told me about Rule Number Two, I thought, as I tried to remember the name of every movie star I'd ever met. Elke Sommer had been seated next to me at a Spago Seder; she headed the list. Gregory Peck had once called asking where to get good steak; he quickly turned into a pal. Kathleen Turner, whom I'd met at a charity function, became a close friend. I had actually been to a party at Henry Winkler's house, and now I wrote down everything I could remember about the evening. I threw in Bob Dylan, who had once been seated next to me at Cirque du Soleil. It wasn't a perfect list, but it would have to do.

▪ ▪ ▪

But my next caller wasn't interested in movie stars. Darlene lived in the panhandle of Texas, and she sounded bone-tired. "This is my fifth," she said wearily. "It was an accident. We can't afford another."

Her husband, Billy, was a mechanic; they'd been trying to save money for their own garage. Listening to her soft southern voice I tried to see the room she was standing in. It would be a small, crowded kitchen with children's toys scattered across the floor and dishes stacked in the sink. "I'm making Hamburger Helper again," she said. "Lots of helper, not much hamburger. What're you having for dinner?"

Chilean sea bass didn't have the right ring. Did lamb chops sound too snooty? Steak? What would she want her baby to eat? "Barbecued chicken," I decided.

"Chicken," she said wistfully. "We don't get chicken much. The kids fight over the drumsticks."

Darlene and I talked for almost an hour. I liked her; she seemed smart and tough and deeply sad about giving her baby to a stranger. "But I know it's for the best," she was saying when she suddenly cried, "You said you were working late!" and slammed down the phone. Did she tell Billy? Did they keep the baby? Or did she decide that her child should be raised on steak?

Over time I learned the right answers, learned to tailor my story to their dreams. The first time I said I was a restaurant critic there was dead silence on the line. By the next call I had turned into a food editor. It was a wise choice. "You must bake a lot of cookies," said Ramona. "Oh yes," I said fervently, "every day. Sometimes twice." Michael's job wasn't very popular either, so I demoted him from news director to weatherman. Amy was the first one I tried that out on. When she said, "You mean like the guy on the TV?" I knew I had done the right thing.

I couldn't dream up a new house because the right woman would eventually see it. But that didn't keep me from embellishing it a bit. I redesigned the kitchen. I redecorated the living room. And day by day the baby's bedroom grew larger.

Meanwhile we ate the same imaginary meal every night: fried chicken, mashed potatoes, green beans, salad, and strawberry shortcake. It was all-American and designed to offend no one (with the possible exception of vegetarians). It might be a little high in cholesterol, but not one of the women I spoke with mentioned that.

The calls made me feel like a teenager talking to boys I wanted to like me, reinventing myself over and over. I was flooded with self-doubt, always certain I had said the wrong thing, convinced that my future was at stake and I had blown it. Though I hadn't smoked in years, I yearned for a cigarette.

Veronica, Joanne, and Louella all hung up when they found out that I was Jewish. Rachel wanted her baby to have a blond mom. Sally didn't like my politics. And April broke my heart; she was like a lover who kept teasing me, leading me on until I was certain that she was the one. And then, suddenly, she just stopped calling. What had I said?

Joshua checked in periodically on our progress. "Take your time," he said. "You can't be too careful. Keep looking. You'll find the right baby. I know you will." And then one day he called my office and his voice sounded different.

"Sit down," he said.

I smoothed my black skirt and said, "Okay."

"Do you want a baby?" he asked.

"Of course," I said.

"Do you *really* want a baby?" he demanded, and I instantly felt guilty, as if he were a preacher asking me to testify about my faith.

"Yes," I answered, trying hard to sound sincere, "I really want a baby. We're writing a new ad—"

"No, no," he interrupted, as if I had not understood him. "I mean do you want a baby right now?"

"Now?" Was this a test? Did he do this to all his clients, just to make sure that they were really motherhood material?

"It's a girl," he said. "Born yesterday. Do you want her?"

"You have a baby girl?" I asked stupidly. "Here in Los Angeles?"

Papers rustled. "Born yesterday at Cedars-Sinai," he read. "Three twenty-two in the afternoon. She got five on her Apgar tests. She's perfect."

"And she doesn't have a mother?"

"It's a long story," he said impatiently, as if I were wasting his time with foolish questions. "I'll gladly tell you the entire tale. But I need to know if you want her. Because if you don't, I have to find another couple."

"You'll have to give me a few details," I insisted.

Joshua sighed, as if I were being unreasonable. "One of my clients," he said slowly, "and I can't tell you her name, contracted to adopt this baby four months ago." His voice indicated his resentment at being forced to go through these banal details when he had a homeless baby on his hands. "Yesterday she coached the birth mother through the delivery. Everything went beautifully."

"There must have been some problem," I said. "Otherwise you wouldn't be calling me."

"I'm getting to that," he said. "This morning my client took the baby home. When she got there her husband was gone. He had left a note saying that he didn't want the baby, and he didn't want to be in the marriage anymore."

"Oh," I said, beginning to understand. "But what about the birth mother?"

"I've just spoken with her," he said. "She doesn't want the baby either. This pregnancy was the result of a rape, and all she wants is to go back to Mexico and forget that any of this ever happened. She doesn't care who gets the baby. She doesn't even want to meet the new parents."

I found that I was unable to talk. It was too fast. After a moment Joshua said, "Ruth, are you there?"

"Yes," I said.

"This is the most perfect situation you could ever have," he said. "Did I mention that the birth mother is beautiful?"

"No," I said. "All you said was that she'd been raped. How old is she?"

"Don't worry," he said. "She's twenty-six. She's a grown-up. She wants to put this all behind her."

"I don't know . . ." I began.

"Call Michael," he said. "Think about it. All you have to do is pay the hospital bills. I'll give you half an hour to think about it. Believe me, if you don't want this baby there are plenty of people who will."

■ ■ ■

Michael was wary. "It's too good to be true," he said. "It doesn't feel right."

I paced around my office, trailing the phone cord behind me. "No more ads," I pleaded. "I don't have to call myself Tammy. We don't even have to meet this woman. It's a gift from heaven, like opening your door one morning and finding the baby you've dreamed of on your doorstep. No waiting. No nothing. We just go get her at the home of the adoptive mother. Please say yes."

"We don't have a cradle," he hedged. "We don't have bottles. We don't have baby clothes." He was down to details. He was going to give in.

"You've made the right decision," said Joshua when I called back. He gave me an address. "You won't be sorry. And don't forget to buy a car seat on the way. In California it's illegal to drive a child without one."

■ ■ ■

We never even went inside. When we rang the bell a maid came out carrying a bundle wrapped in a blue blanket. She handed it over and closed the door. I stood there, terrified. "What if I drop it?" I wailed. "I've never held a baby before."

"Give her to me," said Michael, lifting the baby out of my arms. He peeled back a corner of the blanket and looked down. "How beautiful you are," he crooned to the baby. "Look, she already has hair."

She lay with her eyes closed, her small heart-shaped face framed by straight black hair. Breathing serenely in and out, she was unaware that in twenty hours on earth her fate had already changed. Twice.

■ ■ ■

"Oh, Ruthie," said my mother. "People don't go picking babies up on doorsteps. It's very peculiar."

"It's very lucky," I said. "I still can't quite believe it. And she's such a great baby!"

"Don't tell me she sleeps through the night," my mother replied.

"Not exactly," I admitted. "But I don't seem to mind. I like being with her in the middle of the night, just the two of us, all alone. I love the way she smells. I love the sounds she makes. I can't believe she's mine."

"Is she really yours?" Mom wanted to know. "Are the papers signed?"

"No," I said. "We have to be evaluated by social workers. And the State of California gives the birth mother six months to change her mind. But that's not going to be a problem; she's already gone back to Mexico. Joshua says it's a done deal."

"Well, I think it's very peculiar," my mother repeated. "In the meantime I wish you'd reconsider that name. Gabriella is so odd."

"We call her Gavi for short," I said. "Do you like that any better?"

"No," said my mother.

▪ ▪ ▪

I wished my mother were more enthusiastic, but nothing could puncture my cocoon of happiness. Gavi was funny and portable and easy to love. Michael was entranced; sometimes I'd wake up in the middle of the night and find him in the baby's room, just staring into the crib. Before long we gave up all pretense of putting her into her own room and let her sleep with us; we didn't want her out of our sight.

Overnight we became the obnoxious couple in the restaurant with the baby on the table, the people who walk out of the movies when the baby starts crying, the ones who show up at parties with the baby in a pouch. We were a ridiculous cliché; we didn't care.

I took maternity leave; Michael took her to work. Even the social worker, a large, sarcastic woman who had seen everything, said, "For a formerly childless older couple you are surprisingly comfortable with this baby."

"I don't understand it," I said to my mother. "I've never particularly liked babies. I like them later, after they can talk. But Gavi is different. She's so interesting."

"Your own are always interesting," said Mom. "I'll be happier when you've signed the papers."

"Stop worrying," I said. "It's time you met your granddaughter."

"Not until you sign the papers," she said. "Not until she's really yours."

"Make your reservations," I replied. "It's almost time."

▪ ▪ ▪

When the call came I was mashing bananas. I handed the bowl to Michael and went to the phone. "It's Joshua," said a somber voice. "We have a problem."

"Look!" said Michael, waving a spoon, "Gavi's eating her first solid food!" I gestured for him to be quiet.

"The birth mother wants the baby back," Joshua continued.

"You said she was returning to Mexico!" I cried.

"Well, she didn't," he replied. "She just left my office. She wants to retrieve the baby tomorrow."

"No!" I shouted. "It's absolutely out of the question. She can't have my daughter."

"I don't think you quite understand, Ruth," said Joshua firmly. "You have no rights in this. She hasn't signed any papers."

"I'm this baby's mother," I said. "That woman didn't even care enough to come and meet us! I won't give her Gavi. As far as I'm concerned, that woman relinquished any rights she ever had to this child."

"The state sees it differently," said Joshua coldly. "Of course, you're free to contest it if you like, but I don't do that sort of thing. I'll give you the name of a lawyer who does."

"I thought he'd never had an adoption go wrong," said Michael bitterly as we packed a diaper bag. The pain of this was already etched into his face, and he looked as if he had aged ten years over the last ten minutes. He was already steeling himself for the loss, as if the immense happiness of having this child was undeserved and he had known all along that it would end. My response was different; I expected that somehow, although I could not tell you how, everything would be all right.

"That's what he said," I replied, adding a few cans of Similac. "He also said that this was a perfect situation. He lied about everything. But I don't care what happens. We're not giving Gavi back."

"Of course we're not," he said.

■ ■ ■

Lincoln's office occupied a few cramped rooms in a nondescript mini-mall. It was a long drive. By the time we got there it was almost dark, and the fluorescent lights were bright and harsh, illuminating scuffed furniture that looked as if it had been bought by the truckload at a fire sale. The smell of grease from the burger joint next door hung in the air.

A short, powerfully built man came into the waiting room holding out his hand. His hair was gray, stringy, and so thin you could see the scalp shining beneath it. The right leg of his polyester suit was caught on the stenciled edge of his cowboy boot. I stared at it, mesmerized, as he led us into a windowless office.

But though Lincoln lacked Joshua's smooth charm, he offered hope. Time, he said, was on our side. The birth mother would have to take us to court to get Gavi back. "Show her that you mean business," he said, "and she'll slink back to Mexico and forget the whole thing. I bet she won't even show up." He favored us with a big smile; his teeth were stained with nicotine and his breath was awful. "One day," he predicted. "All it will take is one day in court. The baby will be yours. You'll see."

▪ ▪ ▪

Parents came straggling into the halls of Los Angeles Family Court with their ragged offspring in tow. Children raced through the halls as the bailiffs shouted, "Quiet, quiet, this is a courthouse," and desperate parents cajoled, threatened, and slapped in an attempt to keep order. Men cursed, children wailed, and husbands and wives faced off on hard benches, fighting over money. Bells rang, and public defenders clutched papers as they stumbled from one courtroom to another.

"It's like the third ring of hell," said Michael.

Gabriella slept in her basket, unconcerned by the commotion as we huddled with Lincoln. Years passed. Finally our name was called, and we jumped up and went into a small, hot courtroom.

"The mother doesn't seem to be here," said Lincoln happily. He swiveled around to survey the room. "See? I told you. She's probably gone back to Mexico!"

"Anna Delgardo," said the clerk. "Anna Delgardo, please approach the bench." No one moved. He said it again. "See?" whispered the lawyer. "I told you not to worry!"

Michael beamed, jubilant. "It's over!" he said. "She's ours!" He ran his fingertips gently across Gavi's face.

"It is noted," said the judge, "that the complainant has not made an appearance. Under the circumstances—"

As she spoke a rustling began in the back of the courtroom. A small woman wearing blue jeans and a black T-shirt rushed down the aisle. Her head was down, so all we could see was shiny black hair, but as she came closer she looked up. I caught my breath; her face was shaped like a heart.

"Are you Anna Delgardo?" asked the judge. The woman looked blank. "Eres Anna Delgardo?" asked the clerk in Spanish.

"Sí," said the woman.

The judge switched to Spanish and I listened to the mother of my child explain herself in a detached, dispassionate voice. She worked in a bank in Mexico City. Her boss had raped her. She had told no one, but when she found herself with child she'd come across the border to get an abortion. But she had so little money, and soon it was too late. . . . She had decided to give the baby up.

"But something has changed?" prompted the judge.

"Sí," said the woman. "God has shown me that this was wrong."

"How will you raise the child?" asked the judge. "Do you have family? A green card? An apartment? A job?"

"No," she replied to each question.

"I am going to continue this," said the judge. "I want you to come back to this court in one month with a plan to support your baby. I want to be certain that you do not have another change of heart." She raised her gavel, and that was that.

"She never even looked at Gavi!" Michael raged as we left the courthouse. "There's no way I'm handing my daughter over to that woman."

"Of course not," I said. "How could the judge seriously consider giving Gavi to a woman who let strangers take her infant. A woman who never cared enough to meet her daughter's parents? She must be crazy."

Michael looked down at Gavi, then over at Lincoln. "Is there any possibility that we might lose?" he asked.

Lincoln spread his hands out flat, palms down, like an umpire calling a player safe. "You are not going to lose this baby," he said. "After this it is unlikely that the birth mother will even come back to court. But just in case, we're going to lay the groundwork of the case."

"I'll never give Gavi to that woman," I cried. "Never. Never. I'll do whatever it takes to keep my daughter." I meant it.

▪ ▪ ▪

I had a nightmare. It was the middle of the night. Gavi was crying, calling me to pick her up. I could hear her, but my feet would not move. As I watched, Anna bent over the bed. And then, somehow, it was me in the crib, calling for my mommy. But my mommy had gone away. I cried on and on, bereft. It was the loneliest feeling in the world.

The next day I got a mysterious call. "You must not let Anna take the baby," said a woman in heavily accented English. "She is the bad woman."

"Who is this?" I cried.

"I want to help you keep the baby," said the voice. "I am your friend. She is the bad woman. I will tell the judge."

"Who are you?" I asked again. There was no answer. She had hung up.

"You must get her name," said Lincoln when I reported the call to him. "This could be very helpful when we go back to court."

"But you told me Anna wouldn't come back!" I reminded him.

"She won't. Don't worry. This is going to be unnecessary." But I was now unwilling to believe anything a lawyer said. Joshua had abandoned us completely. Lincoln had been wrong.

■ ■ ■

The mystery voice eventually revealed herself to be Lourdes, who had taken Anna in while she was pregnant. Lourdes was prepared to tell the judge, the court, and the world that Anna had been dealing drugs.

"Good, good," said Lincoln. "This will be helpful."

"Not if we lose Gavi," said Michael. "This only makes things worse. We knew Anna was an irresponsible idiot; now we hear she's a drug dealer too. How can we possibly let her have our daughter?"

"You won't have to," he promised, sending us off to see psychiatrists who would attest that Gavi was so deeply bonded that she would be harmed if she were to be taken away from us. The Department of Children's Services weighed in on our perfection as parents. Lourdes signed a deposition. "Excellent," Lincoln kept saying as he reassured us that all the signs were good and that we had seen the last of Anna.

■ ■ ■

He was wrong again. With her hair coiffed, wearing a simple black sheath and high heels, Gavi's birth mother was barely recognizable as the bedraggled young woman who had stood humbly in front of the judge a month earlier. And this time she was not alone. Head held high, she listened to her lawyer petition for the return of the baby to her rightful parents.

"Parents?" asked the judge.

A man stepped forward. Tall and thin, he was dressed in a gray suit. "I am the baby's father," he announced with natural dignity.

"Am I to understand that you admit to the rape of this woman?" asked the judge.

The young man drew himself proudly up and began to speak.

The lawyer put a hand on his arm. "Your Honor," the lawyer said, "Miss Delgardo—" He stopped and corrected himself. "I mean, the former Miss Delgardo, now admits that she was never raped. She was merely confused. Last month, after leaving your court, she called Mr. Rodriguez in Mexico and told him about their daughter. He immediately flew to Los Angeles; they were married that night. I ask that you return the child to her rightful parents, Mr. and Mrs. Rodriguez."

Stricken, I clutched Gavi and looked at Michael. He clenched his fists, and then he put his arms around me and held me while I cried. The rest was a blur; I sat in the courtroom, head down, holding my daughter as a stream of words decided her future.

"What happened?" I asked later. We were back in the lawyer's office; Gavi was still in my arms.

"The judge ordered a paternity test," said Michael. "The tests take six weeks, and in the meantime they have visitation rights. The judge said they can come see Gavi on Wednesdays and Saturdays. In the end, if that man turns out to be Gavi's father, we have to give her to them."

"I'm not giving her back," I said. "Never. That's all I have to say."

Lincoln made a fist. "We can fight this," he shouted, warriorlike. "Gabriella is an American citizen. She has rights. We could keep those people in court for years!"

Michael ignored him and looked at me. His face was ravaged now, deeply lined. He put his hand on my arm. "Honey," he said gently, "Lincoln may know what he's talking about. He probably does. In this country, money talks. But that doesn't make it right. We're rich Americans. They're poor Mexicans. I don't want to give Gavi up any more than you do, but I don't want to keep her just because we have more money."

"Whose side are you on?" I demanded, clutching Gavi. "Are you seriously telling me that you could, in good conscience, let Gavi go to them?"

Michael looked down at Gavi. "No," he said quietly. "This is killing me. But we may not have a choice. Things have changed. This is about more than you and me and Gavi. You have to be realistic."

"You want to give our daughter to some woman who allowed strangers, people she had never even met, to walk away with her?" I shouted. "Are you crazy?" I was wild with unaccustomed fury. "A woman who acted as if she were some thing instead of a person?"

Lincoln stroked my arm and said soothingly, "You won't have to. We will appeal this all the way to the Supreme Court. It could take years."

■ ■ ■

When we got home we took Gavi for a walk through Griffith Park. "Don't you see, honey," said Michael as we walked, "the lawyers are manipulating you. They want us as a test case. But think what it will mean for Gavi."

"We can win," I said stubbornly.

"But what if he really is her father? What if we don't?" he insisted. "Suppose we fight this for six or seven years and lose. Imagine what it will be like for Gavi to have to leave the only parents she knows, to go to live with strangers in another country. Wouldn't it be better for her if we gave her up now?"

I didn't have an answer. And so I picked Gavi up out of her stroller and held her tightly to me as I shouted at him, over and over, "I hate you, I hate you, I hate you." I didn't know what else to do.

■ ■ ■

The couple arrived on Wednesday wearing the same clothes they had worn in court. I answered the door as politely as I could and took them to Gavi's room. She reached up her arms, asking me to pick her up, but I turned and walked out, closing the door on her cries. I went into the living room and sat there, biting my nails, listening to her wail.

The judge had allowed them two hours, but after forty-five minutes they emerged from the room. The man was holding Gavi, who was still crying. He handed the weary red baby to me, and she immediately subsided; in three seconds she was asleep in my arms.

"Adiós," he said, going to the door. The woman had said nothing. A cab was waiting and I stood at the window watching it drive off.

"She looks like him," said Michael.

"She does not," I insisted. "How can you say that? She looks nothing like him. He's not her father!"

"Maybe you should let me deal with them on Saturday," he said.

"Try to keep me away," I replied.

▪ ▪ ▪

"Good news," said Lincoln the next day. "Lourdes has a friend who is also willing to sign a deposition. She wants the judge to know that the baby will be better off with you. She does not think Anna will be a fit mother!"

"I don't find that comforting," said Michael. "If we lose Gavi, I want to think she'll be okay."

"We're *not* going to lose her," I said.

"Maybe the father will be a good parent," he said.

"If he *is* the father," said Lincoln. "Which I doubt."

"He's *not* the father," I said fiercely.

"He obviously has reason to believe he is," said Michael.

"Why would she even want to keep the baby?" I asked. "I thought that for months all she wanted was an abortion."

"Having a child changes you," said Michael, giving me a significant look. "Nobody should know that better than you."

"We will fight!" said Lincoln. "Gabriella is an American citizen. They are both here illegally. She must be protected. We can fight this all the way to Washington!"

■ ■ ■

"Is this really what you want our life to be?" Michael asked as we drove home from yet another meeting in Lincoln's office. "Do you want to spend the next ten years living and breathing a legal battle?"

"If we have to," I said.

"And what if it takes ten years and we lose?" he asked. "Please think of what this will mean for Gavi. If that man is her father, we have to give her up. For her sake, we have to do it."

"I'm never going to give her up," I screamed at him. "Never. I'll leave the country with her. I'll go without you if I have to."

"I thought I knew you," said Michael. "But I was wrong. I don't know you anymore." How could he? I didn't even know myself.

■ ■ ■

The man's name was Juan. I couldn't look at Anna without loathing, but he seemed decent enough. Whenever they emerged from the bedroom, he was the one holding Gavi. And each time I took her and we watched as her sobs subsided it was he who said, "Thank you for taking such good care of my daughter."

"He'll be good to her," said Michael, who was still steeling himself for the loss.

"He won't have the chance," I replied, still unwilling to face the possibility of life without Gavi.

"I mean, if we have to give her back," he said.

"We're not giving her back," I replied. He bit his lip and said nothing.

■ ■ ■

The blood test was horrible. Gavi screamed and kicked as the nurse struggled to get a needle into her vein. Then it was over, and there was nothing to do but wait.

"I'll make a deal with you," said Michael as we left the hospital. "If Juan does not turn out to be Gavi's father, I'll fight this with you for as long as it takes. But if the blood tests show that he is, you agree to give her back as soon as we get the results."

"Deal," I said, shaking his hand. In my heart I knew that Juan was not Gavi's father. And there were still three weeks until we had to go back to court.

▪ ▪ ▪

Lincoln called a week later. "Now, I want you to remember," he said, "that the blood tests are only ninety-nine percent accurate."

"The results are in?" I asked. "Already?" Michael dashed across the room.

"They're early," he said, taking my hand.

"They indicate," said Lincoln, "a likelihood that Juan Rodriguez is the father."

"They're so early," I moaned.

"And they could be wrong," Lincoln reminded me.

I hung up the phone and picked up Gavi. I took her downstairs to change her diaper, tickling her so that she laughed and wriggled with delight. As I taped the clean diaper closed I tried to imagine what her life would be, living in Mexico with Anna. I saw her, a sturdy toddler, playing outside in the dirt. I saw Anna step out of a pink stucco house, yank her by the arm, and slap her.

Michael came in and bent over, nuzzling the soft skin of Gavi's neck. She cooed. "I'll call and make arrangements to give her back," he said. He was crying.

"No," I replied. "I'm not giving her back. Not now, not ever."

"But you promised that if he was the father . . ."

"I changed my mind," said the ferocious, unfamiliar creature I had become. I knew exactly what I had to do. "I'm not giving her back. Lincoln says we can fight this for years. We owe it to Gavi."

Michael stared at me for a long time, as if wondering where I had come from. He ran his hand softly across Gavi's cheek. Without a word he left the room. I heard the door slam. His car started. And then Gabriella and I were alone.

■ ■ ■

We lived in noisy silence, equally miserable but dealing with it in different ways. Michael worked late and went to bed as soon as he came home. I could feel the bed moving when he got up in the middle of the night to stand, silently, for hours by our daughter's bed. I spent my time with Lincoln, plotting to keep Gabriella. I made bargains with God; I saw signs everywhere. I knew her destiny was with us.

Juan and Anna appeared like clockwork. In spite of myself I could not dislike him. He had dignity and sweetness, and he seemed distraught that Gavi would not stop crying when he held her.

"Duermes, duermes, mi amor," he whispered to her.

"She doesn't want you," I hissed.

But I reserved my hatred for Anna, a princess who never seemed to hold the baby. Why did she even want her, I wondered, this woman who had hoped to abort my child? She would be a horrible mother. Would she get up and sing to Gavi in the middle of the night? Would she tickle her and nuzzle her? Of course not. It would be monstrous to turn Gabriella over to this woman who had walked away without a backward glance. It was out of the question.

"Señora?" Juan was standing next to me, clearing his throat.

"Yes?" I said.

"My mother would like to see her granddaughter—"

"Oh no," I said, "no more visitors."

"I do not make myself clear," he said. "She would like a photograph. I do not have a camera. Do you have a photograph I could send her?"

Relieved, I gave him an entire stack. Michael and I were in most of them; I wanted the grandmother to know that Gavi had a family.

▪ ▪ ▪

Gavi had graduated to peas and carrots. I was feeding her, laughing as she smeared the purées around her face. When the phone rang I answered with one hand, still holding the spoon. It was Michael. "Turn on the television," he said. "The Spanish station, KMEX. Hurry."

I picked Gavi up and took her with me into the living room. When I turned on the television her face, and mine, and Michael's jumped out at me. It was one of the photographs I had given Juan. The Spanish was very rapid, but it was not hard to get the gist of what the anchor was saying: Two American journalists had stolen a Mexican baby. Juan and Anna were in the studio; Anna looked very pretty. She was crying as she said, "Yo quiero mi niña." Juan, looking strong and dignified, said something I could not understand. The picture of me and Michael holding Gavi flashed back on the screen, followed by the logos of the *Los Angeles Times* and CBS.

"Do you get it?" said Michael's voice on the phone. He was hoarse; he had been crying. "Do you finally get it? It's over. We have to give her back. It's not just about us anymore. It's gotten bigger. Now it's become about race, about class. Tomorrow there will be pickets at the paper and the station."

"We can fight it," I said.

▪ ▪ ▪

When the social worker came the next day we gave her Gavi's clothes and toys and bottles. And then there was only Gavi. She looked at me trustingly as I handed her over to the woman. She did not cry when the car door closed. The car drove off, and I watched it until I couldn't see it anymore, and then I watched the last place it had been until I couldn't see anything at all. Blindly I turned and went inside.

Michael and I were like survivors of a shipwreck on a desert island. We bumped around, surprised to be alive, surprised to discover other living beings in the world. We both had nightmares. Neither of us could eat or sleep. Our fragility made us unexpectedly gentle with each other.

Friends shied away from us, and when I showed up at the office Bob roared, "What are you doing here?" He took me to the door and shoved me out. "After what you've been through," he said, "I don't want to see you for at least two weeks."

■ ■ ■

Without diapers, bottles, strollers, or car seats there seemed almost nothing to load into the car. Within minutes we were driving, past Ventura, past Santa Barbara, and up the spine of California.

"I don't want to talk about it," I said. "I want to lie in the sun and drink wine and try not to think about where Gavi is and what she is doing. I want to empty my mind so I don't hear her crying for us, night and day, wondering why we never come."

In the Napa Valley the sky was very blue. We were the only people at the pool. We read, we ate, we drank a great deal. We even made love. We hardly spoke.

Driving home, Michael broke the silence. "I have to tell you something," he said. "I can't do that again. Not now. Not ever. If you want to adopt, you'll have to do it with some other guy. I won't risk my heart like that again."

"I understand," I said.

We were in the hot dry valley between the mountains and the coast. The sun beat down on the parched land. The road stretched before us, relentless and straight. It seemed to be going nowhere.

14

BARCELONA

■ My watch said four A.M. In Los Angeles it was dark. Even the freeways would be deserted, with only an occasional headlight picking out the contours of the road. But in Barcelona the sun was still up, and I had to get through one more night without Gavi. I threw my suitcase on the bed and splashed water on my face. Halfway around the world, this trip had seemed like a perfect escape. Now the idea of spending a week in Barcelona with five famous American chefs just seemed like piling jet lag onto misery.

"Hello, I'm hungry," said Alice, peeking around the door. After years as America's most famous chef, the woman who was called "the mother of California cuisine" was still pretty and petite. "Did you just land? Me too. I ate all the food on the plane, even that terrible tired spinach, but it wasn't much. It's three whole hours until we're supposed to meet the others for dinner, and I can't wait. Let's go out and see what we can find."

It was April, and the air was crisp when we left the hotel, the city too delicious to resist. Rococo buildings were piled onto the sidewalk like pastries on a plate. We walked down the Rambla Catalunya, through lanes of double lime trees and past stalls selling lilacs, lilies, violets, and roses. "Isn't it beautiful?" said Alice, who filled my silence with a running commentary. "And just smell."

In spite of myself I wrinkled my nose and inhaled the city. We walked beneath the beautiful wrought-iron street lamps of the Passeig de Gràcia and turned to twist through smaller streets where each block wore a different perfume. One had the scent of salted fish, the next frying dough, and just beyond that we discovered the ripe yeasty aroma of cheese. And then, halfway down a block, the warm smell of roasting nuts came out to ambush us.

"Look!" said Alice, pointing to a little spice shop on the far side of the street. In the window stood a woman holding a scoop filled with toasted almonds. She smiled, and Alice pulled me across the street.

Inside the shop, saffron, cinnamon, and mint mingled with the aroma of the nuts. The woman gestured, inviting us to come closer as she raked the almonds into a huge pile. Alice and I plunged our hands into the warm mound until they were covered all the way to the wrists. I closed my hand, retracted it, and put an almond in my mouth; the fragrance swelled to fill my entire head.

We munched on almonds as we walked, and then Alice discovered new treats: olives, anchovies, ice cream. "I'm really worried about this dinner," she confided. "We're supposed to cook a meal for absolutely everybody who counts in the Barcelona food world, to show them how American cooking has matured. But these collaboration dinners are always difficult. Doing one in a foreign city, with people you haven't worked with, products you don't know, and no time to practice is insane. I can't believe any of us agreed to it!"

"Yes," I said absently; just in front of us a little girl was toddling down the street with her mother, and my mind was in Mexico, with Gavi.

We walked and fretted; by the time we reached the restaurant in the city's ancient port I was too tired and full to go on. "I'll just meet you guys in the morning," I said, turning back to the hotel. Alice grabbed my arm. "You'll wake up when the food comes," she promised, pulling me inexorably through the door. "You don't want to miss this."

"Yes, I do," I muttered, but I was already inside the worn wooden room. In here, it seemed, nothing had changed for centuries. Chefs in starched white jackets tended a wood-burning oven, separated from the diners by a long zinc-lined bar. Three huge vats of wine roosted beneath it; on top a block of ice slowly dripped onto the wooden floor.

Our fellow travelers were seated at a long table piled with plates of seafood. Mark Miller and Jonathan Waxman looked cool, cosmopolitan, and slightly bored, as if they had been sitting in the restaurant all their lives waiting for the rest of us to arrive. Bradley Ogden, on the other hand, had the eager-beaver air of the American tourist; it was his first trip to Europe, and his eyes darted around as if he were afraid something important would happen while he wasn't watching. Lydia Shire, a comfortable-looking woman with a frank, open face, pointed something out to him. His mouth dropped in astonishment.

Colman was there too, and for a moment I was surprised to see him. Locked inside my own sadness, I had forgotten that it was he who had organized this tour of Barcelona. He had become an authority on Catalan cooking, and he seemed pleased to have us assembled on his turf. I remembered, with a little jolt, that the last time we had shared this continent we had been in love. It seemed so long ago.

"Taste this," he said, barely pausing to say hello. Alice and I sat down, and he passed us each a wooden fork and a small terra-cotta casserole.

"What is it?" asked Alice. The aroma of garlic was so intense it began to wake me up. I shook my head, trying to clear it, and gazed down into a pool of golden oil containing whole cloves of garlic and what looked like small straight pins.

"Taste," he commanded.

Alice and I obediently stuck our wooden forks into the oil and fished out a pin. I put it in my mouth; it was blazingly hot and startlingly tender, with a gentle sweetness tinged with salt. The garlic was subtle, no more than a lingering aftertaste. I had absolutely no idea what I was eating, but it was so delicious that I chased the elusive pins around the dish until there were no more. I looked questioningly at Colman.

"Angulas," he said. "Baby eels."

"They were a surprise," said Bradley.

"There will be a lot of surprises on this trip," promised Colman.

"I hope our dinner doesn't turn out to be one of them," murmured Bradley, but Colman wasn't listening. He was pointing to the platters on the table, saying, "The seafood here is really good," with such a proprietary air that one might have thought that he'd personally snatched these specimens from the ocean. The food on the table actually looked more vegetable than animal, like it had been cut from a garden and not fished from the sea. The tiny squid were the size of blueberries; they were tinged with black and, when I stretched a finger out to touch them, felt as soft as peaches. Grilled sardines were stacked head to tail, like so many logs piled onto the platter. Baby octopuses, their tentacles tightly curled, had the air of prickly little roses basking in the sun, and cuttlefish were tangled into a sofrito of tomatoes and onions, looking like bittersweet growing in a meadow.

Colman picked up the nearest platter and pointed to a small, soft, almost transparent filet with brownish ridges running down the flesh. "Anybody know what this is?" he asked.

"An espardenya," said Mark.

"Right," said Colman. "But do you know what that is?"

"I'll take a wild guess and assume it's a fish," he replied.

From Colman's face I knew that Mark was wrong, but I couldn't imagine what else the filet might be. So I just took a bite. It was supple and slightly sweet. "It's good," I said. Bradley reached for the platter.

"It's a slug," said Colman.

Bradley quickly redirected his hand to the grilled shrimp.

"A slug!" said Mark. "I have to taste that." He speared a filet and bit into it. He chewed for a moment and announced, "I like it."

Awake now, I drank some more wine. It was midnight in Barcelona, and I was eating slugs. And then, unbidden, unwelcome, a thought floated toward me: What time is it right now in Mexico? A shadow crossed my heart.

It was late when we finally left the restaurant. As we walked out the door I stood looking down the cobbled street, thinking how tired I was. It seemed weeks since I had been in bed. "I think I'll turn in," I said.

Alice gave me a sharp look. Did I imagine that she kicked Mark? Perhaps. But I did not imagine that Mark said firmly, "On Bradley's first night in Europe? Impossible! This is Spain. It's early. The bars will be open for hours."

And I certainly did not imagine the nighttime tour of the city, through endless cocktail bars, where beautiful bartenders shook exotic liquors into fabulous potions. We tried drinks with names like pampa, Americano, sidecar. And then, somehow, we were hungry again.

"I know just the place," said Colman, reaching into his inexhaustible knowledge of the city. He led us around a corner and down a flight of stairs into a dark, medieval basement where thick wooden beams hugged small, low tables.

We ordered champagne and local specialties: slices of bread rubbed with tomatoes and drizzled with olive oil, ham made out of duck breast, olives, and anchovies. "Try this," said Colman, offering a platter of sliced, fried meat.

"What is it?" asked Mark.

"Try it," urged Colman. Mark took a tentative taste. "Bull's balls," said Colman.

Mark glared balefully at the platter. "I have to have *something* that I won't eat," he said, taking a big gulp of wine. Sputtering, he spat it out.

"That bad?" asked Jonathan.

"No," said Mark, "but it's not Baby Jesus sliding down your throat in velvet slippers." Colman laughed. I said, "Can we go to bed now?"

"No," they replied in unison, "we're going to look at the cathedral. They light it up at night. It's beautiful."

"Don't you guys ever sleep?" I moaned. "How are you going to cook this dinner if you stay up every night?"

"We're used to it," said Jonathan. "Besides," he added, as if he were about to make a logical case against sleep, "we're in Spain."

It was light when they finally led me back to the hotel. I fell into bed so drunk, so tired that for the first time in weeks I slept without dreaming. It did not occur to me, until much later, that keeping me up had been an act of extraordinary kindness.

▪ ▪ ▪

"We're meeting for cocktails at ten." It was Alice on the phone.

"Cocktails?" I asked. "In the morning?"

"Hurry," she said. "If you get up now you can just make it."

Barcelona is rich in bars, and we began each day in a different one. "Why are we drinking sidecars at ten A.M.?" I asked one morning.

"To try and forget," said Jonathan, "that we have this horrible dinner hanging over our head." He was joking, of course, but when I thought about it afterward it seemed like a premonition. At the time I thought only that I too was trying to forget, and that alcohol was helpful.

Colman had arranged this trip with the firm determination of showing off everything Barcelona had to offer; our schedule was very full. We went to bakeries, wineries, and markets. We were endlessly eating. My body ached from lack of sleep. But the chefs seemed impervious to fatigue, and I was reminded of Wolfgang saying that he worked better when he slept less.

Wolf was now so famous that the year before, when I'd spent a week following him around the country for a story on the life of a celebrity chef, the women at the Hertz counter in Cleveland had squealed at the sight of him and treated him like a major movie star. It seemed to make no difference to him; he still worked as if demons were chasing him. He was in another city every day, cooking charity meals, creating special dinners for wealthy clients, and looking for new places to build restaurants. But although he checked in and out of hotels he rarely rumpled the beds. He snatched his sleep sitting up on airplanes, waking after a couple of hours looking depressingly refreshed. And so when Jonathan said, "If the dinner's a disaster it won't be because we're tired," I believed him.

The chefs wanted to see every site and sample every flavor. We spent hours in an olive store while the owner handed his wares across the counter. First the large obregòns, which are cured in oranges; next the tiny black, purple, and green extremañas; and then, triumphantly, the little grayish arbequines, which are the pride of Catalonia. Colman took us to visit champanerias, vinegar makers, the House of Salt Cod.

"Write this down," said Lydia. "I just ate salt cod with Roquefort sauce. If you had ever told me that I would do such a thing, I would have told you it was impossible."

"Write this down too," said Mark. "Salt cod fried with honey. I can't believe I even tasted it."

"And this," said Alice. "It was good."

"But not that good," said Jonathan.

Surrounded by their noise and banter, sated by a surfeit of food, I gradually became less numb. Sometimes two or three hours would pass when I did not think of Gavi, and most nights, when they finally allowed me to drop into bed, I slept dreamlessly. I was slowly coming back to life; I knew it would be a long time until I could be happy, but I was beginning to understand that such a time might come.

■ ■ ■

For years Barcelona had been forced to speak Spanish; now, freed from the tyranny of language, the city reveled in its own Catalan tongue. If you stopped someone to ask for directions to the Mercado de San José, he would look at you blankly, as if he had no idea what you could possibly be talking about. Ask for La Boqueria, on the other hand, and you got directions not only to the market but also to the nearby sidewalks designed by Miró.

An ornate Art Nouveau roof covers the market. It dates from the last century, but if you look around the edges you find ancient marble columns, the remains of earlier markets in much earlier times. La Boqueria is so rich in history that it feels like a great temple of food, and we all found ourselves becoming quiet as we entered its doors.

Inside, light filtered dimly down from the high ceiling, and we blinked, adjusting our eyes. "Don't forget to make a list of what you find and where you found it," Alice called as we fanned out past neat pyramids of fruit, spiral stacks of mushrooms, and fluffy bouquets of herbs.

At the meat counters the tiny kids were strewn with flowers, which made them look like sacrifices instead of food. The animals were so young that the butchers' knives moved soundlessly through the soft bones. The innards were beautiful too: the tripe so clean and white it might have been spun by spiders, and the great dark blocks of congealed blood laid out like so much marble. Calves' brains, intricate coils, looked like some exotic fungus lying on the counter. "How beautiful they are!" said Lydia, staring at the looping twists. "I want to do something with those brains at the dinner."

Mark stood by the fish stalls, eyeing bright snapper, glistening blue mackerel, and silver sardines. "Raw fish," he murmured, "we should do something with raw fish. That would surprise them, since Catalans always cook their fish."

Across the aisle Alice was cooing over skinny, dark green asparagus. "We'll buy lots and lots of them to cook," she exclaimed. "They're wild!" She moved to the next stack, some fat white asparagus, which she stroked tenderly. "I love their little lavender tips," she explained, leaning over to break one off and stick it into her mouth. The vendor looked on, startled.

Jonathan was mesmerized by clams with brightly patterned shells. "They're called Romeos," he said, staring at them. "Aren't they wonderful? I want to use them for the dinner." The fish woman flirted with him, patting the shells so that all the clams seemed to stick out little red tongues. Jonathan laughed out loud and the fishmonger, delighted, did it again. Then she went behind the counter and picked up a baby. Holding her out toward Jonathan she crooned, "Mi niñiña."

Jonathan squeezed my shoulder. Somewhere in Mexico, I thought, at this very moment, someone is holding Gavi. I hoped, with all my heart, that when she said, "Mi niñiña," she caressed the words in the same way. My eyes filled with tears, and I looked away.

▪ ▪ ▪

The kitchen that the city of Barcelona had selected for the chefs was tiny. It contained two burners, no equipment, and a minuscule sink that rebelled each time it was asked to swallow more than a cup of water. But it would be three more days until the chefs discovered this, and by then it would be too late. As they left the market, they were thinking big. "Colman's bragged about us all over Barcelona," said Alice. "Every winemaker and chef in the region is coming. The Julia Child of Spain will be there. How many courses, do you think?"

Day by day the number grew. "Remember, we don't have a lot of time," said Alice . . . just before adding a quail course to the menu.

"Let's not go crazy," said Jonathan. And then tacked on clams casino as a second course.

"We want to make this as foolproof as possible," suggested Mark, increasing the courses with a poblano pesto. Still to come: the fish course, the meat course, the salad course, dessert.

The menu changed almost hourly as they discovered new foods. But as the days went on, one thing remained constant: Dessert, the chefs had agreed from the start, would be a blood-orange sorbet. "They'll be amazed," said Alice. "The only thing they ever do with blood oranges is use them for juice."

But on the day before the dinner Jonathan suddenly had a terrible thought: "What if there's no ice-cream maker?" he asked.

"Oh, there must be one," said Mark.

"If there's not," said Bradley, "I'll do it by hand." They all turned to stare at him. "With a rubber spatula," he explained, "and a stainless steel bowl set over rock salt and ice."

■ ■ ■

There was no ice-cream maker. There was barely a bowl. As the chefs hauled their purchases into the kitchen they looked at one another with dawning horror. Five people could not possibly work in that kitchen at the same time; five people could barely breathe in there at the same time. The dinner, clearly, was doomed.

"How are we going to cook six courses for forty people on two burners?" asked Alice, staring at the stove.

"We'll grill," said Jonathan.

"But what are you going to grill on?" she asked.

"We'll build a grill," said Mark. "I'll use cobblestones if I have to."

"But it's starting to rain," said Alice.

"Don't worry," said Jonathan, "I can grill in any weather."

They had left behind kitchens stuffed with the latest equipment and staffed with eager assistants. At home they had minions who prepped the food, who cleaned and chopped and shredded. Not one of them had washed a pot in years. Now they were on the far side of the ocean staring at two burners, one small and slightly clogged sink, two pots, one pan, and not nearly enough room. They were staring at disaster. America's most famous chefs took a deep collective breath, pulled on their whites, and went to work.

Bradley commandeered a corner of the kitchen. Knife flashing, he began boning quail; within minutes he was covered in blood. As he finished each bird, Jonathan swept the skeleton into one of the pots for stock; Lydia used the other pot to poach brains. Mark assessed the situation, realized that there was no room for him, and went outside to build a grill.

"I found the most beautiful baby spinach," said Alice, irritably inspecting her purchases, "but when we tried to buy it the woman took this ancient stuff from the back. We tried to get her to sell us the good stuff, but she said it was only for display." Alice gathered up the entire heap, dumped it into the garbage, and turned to the remaining greens. "The asparagus is bitter," she lamented. "The beans aren't very good. There goes one course. We're not going to have enough."

"Alice, Alice," crooned Jonathan. He was now shaking garlic in a pan. The aroma rose up and filled the tiny kitchen. "It's okay."

"Where am I going to sauté the brains?" asked Lydia. In one smooth move Jonathan dumped the garlic out and handed the pan to Lydia.

"I'll put the garlic in the oven," he said. As she took the pan with one hand, her other was already reaching for the oil. They were beginning to move in the same cadence.

"Attention grillmasters," said Mark, standing in the doorway with a puddle forming beneath his feet. "We've got a grill." He shook his soggy hair. "That's the good news. The bad news is, it's pouring."

Alice blanched. "There goes another course," she said.

"Don't worry," said Jonathan, briefly squeezing her shoulder. "I told you. I can grill in any weather."

"In this?" she demanded, pointing at Mark, who had squeezed up to the counter, where he was dripping all over Bradley.

"Pray," he said.

Mark removed his knife from the case and changed the tempo in the room. He and Bradley stood shoulder to shoulder, their knives flashing to a different beat. Mark's was a staccato tattoo that transformed a solid chunk of tuna into a mountain of chopped flesh. He chopped chilies and cilantro and mixed them into the fish. As he squeezed limes over the mixture the aroma in the room changed, becoming piquant and almost tropical.

"Good thing we decided on tuna tartare," he said. "At least we have *something* that doesn't need cooking."

"But we've got to toast the bread to put it on," said Alice, "and we've got to hurry; the guests are beginning to arrive." She pulled open the oven door, and smoke poured into the room.

"We forgot the garlic!" she coughed, peering through the haze, which now enveloped everyone. "Can't anything go right?"

"Alice, Alice," said Jonathan, starting into the refrain, "it's fine."

He pulled out the garlic and began pawing through it as Alice knelt beneath him, toasting bread. She handed the bread to Mark, who had to reach around Jonathan while avoiding Lydia, who was still sautéing brains. The four of them were standing in smoke, occupying a space no larger than a shower stall, but the first course had gone out to the guests and they could hear the applause of the crowd. An air of palpable relief ran through the room. And then Lydia let out a groan.

"We're almost out of olive oil!" she cried.

"Oh no," said Alice, standing up too fast and nearly upsetting the pan. "I can't believe we didn't buy enough."

"The great chefs of America!" said Jonathan. He began to laugh, and as they all joined in there was a moment of near hysteria. Then it was over. Lydia scattered capers into the hot oil; they burst into bloom, becoming crisp little flowers.

"Two courses down," cried Alice, relief evident in her voice as the brains went into the dining room. She picked up a bucket of shrimp and called, "Somebody peel these," as she sent it flying through the air. The confidence of the gesture stunned me; who did she think would catch it?

It was Lydia who held out her hand and grabbed the bucket. With one easy motion she dumped the shrimp out on the counter and began pulling off the heads. The chefs had all caught the rhythm now, moving in a kind of kitchen ballet that did not waste a single gesture. They had become a single ten-armed creature, thinking on its feet with a common goal: to get through the night.

The olive oil held out; the rain stopped. The creature worked silently, piling vegetables, beans, peppers, and clams onto the salad plates, dressing them, getting them out the door.

"It's colorful," said Jonathan. "It's unusual."

"And it's gone," said Alice, watching the last plate disappear into the dining room. Without a word Mark and Lydia went outside to grill quail. Inside, Jonathan reduced stock on one burner to make a sauce while Alice stood next to him, shaking artichokes and pota-toes over the other.

"We could have used that spinach," said Alice, unhappily in-specting the final arrangement. "It's too brown."

The plates were not pretty, but that was a minor detail. The chefs were gritting it out, trying to get the food cooked and the eve-ning to end. There was not quite enough quail to go around—every chef's worst nightmare—but they simply rearranged the plates and made it work. The ordeal was almost over.

Bradley was setting the pace now, his spatula hitting the side of a stainless steel bowl with a relentless *thwack, thwack, thwack,* a vibration reverberating through the kitchen. The beat was strong and so compelling that when he stopped, everything else did too.

In the sudden ringing silence Alice dipped a finger into the sor-bet. We watched her face. "Nothing's right tonight," she said.

Jonathan took a taste. "Terrible," he agreed. And then in an in-stant they had pulled together, desperately trying to make the dish into something they could serve. They macerated strawberries in Muscatel and tumbled them onto the plates.

"We could make circles of blood oranges and put them around the edges," suggested Lydia. She was already slicing as she spoke.

■ ■ ■

The guests applauded. They were polite. "It is so interesting," said the Julia Child of Spain, "to see our own products used in such dif-ferent ways."

"That was a terrible meal," said Alice under her breath. She took a bow.

"It could have been worse," I whispered back, "under the cir-cumstances."

"No," murmured Jonathan, "it was really bad. Accept it. That was no fun."

Lydia, the optimist, did not even lower her voice. "I had a good time," she said. "I liked working together. We fought for it." She looked around at the group and added, "We did our best. Sometimes that is all you can do. And then you move on."

▪ ▪ ▪

The rain had ended, and a gentle mist was rising off the streets when we left. As we walked through the haze we could see that we shared the sidewalks with prostitutes wearing nothing but pantyhose and pumps. In any other city in the world this would have seemed surreal, but framed by Barcelona's fantastic architecture, the women seemed to be appropriately dressed.

We were very hungry; we had worked all night and eaten nothing. But it was so late that even the bars had stopped serving food, and all we could find were flaccid french fries and pallid pizza in an all-night joint. It was our last night in Barcelona, and we had cooked one terrible meal and were eating a worse one. But somehow, we were happy. We had fought for it. We had done our best.

▪ ▪ ▪

"I want to ask a question," said Colman. The sun was coming up, and we all looked blearily across at him. "Why did you come?"

Bradley said for adventure and Jonathan, for the sheer craziness of it all. Lydia had wanted to work with Alice, and Alice had liked the group.

Mark, of course, had had a loftier goal. "I came," he said, "because we need to prove to the Europeans that American cuisine has arrived." He paused for a moment and then added, "And because the thing that gives American cooking its strength is our ability to share ideas and work together." We kept looking at him expectantly, and he finally conceded, "Okay, and also because I thought it would be fun."

Colman turned to me. I knew he had been hoping that we would say we had come to learn about Catalan cooking, and I didn't want to disappoint him.

But that wasn't the truth, and it was too early, or too late, to lie. "When I got on the plane," I said slowly, "I didn't really know why I was coming. But I do now. I needed to find out that sometimes even your best is not good enough. And that in those times you have to give it everything you've got. And then move on."

■ ■ ■

It had been a short trip. It had been forever. When I got home the house seemed less empty and Michael less like a stranger. I was filled with a strange serenity.

"You're crazy," said my mother when I told her what I thought lay behind this extraordinary feeling. "It's all been too much for you. Have you seen a doctor?"

"No," I said. "I don't need to. I know."

"How late are you?" she asked.

"One day," I said.

"Ruthie," she lamented, "stop it. When would you have gotten pregnant?"

"When Michael and I were in the Napa Valley," I said, certain that it was true.

"It's just wishful thinking," my mother insisted.

"I think I'll go get one of those home pregnancy kits," I said dreamily.

"Yes," she replied, "please. Get it over with quickly. The sooner you find out the truth, the less disappointed you will be."

My doctor said much the same thing when I called her. "Those home pregnancy kits are very unreliable." She sighed as if she wished she could wipe them all off the market. "You might as well come in and let us give you a real test."

That one was positive too, but she remained wary. "Don't get your hopes up," she warned. "You're forty-one years old. The chances that you will carry this baby to term are very slim. You've been through a lot. If I were you, I wouldn't tell anyone about this. Not even Michael."

"Of course not," I said. Then I got in my car and drove straight to Michael's office.

"What are you doing here?" he asked when he saw me. "Is something wrong?"

"No," I replied. "For the first time in a very long time, nothing is wrong."

"So why have you come?"

"To tell you that we're going to have a baby."

"Are you sure?" he asked.

This time I had absolutely no doubts.

FRIED CAPERS AND CALVES' BRAINS WITH SHERRY BUTTER SAUCE

I keep telling my son, Nick, that he really ought to try these; that they are, somehow, mixed up with his destiny. So far I haven't been able to convince him of this fact. But then, he's only eleven.

The brains are almost entirely texture—like savory marshmallows in a crisp crust. Tossed with salty capers and drizzled with a sweet, buttery sherry sauce, they play tricks in your mouth. I make them whenever things are going badly. They're a lot of work, but they're worth it. They remind me that life is full of surprises—and that there is always hope.

1 pound calves' brains

6 cups water, plus additional
 salted water for soaking

1½ tablespoons white wine
 vinegar

1 small onion, quartered

1 medium carrot, cut into
 ½-inch pieces

½ celery stalk, cut into
 1-inch pieces

2 sprigs fresh parsley

½ small bay leaf

⅛ teaspoon dried thyme

1½ teaspoons kosher salt

5 black peppercorns

1 large egg

½ teaspoon salt

2 cups fresh bread crumbs

¾ cup olive oil

2 tablespoons large bottled
 capers, drained

salt and paper for seasoning

⅓ cup medium-dry sherry

3 tablespoons unsalted butter

1 teaspoon fresh lemon juice
 or to taste

Accompaniment: lemon wedges

Rinse the brains under cold running water in a colander and transfer them to a bowl of salted cold water to cover by 1 inch. Let the brains soak for 30 minutes; then drain them in a colander and carefully remove the surrounding thin clear membrane and external blood vessels with your fingers.

While the brains are soaking, simmer the remaining 6 cups water with the vinegar, onion, carrot, celery, parsley, bay leaf, thyme, kosher salt, and peppercorns in a 5-quart pot for 15 minutes. Bring the liquid to a boil, add the brains, and simmer gently, covered, for 20 minutes. Use a slotted spoon to transfer the brains to a clean colander. Cool completely.

Put one lobe of the brains in the middle of a piece of plastic wrap and gather the edges of the plastic wrap to form a tight purse. Tightly twist the ends of the plastic wrap so the plastic fits snugly around the brains, folding the ends of the plastic wrap under the purse to prevent them from unraveling. Wrap the remaining lobes in the same manner and chill for 1 hour, or until they are firmer.

Whisk together the egg and salt in a bowl. Put the bread crumbs in a shallow bowl. Unwrap the brains and cut them crosswise into ½-inch-thick pieces. Dip two pieces of brains at a time in the egg, letting the excess drip off, and dredge them in the bread crumbs to coat them, lightly patting the crumbs so they adhere to the brains. Transfer the slices, as coated, to a plate.

Heat the oil in a heavy 10-inch skillet over moderately high heat until hot but not smoking and fry the capers, stirring occasionally, until they open up like flowers and are crisp, 2 to 3 minutes. Use a slotted spoon to transfer the capers to paper towels to drain. Immediately fry the brains, in batches without crowding, until golden brown on both sides, 1 to 2 minutes. Use a slotted spoon to transfer the brains to paper towels to drain. Season the brains with salt and pepper and keep them warm in a low oven.

Drain the oil from the skillet and wipe it clean with a paper towel. Add the sherry and simmer until it's reduced by half. Whisk in the butter, and cook over moderate heat until just incorporated. Remove the skillet from the heat and whisk in the lemon juice. Add salt and pepper to taste.

Serve the brains sprinkled with fried capers and drizzled with sauce.

Serves 6 to 8.

ACKNOWLEDGMENTS

You have to be a little crazy to write a book while editing a magazine. You also have to be blessed with a very indulgent family, friends who put up with never seeing you, and above all, colleagues who can step in and do the work you never quite get to.

I could never have written this book if Laurie Ochoa, Larry Karol, and Diana La Guardia had not been so competent, accommodating, and willing to cover for me at *Gourmet*. They even let me take three weeks off during our biggest issue—and never complained about it. At least not to me.

Michael and Nick were also amazing, letting me disappear into my book every night, every morning, and across entire weekends. They only occasionally mentioned that I was no fun.

My editor, Ann Godoff, and my agent, Kathy Robbins, were both enormously supportive as we raced toward the deadline, making changes up to the very last second. My assistant, Robin Pellicci, never once complained when I handed her yet another page to copy. And Lori Powell did more than test the recipes—she also improved them.

Thanks also to the MacDowell Colony for providing a few weeks of paradise: time to write, endless quiet, and an extraordinarily creative community.

I also want to thank all the people who played such an important part in the tumultuous years I've written about here. Susan Subtle, who practically forced me to write when I insisted I was just a cook. Rosalie Wright, my first editor at *New West* (and still the best boss I've ever had). Bill Broyles, who took over when the magazine became *California*, and pushed me even further. And Donna Warner, who worked with me at *Metropolitan Home*, not only taught me what makes a good photograph but also let me sleep on the floor of her hotel room at all the food conferences I could not afford.

Pat Oleszko, Marion Cunningham, Sherry Virbila, and Elena Fontanari talked me through the painful process of breaking up with Doug. It would have been a whole lot harder without them.

Bruce Henstell was, for many years, my L.A. home. He introduced me to sushi and came to get me the night I was mugged. When I moved to L.A., Mark Peel's and Nancy Silverton's endless generosity made living there fun. Henry Weinstein, Mary Louise Oates, David Shear, Bill Steigerwald, and Kathie Jenkins, my first friends at the *Times*, taught me the difference between writing and journalism. David Shaw and Lucy Stille were wonderful sources of food and friendship. And Steve Wallace changed my life by introducing me to Danny Kaye.

Shelby Coffey gave me the Food Section and let me mold it into something we could all be proud of. Laurie Ochoa and Jonathan Gold did more than help me; they showed me how exhilarating collaboration can be.

Writing about Gavi was hard; living through it was harder. There is still not a day when I don't think about her but over time I came to see that we had played an important role in her life; had we not fought so hard to keep her, she would not have a father. That comforts me. At the time, however, the only comfort came from friends. Stacey Winkler and Howard Weitzman were with us all the way, and Sonia Hernandez was a rock. And I will never, ever, forget Margy Rochlin, Robin Green, and Chris Jonic showing up on Wednesdays and Saturdays to see us through the visits, or Bruce and Barbara Neyers's kindness in lending us their Napa Valley house.

I've tried to be as honest as I can throughout this book. In a few cases I've changed names, and I have occasionally altered the setting or the timing of a story. But all my friends know this about me: I can always eat, and I can always exaggerate.

One more thing. I took the title of this book from the Song of Solomon, which has a lot to say about both food and love.

COMFORT ME WITH APPLES

RUTH REICHL

A Reader's Guide

To print out copies of this
or other Random House Reader's Guides,
visit us at www.atrandom.com/rgg

QUESTIONS
FOR DISCUSSION

1. When Ruth Reichl tells her housemates that she is going to become a restaurant critic, her roommate Nick responds, "You're going to spend your life telling spoiled, rich people where to eat too much obscene food?" Discuss Reichl's transition from chef to critic and the effect it has on her lifestyle. To what degree is Nick's response a reflection of the era (the 1970s)? Thirty years later, does your reaction differ from Nick's?

2. Reichl is known for her restaurant reviews and other food writing. In *Comfort Me with Apples,* do you find her writing about food to be straightforward? Consider her use of metaphor (eggs that taste like sunshine, raspberries like spring) to describe food. Do you find this to be an effective means of conveying her sensations to the reader?

3. How is Reichl's background in journalism reflected in her prose style in this book?

4. Reichl has said that *Comfort Me with Apples* is about women and work. Throughout her personal ups and downs, she always returns to work as a source of solace, continuity, and fulfillment. Consider her trip to Barcleona after she has had to return her adopted daughter to the girl's birth parents. How does the trip console her, and how is she different upon her return?

5. Reichl includes recipes at the end of each chapter, recipes that each signify a specific event in her life and relate to an event in the book. In *Comfort Me with Apples,* cooking is often therapeutic. Think of your own relationship with food and cooking. Are there particular meals that, for you, elicit memories or strong emotional responses?

6. Ruth Reichl's first memoir, *Tender at the Bone,* dealt to a great extent with her often difficult relationship with her mother. How does their relationship evolve and change in *Comfort Me with Apples*? Consider the relationships that dominate her life in this book, including those that intersect with her relationship with her mother, and how they reflect on Reichl's life and character.

7. The author has called *Comfort Me with Apples* "a love story." What is the nature of this love story? Think of the ways in which love pervades the book—love of food, friends, lovers, spouses, chidren, and self.

8. In an interview, Reichl has said, "I believe privacy is overrated. I did hold back when I thought what I was writing would be hurtful for someone else, but I believe that the biggest hope for mankind is for us to learn to know each other, to tell each other the truth." Consider the responsibilities an author has in writing an autobiography. What decisions has Reichl made in shaping her own story, and what effect do they have on the reader's perceptions of her and the other people she features in her book? Is it ever possible to preserve the objective truth (if there is such a thing) in writing a memoir?'

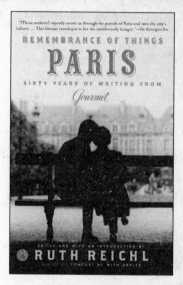

FROM THE MODERN LIBRARY FOOD SERIES

Edited by Ruth Reichl

"[The books] I have chosen for the Modern Library Food Series are all very special, for they each offer more than recipes. . . . These are books for cooks and armchair cooks, for historians, for people who believe that what people eat—and why—is important."

—Ruth Reichl

Perfection Salad: Women and Cooking at the Turn of the Century

Laura Shapiro

Introduction by
Michael Stern

Cooking with Pomiane

Edouard de Pomiane

Introduction by
Elizabeth David

Clémentine in the Kitchen

Samuel Chamberlain

Katish: Our Russian Cook

Wanda L. Frolov

Introduction by
Marion Cunningham

Life à la Henri

Henri Charpentier
and Boyden Sparks

Introduction by
Alice Waters

High Bonnet: A Novel of Epicurean Adventures

Idwal Jones

Introduction by
Anthony Bourdain

www.modernlibrary.com | MODERN LIBRARY